Lessons in

DATE DUE

Boston   Columbus   Indianapolis   New York   San Francisco
Amsterdam   Cape Town   Dubai   London   Madrid   Milan   Munich   Paris   Montreal   Toronto
Delhi   Mexico City   São Paulo   Sydney   Hong Kong   Seoul   Singapore   Taipei   Tokyo

Editor in Chief: Joseph Opiela
Marketing Manager: Allison Arnold
Program Manager: Katharine Glynn
Project Manager: Denise Phillip Grant
Project Coordination, Text Design, and
  Electronic Page Makeup:
  Lumina Datamatics
Program Design Lead/Designer:
  Beth Paquin

Cover Image: Odilion Dimier/
  Getty Images
Senior Manufacturing Buyer:
  Roy L. Pickering, Jr.
Printer/Binder:
  R. R. Donnelley & Sons/
  Crawfordsville
Cover Printer: Phoenix Color/
  Hagerstown

Acknowledgments of third-party content appear on page[s] 240–242, which constitute an extension of this copyright page.

Library of Congress Cataloging-in-Publication Data
Williams, Joseph M., author.
  Style : Lessons in clarity and grace / Joseph M. Williams, The University of
  Chicago ; Revised by Joseph Bizup. — Twelfth Edition.
    pages cm
  Includes index.
  ISBN 978-0-13-408041-3 (alk. paper)— ISBN 0-13-408041-6 (alk. paper)
    1. English language—Style.   2. English language—Technical
English.   3. English language—Business English.   4. English language—
Rhetoric.   5. Technical writing.   6. Business writing.   I. Bizup, Joseph,
(date)- author.   II. Title.
  PE1421.W545 2015
  808'.042—dc23
                                                                    2015031148

3   17

ACC LIBRARY SERVICES
AUSTIN, TX

PEARSON

www.pearsonhighered.com

Student Edition ISBN 10: 0-13-408041-6
Student Edition ISBN 13: 978-0-13-408041-3
A la Carte ISBN 10: 0-13-444207-5
A la Carte ISBN 13: 978-0-13-444207-5

CONTENTS

PREFACE

Most people won't realize that writing is a craft.
You have to take your apprenticeship in it like anything else.
—KATHERINE ANNE PORTER

THE TWELFTH EDITION

This edition of *Style* is my second, but it is the book's twelfth. As I have revised the book a second time, it has inevitably become more my own. But it also remains emphatically Joseph Williams's. I added nothing I believe he would have rejected, and I only made changes I believe he would have embraced. "Writing has consequences," Joe wrote in a 1979 article anticipating his book: "Whatever does not bear on those consequences is irrelevant to our task—to help our students become what they want to be." I have worked with this ideal in mind.

What's New

In preparing this edition, I sought to amplify the book's central point: that good style is a matter of making informed choices in the service of one's readers. Here, specifically, is what's changed:

- I rewrote the section on pronouns and gender-neutral language in Lesson 2. It now focuses less on the problem of gender-biased language than on the many options available to writers who want to write in a gender-neutral fashion.
- I expanded the explanations that accompany the book's hallmark diagrams of the principles of style (Lessons 3–6).
- I revised the section on metadiscourse in Lesson 4 so that it outlines more fully the different ways writers can use this device.
- I included new examples of elegant passages in Lesson 11.
- I rewrote the discussion of sources in Appendix 2. This appendix still addresses plagiarism and the mechanics of citation, but it now

gives more attention to the stylistic effects of different ways of summarizing, paraphrasing, and quoting.

- I modified the book's treatment of revision in two ways. First, I changed language that could seem to suggest that revision is a matter of editing only, that is, of holding the meaning of a sentence or passage constant while adjusting its form. Given his concern with how readers understand texts, Joe naturally focused on how writers could edit their prose to make it clearer for their readers. But he fully understood that writing is a complex, recursive process involving thinking, planning, drafting, rewriting, and editing, and that each of these activities could potentially affect any of the others. The book is now more careful to avoid implying, falsely, that revision means *only* editing. Second, I changed the terms the book uses to discuss revision, replacing *diagnose* and *diagnosis* with *analyze* and *analysis*. The book now presents revision less as a matter of identifying and fixing problems than as a matter of understanding and assessing options.

- I adjusted the book's examples, explanations, and exercises to soften their explicitly American perspective. This change acknowledges the book's global readership and is consistent with the book's core values. The book continues to insist, as it always has, that good style is an ethical and civic virtue.

- I tried to be more precise about the scope of the book's advice. The principles concerning the clarity and coherence of sentences and passages apply to prose of all kinds, but the book's guidance about more global matters of style—motivation (Lesson 8), organization (Lesson 9), using sources (Appendix 2)—is most relevant to various kinds of academic and professional writing.

- Finally, I endeavored throughout to improve and refine the book's explanations of its concepts and principles and to eliminate errors where I found them.

What's the Same
For all these changes, the book continues to address the same questions it always has:

- What is it in a sentence that makes readers judge it as they do?
- How do we analyze our own prose to anticipate their judgments?
- How do we revise a sentence so that readers will think better of it?

Gregory G. Colomb, who revised the tenth edition of *Style,* saw in these questions the essence of the book's "enduring genius": its insight that writers have at their disposal *principles* that allow them to reliably predict readers' responses and to revise accordingly. Although Joe occasionally used the word *rules* to describe his advice, he preferred the word *principles*, because his goal was not to prescribe a correct style but to help writers recognize their options and make informed choices among them.

Following Greg's example, I have preserved Joe's personal voice, not just as a matter of style but because it is crucial to the book's message. Joe knew that every style, even the most transparent, is a choice. In choosing to load his text with what Greg called his "ubiquitous *I*'s," Joe was embracing the limitations and struggles of ordinary writers as his own. If the longevity of *Style* can be attributed to the sound advice Joe gives, the affection the book inspires can be attributed to the solidarity with readers he shows.

How to Use This Book

Here are some suggestions to help you get the most out of this book:

- Be sure you know at least these grammatical terms: SUBJECT, VERB, NOUN, ACTIVE, PASSIVE, CLAUSE, PREPOSITION, and COORDINATION. All grammatical terms are capitalized the first time they appear and are defined in the text or the Glossary.

- If you are using this book for a class, work as much as you can with your fellow students. Discuss the lessons and exercises. Share and comment on one another's writing. Learn from one another.

- If you are using this book on your own, go slowly. Take the lessons a few pages at a time. Do the exercises. Edit someone else's writing. Then edit something you wrote yourself a few weeks ago, then something you wrote that day.

- Understand that as you try to apply the book's principles, you may write more slowly. That's natural, and it passes.

- Finally, remember that the book's principles have less to do with drafting than with revision. If there is a first principle of drafting, it is to ignore most of the advice about it.

Acknowledgments

Many people contributed to this edition, and it is my privilege to recognize them here.

For their guidance and insights as I revised this edition, I thank Joseph Opiela, Katharine Glynn, Samantha Bertschmann, and Denise Phillip Grant at Pearson Education. For their work preparing the text for publication, I thank Prathiba Naveenkumar and Revathi Viswanathan at Lumina Datamatics Ltd.

I thank my colleagues in the College of Arts & Sciences Writing Program at Boston University and elsewhere for our many conversations about Joseph Williams's ideas. I especially thank Deborah Breen, John Brereton, Martin Fido, Cinthia Gannett, Stacey Goguen, Gwen Kordonowy, Sarah Madsen Hardy, Christopher McVey, James Pasto, Thomas Underwood, Anthony Wallace, Christopher Walsh, and Maria Zlateva for sharing their ideas about how the book could be made better; Talia Vestri Croan, Ryan Weberling, and Erica Zimmer for their help preparing the text for this edition; and Jonathan Buehl and William FitzGerald for reading and commenting on sections of this revision. Through his blog, "Lokasenna" led me to the quotation from Mary Wollstonecraft I've added to Lesson 11. I thank also those students who have used the book as well as those readers who have emailed me their often detailed comments and suggestions. It has been a true pleasure to learn what they value in the book and to correspond with them.

I thank the following reviewers for their comments on the eleventh edition: Lee R. Cerling, University of Southern California; Dr. Crystal Elerson, University of Texas at Arlington; Mike Jerbic, San Jose State University; Shirley Kahlert, Merced College; William James Owen, Columbus State University; Sabrina Taylor, Louisiana State University; and Kayla Walker-Edin, Milligan College.

I am deeply grateful to Joe Williams for the time we spent together in 2008, when he visited the writing program I was then directing. And I owe a tremendous debt to Greg Colomb, both for his intellectual and professional guidance and for his friendship. Finally, I thank Annmarie, Grace, and Charlotte for all the love and joy we share together.

In the ninth edition, Joe acknowledged a great many people, including his students at the University of Chicago, other scholars to whom he was intellectually indebted, and the many readers and colleagues who shared observations and ideas with him. These include Theresa Ammirati, Yvonne Atkinson, Margaret Batschelet, Nancy Barendse, Charles Bazerman, Randy Berlin, Cheryl Brooke, Ken Bruffee, Christopher Buck, Douglas Butturff, Donald Byker, Bruce Campbell, Elaine Chaika, Avon Crismore, Constance Gefvert, Darren Cambridge, Mark Canada, Paul Contino, Don Freeman, Jim Garrett, Jill Gladstein, Karen Gocsik, Richard Grande, Jeanne Gunner, Maxine Hairston, Stan Henning, George Hoffman, Rebecca Moore Howard, John Hyman, Sandra Jamieson, Richard Jenseth, Elizabeth Bourque Johnson, Julie Kalish, Seth Katz, Bernadette Longo, Ted Lowe, Brij Lunine, Richard McLain, Joel Margulis, Susan Miller, Linda Mitchell, Ellen Moody, Ed Moritz, Patricia Murray, Neil Nakadate, Janice Neuleib, Ann Palkovich, Matthew Parfitt, Donna Burns Philips, Mike Pownall, Peter Priest, Keith Rhodes, John Ruszkiewicz, Margaret Shaklee, Nancy Sommers, Laura Bartlett Snyder, John Taylor, Mary Taylor, Bill Vande Kopple, James Vanden Bosch, Stephen Witte, Joseph Wappel, Alison Warriner, Wendy Wayman, Patricia Webb, Kevin Wilson, Linda Ziff. I thank them again here on his behalf. I allow Joe to acknowledge his family himself:

> And again, those who contribute to my life more than I let them know: Oliver, Michele, and Eleanor; Chris and Ingrid; Dave, Patty, Owen, and Matilde; Megan, Phil, Lily and Calvin; and Joe, Christine, Nicholas, and Katherine. And at beginning and end still, Joan, whose patience and love flow more generously than I deserve.

JOSEPH BIZUP
BOSTON, MASSACHUSETTS

STUDENT SUPPLEMENT: PEARSON WRITER

Pearson Writer is a digital, mobile-first, all-in-one application intended to assist with all aspects of college writing. When students have questions about writing, grammar, research, or specific disciplines as they work on writing assignments, they can easily search Writer—in their own words, at anytime, from anywhere—and get accurate, easy-to-understand help. A *My Projects* component keeps track of writing assignments for all courses in one place with due dates, monitors where one is in the process, helps at each stage, and provides a place to manage sources, notes, and a bibliography. A *Writing Review* component offers preliminary feedback to help revise and edit writing by automatically highlighting grammar and style issues in one's writing. Students paste their writing into the Review space, and possible errors are automatically highlighted with feedback and suggested revision. In addition, Pearson Writer includes tools to help cite sources in any citation format, and a rich database of sources that can be used for research on any topic for any course.

The mobile version is as usable and effective as the desktop version. Students who register for the desktop version of Writer can download the application onto their smartphone and tablet. Whether working on a laptop, at home or in a computer lab on campus, or using a smartphone or tablet anywhere, students can access guidance and tools for writing, grammar, and research whenever and wherever they want.

To learn more about Pearson Writer and to purchase access online, go to: http://www.writer.pearsonhighered.com.

IN MEMORIAM

Joseph M. Williams, 1933–2008
il miglior fabbro [the best craftsman]
(by Gregory G. Colomb)

On February 22, 2008, the world lost a great scholar and teacher, and I lost a dear friend. For almost thirty years, Joe Williams and I taught together, researched together, wrote together, drank together, traveled together, and argued together and apart. When those "apart" arguments led to what in the last edition he called "our intemperate shouting matches," we grew closer—and wrote more thoughtfully—than ever. I knew his faults, but he was the best man I knew.

My epitaph for Joe—*il miglior fabbro*—puts him in exalted company: I take it from Dante, who applied it to the twelfth-century troubadour Arnaut Daniel, praised by Plutarch as the "Grand Master" of his craft. In the last century, T. S. Eliot famously said it of Ezra Pound. Of course, these poets were all known not for their clarity and grace but for their depth and difficulty. No matter, none have been better than they at their craft, just as none have been better than Joe at his. And Joe has the added distinction that his craft daily multiplies its good a thousand fold and more, in all those papers, reports, memos, and other documents that have served their readers better because of him.

PART ONE

Style as Choice

*. . . English style, familiar but not coarse, and elegant,
but not ostentatious. . . .*
—SAMUEL JOHNSON

Understanding Style

Have something to say, and say it as clearly as you can.
That is the only secret of style.
—MATTHEW ARNOLD

Essentially style resembles good manners. It comes of
endeavouring to understand others, of thinking for them rather
than yourself—or thinking, that is, with the heart as well as
the head.
—SIR ARTHUR QUILLER-COUCH

The great enemy of clear language is insincerity.
—GEORGE ORWELL

FIRST PRINCIPLES

This book rests on two beliefs: it is good to write clearly, and anyone can. The first is self-evident, especially to those who read a lot
of writing like this:

> An understanding of the causal factors involved in excessive drinking
> by students could lead to their more effective treatment.

But the second may seem optimistic to those who want to write
clearly but don't think they can get close to this:

We could more effectively treat students who drink excessively if we understood why they do so.

This book shows you how.

In it, I consider writing from the perspective of reading. None of us can judge our own writing as others will because when we read it, we respond less to the words on the page or screen than to the thoughts in our minds. We see what we thought we said, and we blame our readers for not understanding us as we understand ourselves. This book presents principles—not rules—that you can follow to escape this trap. Once you understand why readers judge one sentence to be dense and abstract and another to be clear and direct, you can use this understanding to serve your readers better. You can also use it to serve yourself as you read. When you encounter writing you find difficult, you will be able to untangle it so that you can grasp (or at least guess at) its meaning.

The difficult, even daunting, task of writing clearly has challenged generations of writers who have hidden their ideas not only from their readers but sometimes even from themselves. Moreover, unclear writing is not just an inconvenience to readers; it is a social ill. When we read such writing in government regulations, we call it *bureaucratese;* in legal documents, *legalese;* in academic writing that inflates small ideas into gassy abstractions, *academese.* Written carelessly or, worse, deliberately, unclear writing is in its extreme forms a language of exclusion that a democracy cannot tolerate. It is also a problem that has afflicted writing in English for almost five hundred years.

A Short History of Unclear Writing

It wasn't until about the middle of the sixteenth century that writers decided that English was eloquent enough to replace Latin and French in serious discourse. But their first efforts were written in a style so complex that it defeated easy understanding:

> If use and custom, having the help of so long time and continuance wherein to [re]fine our tongue, of so great learning and experience which furnish matter for the [re]fining, of so good wits and judgments which can tell how to refine, have griped at nothing in all that time, with all that cunning, by all those wits which they won't let go but hold for most certain in the right of our writing, that then our tongue has no certainty to trust to, but write all at random.
>
> —Richard Mulcaster, *The First Part of the Elementary*, 1582

In the next century, English became the language of science. We might expect that scientists would want to communicate clearly and simply, but the complex style had spread to their writing as well. As one complained,

> Of all the studies of men, nothing may sooner be obtained than this vicious abundance of phrase, this trick of metaphors, this volubility of tongue which makes so great a noise in the world.
>
> —Thomas Sprat, *History of the Royal Society*, 1667

When this continent was settled, writers might have established a new, democratic prose style for a new, democratic nation. In fact, in 1776, the plain words of Thomas Paine's *Common Sense* helped inspire the American Revolution:

> In the following pages I offer nothing more than simple facts, plain arguments, and common sense.

Sad to say, he sparked no such revolution in prose style.

A half century later, James Fenimore Cooper complained about the writing of his day:

> The love of turgid expressions is gaining ground, and ought to be corrected. One of the most certain evidences of a man of high breeding, is his simplicity of speech: a simplicity that is equally removed from vulgarity and exaggeration. . . . Simplicity should be the firm aim, after one is removed from vulgarity. . . . In no case, however, can one who aims at turgid language, exaggerated sentiments, or pedantic utterances, lay claim to be either a man or a woman of the world.
>
> —*The American Democrat*, 1838

Unfortunately, in abusing that style, Cooper adopted it. Had he followed his own advice, he might have written,

> We should discourage those who promote turgid language. A well-bred person speaks simply, in a way that is neither vulgar nor exaggerated. No one can claim to be a man or woman of the world who deliberately exaggerates sentiments or speaks in ways that are turgid or pedantic.

About fifty years later, Mark Twain wrote what we now consider classic American prose. He said this about Cooper's style:

> There have been daring people in the world who claimed that Cooper could write English, but they are all dead now—all dead but Lounsbury [an academic who praised Cooper's style]. . . . [He] says that *Deerslayer* is a "pure work of art." . . . [But] Cooper wrote about the poorest English that exists in our language. . . .
>
> —"Fenimore Cooper's Literary Offenses"

As much as we admire Twain's directness, few of us emulate it.

In the best-known modern essay on English style, "Politics and the English Language," George Orwell anatomized the turgid language of politicians, bureaucrats, academics, and others:

> The keynote [of a pretentious style] is the elimination of simple verbs. Instead of being a single word, such as *break, stop, spoil, mend, kill,* a verb becomes a phrase, made up of a noun or adjective tacked on to some general-purposes verb such as *prove, serve, form, play, render.* In addition, the passive voice is wherever possible used in preference to the active, and noun constructions are used instead of gerunds (*by examination of* instead of *by examining*).

But as Cooper did, in abusing that style Orwell adopted it. He could have written more concisely:

> Pretentious writers avoid simple verbs. Instead of using one word, such as *break, stop, spoil, mend, kill,* they turn the verb into a noun or adjective, and tack it onto some general-purpose verb such as *prove, serve, form, play, render.* Wherever possible, they use the passive voice instead of the active and noun constructions instead of gerunds (*by examination of* instead of *by examining*).

If the best-known critic of an opaque style could not resist it, we shouldn't be surprised that politicians and academics embrace it. On the language of the social sciences:

> A turgid and polysyllabic prose does seem to prevail in the social sciences. . . . Such lack of ready intelligibility, I believe, usually has little or nothing to do with the complexity of subject matter, and nothing at all to do with profundity of thoughts. It has to do almost entirely with certain confusions of the academic writer about his own status.
>
> —C. Wright Mills, *The Sociological Imagination*

On the language of medicine:

> It now appears that obligatory obfuscation is a firm tradition within the medical profession. . . . This may explain why only the most eminent physicians, the Cushings and Oslers, feel free to express themselves lucidly.
>
> —Michael Crichton, "Medical Obfuscation: Structure and Function," *New England Journal of Medicine*

On the language of law:

> But now, in law journals, in speeches, in classrooms and in court-rooms, lawyers and judges are beginning to worry about how often they have been misunderstood, and they are discovering that sometimes they cannot even understand each other.
>
> —Tom Goldstein, *New York Times*

On the language of science:

> But there are times when the more the authors explain [about ape communication], the less we understand. Apes certainly seem capable of using language to communicate. Whether scientists are remains doubtful.
>
> —Douglas Chadwick, *New York Times*

Most of us first confront that kind of writing in textbook sentences like this one:

> Recognition of the fact that systems [of grammar] differ from one language to another can serve as the basis for serious consideration of the problems confronting translators of the great works of world literature originally written in a language other than English.

In about half as many words, that means:

> When we recognize that languages have different grammars, we can consider the problems of those who translate great works of literature into English.

Generations of students have struggled with dense writing, many thinking they weren't smart enough to grasp a writer's deep ideas. Some have been right about that, but more could have blamed the writer's inability (or refusal) to write clearly. Many students, sad to say, give up. Sadder still, others learn not only to read that style but to write it, inflicting it in turn on their readers and thereby sustaining a 450-year-old tradition of unreadable writing.

Some Private Causes Of Unclear Writing

Unclear writing is a social problem, but it often has private causes. Michael Crichton mentioned one: some writers plump up their prose, hoping that complicated sentences indicate deep thought. And when we want to hide the fact that we don't know what we're talking about, we typically throw up a tangle of abstract words in long, complex sentences.

Others write graceless prose not deliberately but because they are seized by the idea that good writing must be free of the kind of errors that only a grammarian can explain. They approach a blank page not as a space to explore ideas, but as a minefield of potential errors. They creep from word to word, concerned less with their readers' understanding than with their own survival. I address that issue in Lesson 2.

Others write unclearly because they freeze up, especially when they are learning to think and write in a new academic or professional setting. As we struggle to master new ideas, most of us write worse than we do when we write about things we understand better. If that sounds like you, take heart: you will write more clearly when you more clearly understand what you are writing about.

But the biggest reason most of us write unclearly is that we don't know when readers will think we are unclear, much less why. Our own writing always seems clearer to us than to our readers because we read into it what we want them to get out of it. And so instead of revising our writing to meet their needs, we send it off the moment it meets ours.

In all of this, of course, is a great irony: we are likely to confuse others when we write about a subject that confuses us. But when we become confused by a complex style, we too easily assume that its complexity signals deep thought, and so we try to imitate it, making our already confused writing even worse.

ON DRAFTING AND REVISING

A warning: if you think about the principles presented in this book *as you draft*, you may never finish drafting. Most experienced writers like to get something down on paper or up on the screen as fast as they can. Then as they revise that first draft into something clearer, they understand their ideas better. And when they understand their ideas better, they express them more clearly, and the more clearly they express them, the better they understand them ... and so it goes, ending only when they run out of energy, interest, or time.

For a fortunate few, that end comes weeks, months, even years after they begin. For most of us, though, the deadline is closer to tomorrow morning. And so we have to settle for prose that is less than perfect but as good as we can make it in the time we have. (Perfection may be the ideal, but it is the death of done.)

So when you draft, concentrate first on getting your ideas into words. Then use the principles here both to help you refine your ideas and to identify and quickly revise sentences and passages likely to give your readers a problem.

As important as clarity is, though, some occasions call for more:

> Now the trumpet summons us again—not as a call to bear arms, though arms we need—not as a call to battle, though embattled we are—but a call to bear the burden of a long twilight struggle, year in and year out, "rejoicing in hope, patient in tribulation"—a struggle

against the common enemies of man: tyranny, poverty, disease and war itself.

—John F. Kennedy, Inaugural Address, January 20, 1961

Few of us are called upon to write a presidential address, but even on less lofty occasions, some of us take a private pleasure in writing a shapely sentence, even if no one will notice. If you enjoy not just writing a sentence but crafting it, you will find suggestions in Part Four.

Writing is also a social act that might or might not serve the best interests of readers, so in Lesson 12, I address some issues about the ethics of style. In Appendix I, I discuss styles of punctuation. In Appendix II, I explain how to use and cite quotations and other material from sources.

Many years ago, H. L. Mencken wrote this:

> With precious few exceptions, all the books on style in English are by writers quite unable to write. The subject, indeed, seems to exercise a special and dreadful fascination over school ma'ams, bucolic college professors, and other such pseudoliterates. . . . Their central aim, of course, is to reduce the whole thing to a series of simple rules—the overmastering passion of their melancholy order, at all times and everywhere.
>
> —"The Fringes of Lovely Letters"

Mencken was right: no one learns to write well by rule, especially those who cannot see or feel or think. But I know that many who do see clearly, feel deeply, and think carefully still cannot write sentences that make their thoughts, feelings, and visions clear to others. I also know that the more clearly we write, the more clearly we see and feel and think. Rules help no one do that, but some principles can.

Here they are.

2

Correctness

God does not much mind bad grammar, but He does not take any particular pleasure in it.
—ERASMUS

Established custom, in speaking and writing, is the standard to which we must at last resort for determining every controverted point in language and style.
—HUGH BLAIR

English usage is sometimes more than mere taste, judgment, and education—sometimes it's sheer luck, like getting across the street.
—E. B. WHITE

UNDERSTANDING CORRECTNESS

To careful writers, nothing is more important than choice, for choice is what allows them to express themselves clearly and precisely. Which of these sentences would you choose to give to your readers?

1. Lack of media support was the cause of our election loss.
2. We lost the election because the media did not support us.

Most of us would choose (2).

Correctness, though, seems a matter not of choice but of obedience. That does seem to simplify things: "correctness" requires not sound judgment but only a good memory. Some teachers and editors, in fact, think we can stay safe by memorizing and following dozens of alleged "rules" of correct grammar and usage: the truth, however, is more complicated. Some rules are real—if we ignore them, we risk being labeled at least unschooled: VERBS must agree with their SUBJECTS. (Words set in small capitals are defined in the glossary.) There are numerous others. But many often-repeated rules are less important than many think, and some are not even real:

- Never begin a sentence with *and* or *but*.
- Never use double negatives.
- Never split INFINITIVES.

If you obsess over them all, you prevent yourself from writing quickly and clearly. That's why I address correctness now, before clarity, because I want to put it where it belongs—behind us.

THE SOCIAL AUTHORITY OF GRAMMAR RULES

Opinion is split on the social role of grammar rules. To some, they are just another device that the Ins use to control the Outs by stigmatizing their language and thereby suppressing their social and political aspirations. To others, the rules of Standard English have been so refined by generations of educated speakers and writers that they must be observed by all the best writers of English.

Both views are correct, partly. For centuries, those governing our affairs have used grammatical "errors" to screen out those unwilling or unable to acquire the habits of the schooled middle class. But the critics are wrong to claim that those rules were *devised* for that end. Standard forms of a language originate in accidents of geography and economic power. When a language has different regional dialects, that of the most powerful speakers usually becomes the most prestigious and the basis for a nation's "correct" writing.

Thus if Edinburgh rather than London had become the center of Britain's economic, political, and literary life, we would speak and write less like Shakespeare and more like the Scottish poet Robert Burns:

A ye wha are sae guid yourself   (All you who are so good yourselves
Sae pious and sae holy,   So pious and so holy,

Ye've nought to do but mark You've nothing to do but talk
  and tell about
Your neebours' fauts and folly! Your neighbors' faults and folly!)

Conservatives, on the other hand, are right that many rules of Standard English originated in efficient expression. For example, we no longer use all the endings that our verbs required a thousand years ago. We now omit present tense inflections in all but one context (and we don't need it there):

	1ST PERSON	2ND PERSON	3RD PERSON
Singular	I know + ø.	You know + ø.	She know + **S**.
Plural	We know + ø.	You know + ø.	They know + ø.

But those conservatives are wrong when they claim that Standard English has been refined by the logic of educated speakers and writers and, therefore, must be socially and morally superior to the debased language of their alleged inferiors.

Here's the point: Those determined to discriminate will seize on any difference. But our language seems to reflect the quality of our minds more directly than do our ZIP codes, so it's easy for those inclined to look down on others to think that grammatical "errors" indicate mental or moral deficiency. That belief is not just factually wrong; in a democracy, it is also socially destructive. Yet even if *ain't* is logically correct, so great is the power of social convention that we avoid it, at least if we hope to be taken seriously when we write for serious purposes.

THREE KINDS OF RULES

These corrosive social attitudes about correctness have been encouraged by generations of grammarians who, in their zeal to codify "good" English, have confused three kinds of "rules."

1. Real Rules

Real rules define what makes English English: ARTICLES must precede NOUNS: *the book,* not *book the.* Speakers born into English don't think about these rules at all when they write, and they violate them only when tired or distracted.

2. Social Rules

Social rules distinguish Standard English from nonstandard: *He doesn't have any money* versus *He don't have no money.* Schooled writers observe these rules as naturally as they observe the Real Rules and think about them only when they notice others violating them. The only writers who *self-consciously* try to follow them are those not born into Standard English who are striving to associate themselves with the English-speaking educated classes.

3. Invented Rules

Finally, some grammarians have invented a handful of rules that they think we all *should* observe. These are the rules that the grammar police love to enforce and that too many educated writers obsess over. Most date from the last half of the eighteenth century:

> Don't split infinitives, as in *to **quietly** leave.*
>
> Don't end a sentence with a PREPOSITION.

A few date from the twentieth century:

> Don't use *hopefully* for *I hope*, as in ***Hopefully**, it won't rain.*
>
> Don't use *which* for *that*, as in *a car **which** I sold.*

For almost 300 years, grammarians have accused the best writers of violating rules like these, and the best writers have consistently ignored them. Which is lucky for the grammarians, because if writers did obey all the rules, grammarians would have to keep inventing new ones, or find another line of work. The fact is, none of these invented rules reflects the unself-conscious usage of our best writers. In this lesson, we focus on this third kind of rule, the handful of invented ones, because only they vex those who already write Standard English.

OBSERVING RULES THOUGHTFULLY

It is no simple matter to deal with these invented rules if you want to be thought of as someone who writes "correctly." You could choose the worst-case policy: follow all the rules all the time because sometime, someone will criticize you for something—for beginning a sentence with *and* or ending it with *up*. But if you try to obey all the rules all the time, you risk becoming so obsessed with rules that you tie yourself in knots. And sooner or later, you will impose those rules—real or not—on others.

The alternative to blind obedience is selective observance. But then you have to decide which rules to observe and which to ignore. And if you ignore an alleged rule, you may have to deal with someone whose passion for "good" grammar makes her see in your split infinitive a sign of intellectual flabbiness, moral corruption, and social decay.

If you want to avoid being accused of "lacking standards" but refuse to submit to whatever "rule" someone can dredge up from ninth-grade English, you have to know more about these invented rules than the rule-mongers do. The rest of this lesson helps you do just that.

TWO KINDS OF INVENTED RULES

We can sort most invented rules into two groups: Folklore and Elegant Options.

Folklore

These rules include those that most careful readers and writers ignore. You may not yet have had some of them inflicted on you, but chances are that you will. In what follows, the quotations that illustrate "violations" of these rules are from writers of considerable intellectual and scholarly stature or who, on matters of usage, are reliable conservatives (some are both). A check mark indicates acceptable Standard English, despite what some grammarians claim.

1. **"Don't begin sentences with *and* or *but*."** This passage ignores the "rule" twice:

   ✓ **But,** it will be asked, is tact not an individual gift, therefore highly variable in its choices? **And** if that is so, what guidance can a manual offer, other than that of its author's prejudices—mere impressionism?

   —Wilson Follett, *Modern American Usage:*
   A Guide, edited and completed by
   Jacques Barzun et al.

   Some inexperienced writers do begin too many sentences with *and*, but that is an error not in grammar but of style.

Some insecure writers also think they should not begin a sentence with *because*. Allegedly not this:

✓ **Because** we have access to so much historical fact, today we know a good deal about changes within the humanities which were not apparent to those of any age much before our own and which the individual scholar must constantly reflect on.

—Walter Ong, S. J., "The Expanding Humanities and the Individual
Scholar," *Publication of the Modern Language Association*

This folklore about *because* appears in no handbook I know of, but it is gaining currency. It probably stems from advice aimed at avoiding sentence FRAGMENTS like this one:

The plan was rejected. **Because** it was incomplete.

QUICK TIP   At best, this rule reflects a small truth of style. As you will see in Lesson 5, readers prefer sentences to begin with information they know and to proceed to information they don't. But SUBORDINATE CLAUSES beginning with *because* usually convey new information, and so putting one at the beginning of a sentence can be mildly awkward. To begin a sentence with a CLAUSE expressing familiar information about causation, use *since* rather than *because*, because *since* implies that the reader already knows what's in the clause:

✓ Since our language seems to reflect our quality of mind, it is easy for those inclined to look down on others to think that grammatical "errors" indicate mental or moral deficiency.

There are exceptions to this principle, but it's generally sound.

2. **"Use the RELATIVE PRONOUN *that*—not *which*—for RESTRICTIVE CLAUSES."** Allegedly not this:

✓ Next is a typical situation **which** a practiced writer corrects "for style" virtually by reflex action.

—Jacques Barzun, *Simple and Direct*

Yet just a few sentences before, Barzun himself (one of our most eminent intellectual historians and critics of style) had asserted:

Us[e] *that* with defining [i.e., restrictive] clauses except when stylistic reasons interpose.

(In the sentence quoted above, no such reasons interpose.)

This "rule" is relatively new. It first appeared in 1906 in Henry and Francis Fowler's *The King's English.* The Fowlers thought that the random variation between *that* and *which* to begin a restrictive clause was messy, so they just asserted that henceforth writers should (with some exceptions) limit *which* to NONRESTRICTIVE CLAUSES.

A nonrestrictive clause modifies a noun naming a referent that you can identify unambiguously without the information in that clause. For example:

✓ ABCO Inc. ended its first bankruptcy, **which** it had filed in 2012.

A company can have only one first bankruptcy, so we can unambiguously identify the bankruptcy without the information in the following clause. We therefore call that clause *nonrestrictive,* because it does not further "restrict" or identify what the noun names. In that context, we put a comma before the modifying clause and begin it with *which.* This rule is based on historical and contemporary usage.

But the Fowlers sought to limit *which* to nonrestrictive clauses only. For restrictive clauses, they prescribed *that.* For example:

✓ ABCO Inc. sold a product **that** [*not* **which**] made millions.

Since ABCO presumably makes many products, the clause *that made millions* "restricts" the product to the one that made millions, and so, according to the Fowlers, it should begin with *that.* (For another allegedly incorrect *which,* see the passage by Walter Ong on p. 14.)

Francis died in 1918, but Henry continued the family tradition with his 1926 *A Dictionary of Modern English Usage.* In that landmark work, he discussed the finer points of *which* and *that,* and then made this wistful observation:

> Some there are who follow this principle now; but it would be idle to pretend that it is the practice either of most or of the best writers.

I confess I follow the Fowlers' advice, not because a restrictive *which* is an error, but because *that* has a softer sound. I do sometimes choose a *which* when it's within a word or two of a *that,* because I don't like the sound of two *that*s close together:

✓ We all have **that** one rule **that** we will not give up.

✓ We all have **that** one rule **which** we will not give up.

3. **"Use *fewer* with nouns you count, *less* with nouns you cannot."** Allegedly not this:

    ✓ I can remember no **less** than five occasions when the correspondence columns of *The Times* rocked with volleys of letters. . . .

    > —Noel Gilroy Annan, Lord Annan, "The Life of the Mind in British Universities Today," *American Council of Learned Societies Newsletter*

    No one uses *fewer* with mass nouns (*fewer dirt*) but educated writers often use *less* with countable plural nouns (*less resources*).

4. **"Use *since* and *while* to refer only to time, not to mean *because* or *although*."** Most careful writers use *since* with a meaning close to *because* but, as mentioned above, with an added sense of "What follows I assume you already know":

    ✓ **Since** asbestos is dangerous, it should be removed carefully.

    Nor do most careful writers restrict *while* to its temporal sense (*We'll wait while you eat*). They use it also with a meaning close to "I assume you know what I state in this clause, but what I assert in the next will qualify it":

    ✓ **While** we agree on a date, we disagree about the place.

Here's the point: If writers whom we judge to be competent regularly violate some alleged rule and most careful readers never notice, then the rule has no force. In those cases, it is not writers who should change their usage, but grammarians who should change their rules.

Elegant Options

These next "rules" complement the Real Rules. Most readers do not notice when you observe these Real Rules, but does when you violates them (like that). On the other hand, few readers notice when you violate these elegant options, but some do when you observe them, because doing so makes your writing seem just a bit more self-consciously formal.

1. **"Don't split infinitives."** Purists condemn Dwight Macdonald, himself a linguistic archconservative, for this sentence (my emphasis in all the examples that follow):

✓ One wonders why Dr. Gove and his editors did not think of labeling *knowed* as substandard right where it occurs, and one suspects that they wanted **to slightly conceal** the fact. . . .

—"The String Untuned," *The New Yorker*

They would require

they wanted **to conceal slightly** the fact. . . .

Infinitives are split so often that when you avoid splitting one, careful readers may think you are trying to be especially correct, whether you are or not.

2. **"Use *whom* as the OBJECT of a verb or preposition."** Purists would condemn William Zinsser for this use of *who*:

✓ Soon after you confront this matter of preserving your identity, another question will occur to you: "**Who** am I writing for?"

—*On Writing Well*

They would insist on

another question will occur to you: "For **whom** am I writing?"

Here is an actual rule: use *who* when it is the subject of a verb in its own clause; use *whom* only when it is an object in its own clause.

3. **"Don't end a sentence with a preposition."** Purists condemn Sir Ernest Gowers, editor of the second edition of Fowler's *Dictionary*, for this:

✓ The peculiarities of legal English are often used as a stick to beat the official **with.**

—*The Complete Plain Words*

They insist on this:

. . . a stick **with which** to beat the official.

The first is correct; the second is more formal. (Again, see the Ong passage on p. 14.) And when you choose to shift both the preposition and its *whom* to the left, your sentence seems more formal yet. Compare:

✓ The man I met **with** was the man I had written **to.**

✓ The man **with whom** I met was the man **to whom** I had written.

A preposition can, however, end a sentence weakly (see pp. 82–83). George Orwell may have chosen to end this next sentence with *from* to make a sly point about English grammar, but I suspect it just ended up there (and note the "incorrect" *which*):

> [The defense of the English language] has nothing to do with . . . the setting up of a "standard English" **which** must never be departed **from.**

—"Politics and the English Language"

This would have been less awkward and more emphatic:

> We do not defend English just to create a "standard English" whose rules we must always obey.

4. **"Use the singular with *none* and *any*."** *None* and *any* were originally singular, but today most writers use them as plural, so if you use them as singular, some readers will notice. The second sentence is a bit more formal than the first:

✓ **None** of the reasons **are** sufficient to end the project.

✓ **None** of the reasons **is** sufficient to end the project.

When you are under close scrutiny, you might choose to observe all these optional rules. Ordinarily, though, most careful writers ignore them, which is to say they are not rules at all but rather stylistic choices that create a formal tone. If you adopt the worst-case approach and observe them all, all the time, few readers will give you credit but many will notice how formal you seem.

HOBGOBLINS

For some unknown reason, a handful of items have become the object of particularly zealous abuse. There's no explaining why; none of them interferes with clarity or concision.

1. **"Never use *like* for *as* or *as if*."** Allegedly, not this:

✓ These operations failed **like** the earlier ones did.

But this:

✓ These operations failed **as** the earlier ones did.

Like became a SUBORDINATING CONJUNCTION in the eighteenth century when writers began to drop *as* from the conjunctive PHRASE *like as*, leaving just *like* as the CONJUNCTION.

This process is called *elision*, and it is a common linguistic change. It is telling that when editing the second edition of Fowler's *Dictionary* (the one favored by conservatives), Gowers deleted *like* for *as* from Fowler's list of "Illiteracies" and moved it into the category of "Sturdy Indefensibles."

2. **"Don't use *hopefully* to mean 'I hope.'"** Allegedly, not this:

   ✓ Hopefully, it will not rain.

   But this:

   ✓ I hope that it will not rain.

   This "rule" dates from the middle of the twentieth century. It has no basis in logic or grammar, as the allegedly incorrect use of *hopefully* parallels the usage of other words that no one complains about, words such as *candidly, frankly, sadly*, and *happily*:

   ✓ Candidly, we may fail. (That is, *I am candid when I say we may fail.*)

   ✓ Sadly, we must go. (That is, *I am sad when I say we must go.*)

3. **"Don't use *finalize* to mean 'finish' or 'complete.'"** But *finalize* doesn't mean just "finish." It means "to clean up the last few details," a sense captured by no other word.

4. **"Don't use *impact* as a verb but only as a noun."** Some would object to this:

   ✓ The survey impacted our strategy.

   And insist on this:

   ✓ The survey had an impact on our strategy.

   Impact has been a verb for 400 years, but on some people, historical evidence has none.

5. **"Don't modify absolute words such as *perfect, unique, final*, or *complete* with *very, more, quite*, and so on."** That rule would have deprived us of this familiar sentence:

   ✓ We the People of the United States, in order to form a **more perfect** union. . . .

   (Even so, this is a rule generally worth following.)

6. **"Never ever use *irregardless* for *regardless* or *irrespective*."** However arbitrary this rule is, follow it. Use *irregardless* and some will judge you irredeemable.

SOME WORDS THAT ATTRACT SPECIAL ATTENTION

Some words are so often confused with others that careful readers are likely to note when you correctly distinguish them. Here are some:

aggravate means "to make worse." Fastidious readers may object if you use it to mean "annoy."

anticipate means "to prepare for a contingency." It does not mean just "expect." You anticipate a question when you prepare its answer before it's asked; if you know it's coming but don't prepare, you only expect it.

anxious means "uneasy" not "eager." You're eager to leave if you're happy to go. You're anxious about leaving if it makes you nervous.

blackmail means "to extort by threatening to reveal damaging information." It does not mean simply "coerce." One country cannot blackmail another with nuclear weapons when it only threatens to use them.

cohort means "a group who attends on someone." It does not mean a single accompanying person. When Prince William married Kate Middleton, she became his consort; his hangers-on are still his cohort.

comprise means "to include all parts in a single unit." It is not synonymous with *compose* or *constitute*. The alphabet is not comprised by its letters; it comprises them. Letters constitute the alphabet, which is thus constituted by them.

continuous means "without interruption." It is not synonymous with *continual*, which means an activity continued through time, with interruptions. If you continuously interrupt someone, that person will never say a word because your interruption will never stop. If you continually interrupt, you let the other person finish a sentence from time to time.

disinterested means "neutral." It does not mean "uninterested." A judge should be disinterested in the outcome of a case but not uninterested in it. (Incidentally, the original meaning of *disinterested* was "to be uninterested.")

enormity means "hugely bad." It does not mean "enormous." In private, a belch might be enormous, but at a state funeral, it would also be an enormity.

flaunt means "to display conspicuously." It is not synonymous with *flout*, which means "to scorn a rule or standard." If you choose to scorn this distinction, you would not flout your flaunting it but flaunt your flouting it.

fortuitous means "by chance." It does not mean "fortunate." You are fortunate when you fortuitously pick the right number in the lottery.

fulsome means "sickeningly excessive." It does not mean just "much." We all enjoy praise, except when it becomes fulsome.

notorious means "known for bad behavior." It does not mean "famous." Frank Sinatra was a famous singer but a notorious bully.

simplistic does not mean merely "simple." It means "overly simple" and is usually used in a pejorative sense. A simple solution to a problem is often best; a simplistic solution never is.

These days, many readers won't care about these distinctions, but some will. And they may be just those whose judgment carries weight when it matters most.

On the other hand, as an educated writer, you are expected to correctly distinguish *imply* and *infer, principal* and *principle, accept* and *except, capital* and *capitol, affect* and *effect, proceed* and *precede, discrete* and *discreet.* Most careful readers also notice when a Latinate or Greek plural noun is used as a singular, so you might want to keep these straight, too:

Singular	datum	criterion	medium	stratum	phenomenon
Plural	data	criteria	media	strata	phenomena

Here's the point: You can't predict good grammar or correct usage by logic or general rule. You have to learn the rules one-by-one and accept the fact that many of them are arbitrary and idiosyncratic.

PRONOUNS AND GENDER-NEUTRAL LANGUAGE

Pronouns and Their Referents

Just as we expect verbs to agree with their subjects, so we expect pronouns to agree with their antecedents. Not this:

> Early **efforts** to oppose surveillance of ordinary citizens failed because **it** ignored political issues. **No one** wanted to expose **themselves** to the charge of being unpatriotic.

But this:

> ✓ Early **efforts** to oppose surveillance of ordinary citizens failed because **they** ignored political issues. **No one** wanted to expose **himself** to the charge of being unpatriotic.

But making pronouns agree with their referents, you might have noticed, raises two problems.

First, do we use a singular or plural pronoun when referring to a noun that is singular in grammar but plural in meaning? Some writers use a singular verb and pronoun when the group acts as a single entity:

> ✓ The **committee** HAS met but has not yet made **its** decision.

But they use a plural verb and pronoun when its members act individually:

> ✓ The **faculty** HAVE the memo, but not all of **them** have read it.

These days plurals are irregularly used in both senses (but the plural is the rule in British English).

Second, what pronoun do we use to refer to singular common nouns that signal no gender, such as *teacher, doctor,* or *student,* or to pronouns that are singular in form but indeterminate or plural in meaning, such as *someone, anyone,* or *everyone?* We casually use *they:*

> Every **student** knows that to get good grades, **they** must take **their** classes seriously. If **someone** won't do **their** work, it is very hard for **them** to succeed.

In formal writing, though, most careful writers and readers still want a singular pronoun. The convention was once that a feminine third-person singular pronoun (*she, her, hers*) could be used only when its referent was unambiguously female and that the masculine pronoun (*he, him, his*) should be used in all other cases. But that rule leads to sentences that today seem socially and stylistically awkward:

> Every **student** knows that to get good grades, **he** must take **his** classes seriously. If **someone** won't do **his** work, it is very hard for **him** to succeed.

If, however, we reject the singular *they* because some (including me) consider it improper in formal writing, and we likewise reject *he* because some (also including me) regard it as biased, we are then confronted with a tricky problem of style. The thing to remember is that we have choices.

Gender-Neutral Options

We wouldn't have to face such conundrums if, like many other languages, English had a gender-neutral third-person singular pronoun. Luckily, English offers good options to careful writers who want to write in a gender-neutral fashion. Here are four, in detail.

1. **Replace the gendered pronoun with another pronoun or with a noun.** In English, only third-person singular pronouns are explicitly gendered, and you can often simply replace them.

Use both the masculine and feminine pronouns: You can replace a masculine pronoun with the masculine and feminine pronouns together.

A careful **writer** will always consider the needs of **his** readers.

✓ A careful **writer** will always consider the needs of **his or her** readers.

But this solution is not entirely inclusive, as some people identify as neither male nor female. And it can be cumbersome if a sentence contains several pronouns.

Substitute plurals for singulars: In English, plural pronouns are gender neutral and can refer to categories or classes.

A **writer** should use gender-neutral language if **he** wants **his** readers to see **him** as modern and progressive.

✓ **Writers** should use gender-neutral language if **they** want **their** readers to see **them** as modern and progressive.

But since we usually expect abstractions to be singular, using the plural can sometimes change the meaning.

Substitute the first-person plural pronoun: In English, first-person pronouns are gender-neutral, and we can use them in their plural form generically.

A **writer** should use gender-neutral language if **he** wants **his** readers to see **him** as modern and progressive.

✓ **We** should use gender-neutral language in **our** writing if **we** want **our** readers to see **us** as modern and progressive.

But *we* can be ambiguous, and in some contexts, it can sound too formal.

Substitute the indefinite pronoun "one": This pronoun is also gender neutral, so one may use it as well.

A **writer** should use gender-neutral language if **he** wants to seem modern and progressive.

✓ **One** should use gender-neutral language if **one** wants to seem modern and progressive.

But even more than *we*, *one* can sound stiff.

Repeat the noun: In English, nouns aren't gendered, so you can avoid pronouns by repeating those nouns.

If a **writer** wants to seem modern and progressive, **he** should use gender-neutral language.

✓ If a **writer** wants to seem modern and progressive, **the writer** should use gender-neutral language.

But repeating a noun, especially more than once, can sound stiff.

2. **Cut a gendered pronoun when that doesn't change the meaning.** You can sometimes replace a pronoun with another kind of word or cut it altogether.

Replace a possessive pronoun with an article or other determiner: If you want to use a singular count noun, you can replace a possessive pronoun with another DETERMINER (italicized) such as an article or quantifier.

A **writer** can impress *his* **reader** by using gender-neutral language.

✓ A **writer** can impress *a* **reader** by using gender-neutral language.

✓ A **writer** can impress *each* **reader** by using gender-neutral language.

Cut the pronoun: If you use a plural noun, you can sometimes simply cut a redundant POSSESSIVE.

✓ A **writer** can impress **readers** by using gender-neutral language.

But not all possessives are redundant. Compare these:

A passionate **writer** treasures **his books**.

✓ A passionate **writer** treasures **books**.

3. *Avoid a gendered pronoun by choosing a different grammatical construction.* If you can't replace or cut a gendered pronoun, you will have to make a more ambitious revision. In particular, look for opportunities to eliminate a gendered pronoun that is the subject of a subordinate or MAIN CLAUSE, as in these next sentences (pronouns and referents boldfaced, subordinate clauses italicized):

A **writer** should use gender-neutral language *if* **he** *wants to seem modern and progressive.*

If a **writer** *wants to seem modern and progressive,* **he** should use gender-neutral language.

But be careful with these next options, because when you eliminate subjects of sentences and clauses, you risk cutting "doers" or characters and making your writing unclear (see Lessons 3 and 4).

Rephrase using a relative clause: You can replace a subordinate clause with a RELATIVE CLAUSE (underlined) introduced by *who*, *whom*, or *whose*.

✓ A **writer** who wants to seem modern and progressive should use gender-neutral language.

Rephrase using a gerund or nominalization: You can use a GERUND (a word of the form verb+*ing* that acts as a noun) or NOMINALIZATION (a verb turned into a noun) to avoid repeating a "doer" or to cut it entirely (main subject underlined, gerund and nominalization italicized).

✓ *Using* gender-neutral language makes a **writer** seem modern and progressive.

✓ The *use* of gender-neutral language makes a **writer** seem modern and progressive.

Rephrase using the passive voice: You can also switch from the ACTIVE to the PASSIVE voice (passive verb capitalized).

✓ Gender-neutral language should BE USED if a **writer** wants to seem modern and progressive.

Rephrase using an infinitive phrase: You can use an infinitive phrase (underlined).

✓ To seem modern and progressive, a **writer** should use gender-neutral language.

But watch out for DANGLING MODIFIERS (see p. 155). In that last sentence, the modifier doesn't dangle, because the infinitive phrase modifies *writer*, the subject of the main clause. In this one, it does:

> To seem modern and progressive, gender-neutral language should be used.

It is the *writer* (not *gender-neutral language*) who wants to seem modern and progressive.

4. **Alternate between masculine and feminine pronouns.** Finally, you can alternate between *he* and *she*, as I have in this book. Some readers find this solution stylistically intrusive, but it is an option that is becoming increasingly popular.

The Future

Some argue that we should tackle the problem head-on and just invent an inclusive third-person singular pronoun. Such attempts at linguistic engineering, however, are rarely successful, especially when they concern the basic structures of a language. But if engineering won't work, evolution eventually will. The one constant with language is that it changes to meet its users' needs, and I suspect that in time we will come to accept *they* as an inclusive third-person singular pronoun. The fact is, eminent writers have used *they* in this way since at least the fourteenth century. But whatever the past and whatever the future, we have choices now, and that's what matters most.

SUMMING UP

We must write correctly, but if in defining correctness we ignore the difference between fact and folklore, we risk overlooking what is really important—the choices that make our writing dense and wordy or clear and concise. We are not precise merely because we get right *which* and *that* and avoid *finalize* and *hopefully*. Many who obsess over such details are oblivious to this more serious kind of problem:

> Too precise a specification of information processing requirements incurs the risk of overestimation resulting in unused capacity or inefficient use of costly resources or of underestimation leading to ineffectiveness or other inefficiencies.

That means:

> ✓ When you specify too precisely the resources you need to process information, you may overestimate. If you do, you risk having more capacity than you need or using costly resources inefficiently.

Both sentences are grammatically correct, but who would choose the first over the second?

I suspect that those who observe all the rules all the time do so not because they want to protect the integrity of the language but because they want to assert a style of their own. Some of us are straightforward and plain speaking; others take pleasure in a bit of formality, in a touch of fastidiously self-conscious "class." We should not scorn this impulse, so long as it is not a pretext for social discrimination and so long as it remains subordinated to the more important matters to which we now turn: the choices that define not "good grammar" but clarity and grace.

PART TWO

Clarity

*Everything that can be thought at all
can be thought clearly.
Everything that can be said can be said clearly.*
—LUDWIG WITTGENSTEIN

*It takes less time to learn to write nobly than to
learn to write lightly and straightforwardly.*
—FRIEDRICH NIETZSCHE

Lesson

3

Actions

Suit the action to the word, the word to the action.
—WILLIAM SHAKESPEARE, *HAMLET*, 3.2

I am unlikely to trust a sentence that comes easily.
—WILLIAM GASS

UNDERSTANDING JUDGMENTS

We have words enough to praise writing we like—*clear, direct, concise*—and more than enough to abuse writing we don't: *unclear, indirect, abstract, dense, complex.* We can use those words to distinguish these two sentences:

> 1a. The cause of our schools' failure at teaching basic skills is not understanding the influence of cultural background on learning.

> 1b. Our schools have failed to teach basic skills because they do not understand how cultural background influences the way a child learns.

Most of us would call (1a) too complex, (1b) clearer and more direct. But those words don't refer to anything *in* those sentences; they describe how those sentences make us *feel.* When we say that (1a) is unclear, we mean that *we* have a hard time understanding it; we say it's dense when *we* struggle to read it.

The problem is to understand what is in those two sentences that makes readers feel as they do. Only then can you rise above your too-good understanding of your own writing to know when your readers will think it needs revising. To do that, you have to know what counts as a well-told story. (To profit from this lesson and the next three, you must be able to identify verbs, SIMPLE SUB-JECTS, and WHOLE SUBJECTS. See the Glossary.)

TELLING STORIES: CHARACTERS AND ACTIONS

This story has a problem:

> 2a. Once upon a time, as a walk through the woods was taking place on the part of Little Red Riding Hood, the Wolf's jump out from behind a tree occurred, causing her fright.

We prefer something closer to this:

> ✓ 2b. Once upon a time, Little Red Riding Hood was walking through the woods, when the Wolf jumped out from behind a tree and frightened her.

Most readers think (2b) tells the story more clearly than (2a) because it follows two principles:

- The main characters are subjects of verbs.
- Those verbs express specific actions.

Principle of Clarity 1: Make Main Characters Subjects

Look at the subjects in (2a). The simple subjects (underlined) are *not* the main characters (italicized):

> 2a. Once upon a time, as a <u>walk</u> through the woods was taking place on the part of *Little Red Riding Hood*, the *Wolf's* <u>jump</u> out from behind a tree occurred, causing *her* fright.

Those subjects name not characters but actions expressed in abstract nouns, *walk* and *jump:*

SUBJECT	VERB
a <u>walk</u> through the woods	was taking place
the *Wolf's* <u>jump</u> out from behind a tree	occurred

The whole subject of *occurred* does have a character in it: the possessive noun *Wolf's jump*. But the Wolf is not *the* subject. It is only attached to the simple subject *jump*.

Contrast those abstract subjects with these, where the characters (italicized) are also the simple subjects (underlined):

✓ 2b. Once upon a time, <u>*Little Red Riding Hood*</u> was walking through the woods, when the <u>*Wolf*</u> jumped out from behind a tree and frightened *her.*

The subjects and the main characters are now the same words:

SUBJECT/CHARACTER	VERB
Little Red Riding Hood	was walking
Wolf	jumped

Principle of Clarity 2: Make Important Actions Verbs

Now look at how the actions and verbs differ in (2a): the characters' actions are expressed not in verbs but in abstract nouns (actions are boldfaced; verbs are capitalized):

2a. Once upon a time, as a **walk** through the woods WAS TAKING place on the part of Little Red Riding Hood, the Wolf's **jump** out from behind a tree OCCURRED, causing her **fright.**

Note how vague the verbs are: *was taking, occurred.* The story isn't about *taking* and *occurring* but about *walking* and *jumping* and *frightening.* In (2b), the clearer sentence, the verbs name these important story actions:

✓ 2b. Once upon a time, Little Red Riding Hood WAS WALKING through the woods, when the Wolf JUMPED out from behind a tree and FRIGHTENED her.

> *Here's the point:* In (2a), the sentence that seems wordy and indirect, the two main characters, Little Red Riding Hood and the Wolf, are *not* subjects, and their actions—walking, jumping, and frightening—are *not* verbs. In (2b), the more direct sentence, those two main characters *are* subjects and their main actions *are* verbs. That's why we prefer (2b).

FAIRY TALES AND "SERIOUS" WRITING

Writing in college or on the job may seem distant from fairy tales like "Little Red Riding Hood." But it's not, because in every kind of writing, most sentences still tell stories. That is, they are still about characters doing things. Compare these two:

> 3a. The Federalists' argument in regard to the destabilization of government by popular democracy was based on their belief in the tendency of factions to further their self-interest at the expense of the common good.

> ✓ 3b. The Federalists argued that popular democracy destabilized government, because they believed that factions tended to further their self-interest at the expense of the common good.

We can analyze those sentences as we did the ones about Little Red Riding Hood.

Sentence (3a) feels dense for two reasons. First, its characters are not subjects. Its simple subject (underlined) is *argument*, but the characters (italicized) are *Federalists, popular democracy, government*, and *factions:*

> 3a. The *Federalists'* <u>argument</u> in regard to the destabilization of *government* by *popular democracy* was based on *their* belief in the tendency of *factions* to further *their* self-interest at the expense of the common good.

Second, the important actions (boldfaced) are not verbs (capitalized) but abstract nouns:

> 3a. The Federalists' **argument** in regard to the **destabilization** of government by popular democracy WAS BASED on their **belief** in the **tendency** of factions to FURTHER their self-interest at the expense of the common good.

Notice how long and complex is the whole subject of (3a) and how little meaning is expressed by its main verb *was based:*

WHOLE SUBJECT	VERB
The Federalists' argument in regard to the destabilization of government by popular democracy	was based

Readers think (3b) is clearer for two reasons: most of the characters (italicized) are subjects (underlined), and the actions (boldfaced) are verbs (capitalized):

> ✓ 3b. The <u>*Federalists*</u> ARGUED that <u>*popular democracy*</u> DESTABILIZED government, because <u>*they*</u> BELIEVED that <u>*factions*</u> TENDED TO FURTHER *their* self-interest at the expense of the common good.

Note as well that when we make a character the simple subject, the whole subject (*The Federalists*) also becomes short and concrete.

In the rest of this lesson, we look at verbs and actions; in the next, at subjects and characters.

Verbs and Actions

Our principle is this: a sentence seems clear when its important actions are in verbs. Look at how sentences (4a) and (4b) express their actions. In (4a), most of the actions (boldfaced) are not verbs (capitalized); they are nouns:

> 4a. Our **lack** of data PREVENTED **evaluation** of UN **actions** in **targeting** funds to areas most in **need** of **assistance**.

In (4b), on the other hand, the actions are almost all verbs:

> ✓ 4b. Because we LACKED data, we could not EVALUATE whether the UN HAD TARGETED funds to areas that most NEEDED **assistance**.

Readers will think your writing is dense if you use lots of abstract nouns, especially those derived from verbs and ADJECTIVES, nouns ending in *-tion, -ment, -ence*, and so on, and especially when you make those abstract nouns the subjects of verbs.

A noun derived from a verb or adjective has a technical name: nominalization. The word illustrates its meaning: when we nominalize *nominalize*, we create the nominalization *nominalization*. Here are a few examples:

VERB	→	NOMINALIZATION	ADJECTIVE	→	NOMINALIZATION
discover	→	discovery	careless	→	carelessness
resist	→	resistance	different	→	difference
react	→	reaction	proficient	→	proficiency

We can also nominalize a verb by adding *-ing* (making it a gerund):

> She flies → her flying   We sang → our singing

Some nominalizations and verbs are identical:

> hope → hope   result → result   repair → repair

> We REQUEST that you REVIEW the data.

> Our **request** IS that you DO a **review** of the data.

(Some actions also hide out in adjectives: *It is applicable → it applies.* Some others: *indicative, dubious, argumentative, deserving.*)

No element of style more characterizes writing that feels dense, abstract, indirect, and difficult than lots of nominalizations, especially as the subjects of verbs.

Here's the point: In grade school, we learned that subjects *are* characters (or "doers") and that verbs *are* actions. That's often true:

subject	verb	object
We	discussed	the problem.
doer	action	

But it is not true for this almost synonymous sentence:

subject	verb		
The problem	was	the topic	of our discussion.
		doer	action

We can move characters and actions around in a sentence, and subjects and verbs don't have to name any particular kind of thing at all. But when you match characters to subjects and actions to verbs in most of your sentences, readers are likely to think your prose is clear, direct, and readable.

Exercise 3.1

If you aren't sure whether you can distinguish verbs, adjectives, and nominalizations, practice on the list below. Turn verbs and adjectives into nominalizations, and nominalizations into adjectives and verbs. Remember that some verbs and nominalizations have the same form:

Heavy rains CAUSE flooding.

Heavy rains ARE a **cause** of flooding.

analysis	believe	attempt	conclusion	evaluate
suggest	approach	comparison	define	discuss
expression	failure	intelligent	thorough	appearance
decrease	improve	increase	accuracy	careful
emphasize	explanation	description	clear	examine

Exercise 3.2

Identify the subject, character, verb, and action in these pairs of sentences. The unclear sentence is first; the improved sentence follows. What do you notice about how characters and subjects, and actions and verbs, are aligned in each?

1a. There is opposition among many voters to nuclear power plants based on a belief in their threat to human health.

1b. Many voters oppose nuclear power plants because they believe that such plants threaten human health.

2a. Growth in the market for electronic books is driven by the frequent preference among customers for their convenience and portability.

2b. The market for electronic books has grown because customers frequently prefer their convenience and portability.

3a. There is a belief among some researchers that consumers' choices in fast food restaurants are healthier because there are postings of nutrition information in menus.

3b. Some researchers believe that consumers are choosing healthier foods because fast food restaurants are posting nutrition information in their menus.

4a. The design of the new roller coaster was more of a struggle for the engineers than had been their expectation.

4b. The engineers struggled more than they expected when designing the new roller coaster.

5a. Because the student's preparation for the exam was thorough, none of the questions on it were a surprise.

5b. Because the student prepared thoroughly for the exam, she was not surprised by any of the questions on it.

Exercise 3.3

Create three sentences using verbs and adjectives from Exercise 3.1. Then rewrite them using the corresponding nominalizations (keep the meaning the same). For example, using *suggest, discuss*, and *careful*, write:

I SUGGEST that we DISCUSS the issue CAREFULLY.

Then rewrite that sentence into its nominalized form:

My **suggestion** is that our **discussion** of the issue be done with **care**.

Only when you see how a clear sentence can be made unclear will you understand why it seemed clear in the first place.

The Problem of Familiarity

Writers tend to write badly when they are unsure about what they want to say or how to say it. But they also tend to write badly because they are too familiar with their own writing to accurately judge how readers will respond to it.

You've probably had this experience: you think you've written something good, but your reader thinks otherwise. You wonder whether that person is just being difficult, but you bite your tongue and try to fix it, even though you think it should already be clear to anyone who can read Dr. Seuss. When that happens to me (regularly, I might add), I almost always realize—eventually—that my readers are right, that they see where my writing needs work better than I do.

Why are we so often right about the writing of others and so often wrong about our own? It is because we all read into our own writing what we want readers to get out of it. That explains why two readers can disagree about the clarity of the same piece of writing: the reader who is most familiar with its content will likely find it clearest. Both are right, because clarity is not a property of sentences but an impression of readers. It is in the eye of the beholder.

That is why we need to look at our own writing in a way that is almost mechanical, that sidesteps our too-good understanding of it. The quickest way is to follow the procedure below.

How to Revise: Characters and Actions

You can use the two principles of clarity (make main characters subjects; make important actions verbs) to explain why your readers judge your prose as they do. But more important, you can also use them to identify and revise sentences that seem clear to you but will not to your readers. Revision is a three-step process: analyze, assess, rewrite.

1. **Analyze**

    a. Ignoring short (four- or five-word) introductory phrases, underline the first seven or eight words in each sentence.

    > The automation of manufacturing, assembly, and shipping processes by corporations means the loss of jobs for many blue-collar workers.

    b. Then ask two questions:

    - Did you underline any abstract nouns as simple subjects?

The **automation** of manufacturing, assembly, and shipping processes by corporations means the loss of jobs for many blue-collar workers.

- Did you underline seven or eight words before getting to a verb?

The automation of manufacturing, assembly, and shipping processes by corporations (10 words) **means** the loss of jobs for many blue-collar workers.

If you answer *yes* to either, you should probably revise.

2. **Assess**

  a. Decide who or what your main characters are (more about this in the next lesson).

The automation of manufacturing, assembly, and shipping processes by **corporations** means the loss of jobs for many **blue-collar workers.**

  b. Then look for the actions that those characters perform, especially actions hidden in nominalizations, those abstract nouns derived from verbs.

The **automation** of manufacturing, assembly, and shipping processes by corporations means the **loss** of jobs for many blue-collar workers.

3. **Rewrite**

  a. If the actions are nominalizations, make them verbs.

automation → automate   loss → lose

  b. Make the characters the subjects of those verbs.

corporations automate   blue-collar workers lose

  c. Rewrite the sentence with characters as subjects and actions as verbs, using subordinating conjunctions such as *because, if, when, although, why, how, whether,* or *that* to show relationships among ideas.

  ✓ Many blue-collar workers are losing their jobs **because** corporations are automating their manufacturing, assembly, and shipping processes.

SOME COMMON PATTERNS

You can quickly spot and revise five common patterns of nominalizations.

1. **The nominalization is the subject of an empty verb such as *be, seems, has,* etc.:**

    The **intention** of the committee IS to audit the records.

    a. Change the nominalization to a verb:

    intention → intend

    b. Find a character that would be the subject of that verb:

    The intention of the *committee* is to audit the records.

    c. Make that character the subject of the new verb:

    ✓ The *committee* INTENDS to audit the records.

2. **The nominalization follows an empty verb:**

    The *agency* CONDUCTED an **investigation** into the matter.

    a. Change the nominalization to a verb:

    investigation → investigate

    b. Replace the empty verb with the new verb:

    conducted → investigated

    ✓ The *agency* INVESTIGATED the matter.

3. **One nominalization is the subject of an empty verb and a second nominalization follows it:**

    Our **loss** in sales WAS a result of their **expansion** of outlets.

    a. Revise the nominalizations into verbs:

    loss → lose   expansion → expand

    b. Identify the characters that would be the subjects of those verbs:

    Our **loss** in sales was a result of *their* **expansion** of outlets.

    c. Make those characters subjects of those verbs:

    we lose   they expand

    d. Link the new clauses with a logical connection:
    - To express simple cause: *because, since, when*
    - To express conditional cause: *if, provided that, so long as*
    - To contradict expected causes: *though, although, unless*

Our **loss** in sales	→	*We* **LOST** sales
was the result of	→	because
their **expansion** of outlets	→	*they* **EXPANDED** outlets

4. A nominalization follows *there is* or *there are:*

There IS no **need** for our further **study** of this problem.

a. Change the nominalization to a verb:

need → need   study → study

b. Identify the character that should be the subject of the verb:

There is no **need** for *our* further **study** of this problem.

c. Make that character the subject of the verb:

no need → we need not   our study → we study

✓ *We* **NEED** not **STUDY** this problem further.

5. Two or three nominalizations in a row are joined by prepositions:

We did a **review** of the **evolution** of the brain.

a. Turn the first nominalization into a verb:

review → review

b. Either leave the second nominalization as it is, or turn it into a verb in a clause beginning with *how* or *why:*

evolution of the brain → how the brain evolved

✓ First, *we* **REVIEWED** the **evolution** of the *brain*.

✓ First, *we* **REVIEWED** how the *brain* EVOLVED.

QUICK TIP   When you revise a complicated sentence, you will have more than one character-action clause. Decide how the clauses fit together, then try out these patterns: *X because Y; Since X, Y; If X, then Y; Although X, Y; X and/but/ so Y.*

Some Happy Consequences

When you consistently rely on verbs to express important actions, your readers benefit in many ways:

1. Your sentences are more concrete. Compare:

   There WAS an affirmative **decision** for **expansion**.

   ✓ *The director* DECIDED to EXPAND the program.

2. Your sentences are more concise. When you use nominalizations, you have to add articles like *a* and *the* and prepositions such as *of, by,* and *in.* You don't need them when you use verbs and conjunctions:

   A **revision** *of* the program WILL RESULT *in* **increases** *in* our **efficiency** *in the* **servicing** *of* clients.

   ✓ *If* we REVISE the program, we CAN SERVE clients more EFFICIENTLY.

3. The logic of your sentences is clearer. When you nominalize verbs, you link actions with fuzzy prepositions and phrases such as *of, by,* and *on the part of.* But when you use verbs, you link clauses with precise subordinating conjunctions such as *because, although,* and *if:*

   Our more effective presentation of our study resulted in our success, despite an earlier start by others.

   ✓ **Although** others started earlier, we succeeded **because** we presented our study more effectively.

4. Your sentences tell more coherent stories. Nominalizations let you distort the sequence of actions. (The numbers refer to the real sequence of events.)

   Decisions[4] in regard to administration[5] of medication despite inability[2] of irrational patients appearing[1] in a Trauma Center to provide legal consent[3] rest with the attending physician alone.

   ✓ When patients appear[1] in a Trauma Center and behave[2] so irrationally that they cannot legally consent[3] to treatment, only the attending physician can decide[4] whether to medicate[5] them.

Exercise 3.4

One sentence in each of these pairs is clear, expressing characters as subjects and actions as verbs; the other is less clear, with actions in nominalizations and characters often not in subjects. First, decide which is which. Then underline subjects, bracket verbs, box actions, and circle characters. What do you notice about where these words appear in the sentences?

1a. Some people argue that atmospheric carbon dioxide does not elevate global temperature.

1b. There has been speculation by educators about the role of the family in improving educational achievement.

2a. The store's price increases led to frustration among its customers.

2b. When we write concisely, readers understand easily.

3a. Researchers have identified the AIDS virus but have failed to develop a vaccine to immunize those at risk.

3b. Attempts by economists at defining full employment have been met with failure.

4a. Complaints by editorial writers about voter apathy rarely offer suggestions about dispelling it.

4b. Although critics claim that children who watch a lot of television tend to become less able readers, no one has demonstrated that to be true.

5a. The loss of market share to Japan by domestic automakers resulted in the disappearance of hundreds of thousands of jobs.

5b. When educators embrace new-media technology, our schools will teach complex subjects more effectively.

6a. We need to know which parts of our national forests are being logged most extensively so that we can save virgin stands at greatest risk.

6b. There is a need for an analysis of library use to provide a reliable base for the projection of needed resources.

Exercise 3.5

Now revise the nominalized sentences in Exercise 3.4 into sentences in which the actions are verbs. Use its paired verbal version as a model. For example, if the verbal sentence begins with *when*, begin your revision with *when:*

Sentence to revise: 2a. The store's price **increases** led to **frustration** among its customers.

Model: 2b. When we WRITE concisely, readers UNDERSTAND more easily.

Your revision: 2a. When the store INCREASED prices, . . .

Exercise 3.6

Revise these next sentences so that the nominalizations are verbs and characters are their subjects. In (1) through (4), characters are italicized and nominalizations are boldfaced.

1. *Lincoln's* **hope** was for the **preservation** of the Union without war, but the *South's* **attack** on Fort Sumter made war an **inevitability**.

2. Attempts were made on the part of the *president's aides* to assert *his* **immunity** from a *congressional* subpoena.

3. There were **predictions** by *business executives* that the **economy** would experience a quick **revival**.

4. Your **analysis** of *my* report omits any data in **support** of *your* **criticism** of *my* **findings**.

In sentences 5 through 8, the characters are italicized; find the actions and revise.

5. Attempts at explaining increases in *voter* participation in this year's elections were made by *several candidates*.

6. The agreement by the *class* on the reading list was based on the assumption that there would be tests on only certain selections.

7. There was no independent *business-sector* study of the cause of the sudden increase in the trade surplus.

8. An understanding as to the need for controls over drinking on campus was recognized by *fraternities*.

A QUALIFICATION: USEFUL NOMINALIZATIONS

I have so relentlessly urged you to turn nominalizations into verbs that you might think you should never use them. But in fact, you can't write well without them. The trick is to know which to keep and which to revise. Keep these:

1. **A nominalization that is a short subject that refers to a previous sentence:**

   ✓ **These arguments** all depend on a single unproven claim.

   ✓ **This decision** can lead to positive outcomes.

Those nominalizations link one sentence to another in a cohesive flow, an issue I'll discuss in more detail in Lesson 5.

2. **A short nominalization that replaces an awkward** *The fact that:*

> The fact that she ADMITTED guilt impressed me.

> ✓ Her **admission** of guilt impressed me.

> But then, why not this?

> ✓ She IMPRESSED me when she ADMITTED her guilt.

3. **A nominalization that names what would be the object of the verb:**

> I accepted what she REQUESTED [that is, *She requested **something***].

> ✓ I accepted her **request.**

Familiar nominalizations such as *request* feel more concrete than abstract ones. But when you can, you should still express actions as verbs:

> Her **request** for **assistance** CAME after the deadline.

> ✓ She REQUESTED **assistance** after the deadline.

4. **A nominalization that refers to a concept so familiar to your readers that to them, it is a virtual character (more about this in the next lesson):**

> ✓ Few problems have so divided us as **abortion** on **demand.**

> ✓ The Equal Rights **Amendment** was an issue in past **elections.**

> ✓ **Taxation** without **representation** did not spark the American **Revolution.**

Those nominalizations name familiar concepts: *abortion* on *demand, amendment, election, taxation, representation, revolution.* You must develop an eye for distinguishing nominalizations expressing common ideas from those you can revise into verbs:

> There is a **demand** for a **repeal** of the **inheritance** tax.

> ✓ We DEMAND that Congress REPEAL the **inheritance** tax.

CLARITY, NOT SIMPLEMINDEDNESS

Your readers want you to write clearly, even simply—but not simplistically (see p. 21). Some argue that all sentences should be short, no more than fifteen words or so. But many mature ideas cannot be expressed so compactly. In Lessons 10 and 11 we look at ways to write longer sentences that communicate complex ideas but are still readable.

IN YOUR OWN WORDS

Exercise 3.7

Go through a page of your own writing. Underline whole subjects and bracket verbs. Now, think about the story you are telling. Circle the main characters and box their actions, wherever they appear. Look especially for actions hidden in nominalizations. What do you notice? How clear will a reader likely find your writing? If necessary, revise to align characters with subjects and specific actions with verbs.

Exercise 3.8

Writers tend to think their writing is clearer than their readers do. Select a page of your writing and share it with a reader. Both of you rate its clarity on a scale of 1–10, with 10 being perfectly clear and 1 being incomprehensible. Use the procedures for analyzing sentences on pages 35–36 to explain any differences in your ratings. Revise your writing if necessary.

SUMMING UP

The two most general principles for clear sentences are these: make main characters the subjects of your verbs; make those characters' important actions your verbs.

We can represent these principles graphically. Readers must mentally integrate two levels of sentence structure. One, the grammatical level, is the relatively fixed sequence of subject and verb (the empty box is for everything that follows the verb):

| Fixed Positions | Subject | Verb | _____ | Grammar Level |

The other, the story level, is based on characters and their actions and has no fixed order. Characters and actions can appear anywhere in a sentence, because writers can move them around.

But readers prefer them to align with subjects and verbs. We can represent this preference graphically:

Fixed Positions	Subject	Verb	_____	Grammar Level
Movable Elements	Character	Action	_____	Story Level

Keep in mind that readers want to see characters not just *in* a subject, but *as* the subject. Not this:

> The *president's* veto of the bill INFURIATED Congress.
>
> The veto of the bill by the *president* INFURIATED Congress.

But this:

> ✓ When the *president* VETOED the bill, *he* INFURIATED Congress.

When you frustrate those expectations, you make readers work harder than necessary. So keep these principles in mind as you revise:

1. Express actions in verbs:

   > The **intention** of the committee is to improve morale.
   >
   > ✓ The committee **INTENDS** to improve morale.

2. Make the subjects of those verbs the characters associated with those actions:

   > A decision by the *dean* in regard to the funding of the program by the *department* is necessary for adequate *staff* preparation.
   >
   > ✓ The *staff* CAN PREPARE adequately, only after the *dean* DECIDES whether the *department* WILL FUND the program.

3. Don't revise nominalizations when:

   a. they refer to a previous sentence:

      > ✓ **These arguments** all depend on a single unproven claim.

   b. they replace an awkward *the fact that:*

      > **The fact that she strenuously objected** impressed me.
      >
      > ✓ **Her strenuous objections** impressed me.

c. they name what would be the object of a verb:

> I do not know **what she INTENDS.**
> ✓ I do not know **her intentions.**

d. they name a concept so familiar to your readers that it is a virtual character:

> ✓ Few issues have so divided us as **abortion** on **demand.**
> ✓ The Equal Rights **Amendment** was an issue in past **elections.**

Lesson

4

Characters

*Whatever is translatable in other and simpler words of the same
language, without loss of sense or dignity, is bad.*
—SAMUEL TAYLOR COLERIDGE

When character is lost, all is lost.
—ANONYMOUS

UNDERSTANDING CHARACTERS

Readers think sentences are clear and direct when they see key
actions in their verbs. Compare (1a) with (1b):

> 1a. The EPA feared the president would recommend to Congress that
> it reduce its budget.

> 1b. The EPA had fears that the president would send a recommenda-
> tion to Congress that it make a reduction in its budget.

Most readers think (1b) is a bit less clear than (1a), but not much.
Now compare (1b) to (1c):

> 1c. The fear of the EPA was that a recommendation from the presi-
> dent to Congress would be for a reduction in its budget.

Most readers think that (1c) is much less clear than either (1a)
or (1b).

The reason is this: In both (1a) and (1b), the important characters (italicized) are subjects (underlined) of verbs (capitalized):

1a. The _EPA_ FEARED the _president_ WOULD RECOMMEND to _Congress_ that it REDUCE its budget.

1b. The _EPA_ HAD fears that the _president_ WOULD SEND a recommendation to _Congress_ that _it_ MAKE a reduction in its budget.

But in (1c) the two simple subjects (underlined) are not concrete characters but abstractions (boldfaced):

1c. The **fear** of the _EPA_ WAS that a **recommendation** from the _president_ to _Congress_ WOULD BE for a **reduction** in its budget.

The different verbs in (1a) and (1b) matter somewhat, but the abstract subjects in (1c) matter more. Even worse, characters can be deleted entirely, like this:

1d. There WAS **fear** that there WOULD BE a **recommendation** for a budget **reduction**.

Who fears? Who recommends? The sentence's context may help readers guess correctly, but if the context is ambiguous, you risk them guessing wrongly.

> _Here's the point:_ Readers want actions in verbs, but they want characters as subjects even more. We create a problem for readers when for no good reason we fail to name characters in subjects or, worse, delete them entirely. It is important to express actions in verbs, but the _first_ principle of a clear style is this: make the subjects of most of your verbs the main characters in your story.

HOW TO REVISE: CHARACTERS AND ACTIONS (AGAIN)

To get characters into subjects, you have to know three things:

1. when your subjects are not characters
2. if they aren't, where you should look for characters
3. what you should do when you find them (or don't)

The Basic Procedure

This sentence feels indirect and impersonal:

> Governmental intervention in fast-changing technologies has led to the distortion of market evolution and interference in new product development.

We can analyze and revise it according to our procedure from Lesson 3:

1. **Underline the first seven or eight words:**

   <u>Governmental intervention in fast-changing technologies has</u> led to the distortion of market evolution and interference in new product development.

   In those first words, readers want to see characters not just *in* the whole subjects of verbs, as *government* is implied in *governmental*, but *as* their simple subjects. Here they aren't.

2. **Find the main characters.** They may be possessive nouns or pronouns attached to nominalizations, objects of prepositions (particularly *by* and *of*), or only implied. In that sentence, one main character is in the adjective *governmental;* the other, *market*, is in the object of a preposition: *of market evolution.*

3. **Skim the passage for actions involving those characters, particularly actions buried in nominalizations.** Ask *Who is doing what?*

governmental **intervention**	→ ✓ *government* **intervenes**
distortion	→ ✓ *[government]* **distorts**
market **evolution**	→ ✓ *markets* **evolve**
interference	→ ✓ *[government]* **interferes**
development	→ ✓ *[markets]* **develop**

   To revise, reassemble those new subjects and verbs into a sentence, using conjunctions such as *if, although, because, when, how*, and *why:*

   ✓ When a *government* **INTERVENES** in fast-changing technologies, *it* **DISTORTS** how *markets* **EVOLVE** and **INTERFERES** with their ability to **DEVELOP** new products.

   Be aware that just as actions can be in adjectives (*reliable* → *rely*), so can characters:

   Medieval *theological* debates often addressed issues considered trivial by modern *philosophical* thought.

   When you find a character implied in an adjective, revise in the same way:

   ✓ *Medieval theologians* often debated issues that *modern philosophers* consider trivial.

Here's the point: The first step in analyzing a dense style is to look at subjects. If you do not see main characters as simple subjects, you have to look for them. They can be in objects of prepositions, in possessive pronouns, or in adjectives. Once you find them, look for actions they are involved in. When you are revising, make those characters the subjects of verbs naming those actions. When you are reading a dense passage, try to find characters and their actions, and retell the story to yourself.

RECONSTRUCTING ABSENT CHARACTERS

Readers have the biggest problem with sentences devoid of *all* characters:

> A decision was made in favor of doing a study of the disagreements.

That sentence could mean either of these, and more:

> We decided that I should study why they disagreed.
>
> I decided that you should study why he disagreed.

The writer may know who is doing what, and readers may be able to guess from context. But often they can't and will need help.

Sometimes we omit characters to make a general statement:

> Research strategies that look for more than one variable are of more use in understanding factors in psychiatric disorder than strategies based on the assumption that the presence of psychopathology is dependent on a single gene or on strategies in which only one biological variable is studied.

But when we try to revise that into something clearer, we have to invent characters and then decide what to call them. Do we use *one, we* or *you?* Do we name a generic "doer"?

> ✓ If *one/we/you/researchers* are to understand what causes psychiatric disorder, *one/we/you/they* should use research strategies that look for more than one variable rather than assume that a single gene is responsible for a psychopathology or adopt a strategy in which *one/we/you/they* study only one biological variable.

To most of us, *one* feels stiff, but *we* may be ambiguous because it can refer just to the writer, or to the writer and others but not the reader, or to the reader and writer but not others, or to everyone.

And if you are not directly addressing your reader, *you* is usually inappropriate.

But if you avoid both nominalizations and vague pronouns, you can slide into passive verbs (I'll discuss them in a moment):

> To understand what makes patients vulnerable to psychiatric disorders, strategies that look for more than one variable SHOULD BE USED rather than strategies in which a gene IS ASSUMED to cause psychopathology or only one biological variable IS STUDIED.

To reconstruct missing characters, you have to use your judgment. In general, choose the most specific characters you can find.

QUICK TIP   When you are explaining a complicated issue to someone involved in it, imagine sitting across the table from that person, saying *you* as often as you can:

> Taxable intangible property includes financial notes and municipal bonds. A one-time tax of 2% on its value applies to this property.

> ✓ **You** have to pay tax on **your** intangible property, including **your** financial notes and municipal bonds. On this property, **you** pay a one-time tax of 2%.

If *you* is not appropriate, change it to a character that is:

> **Taxpayers** have to pay tax on their intangible property, including **their** financial notes and municipal bonds. **They** pay . . .

ABSTRACTIONS AS CHARACTERS

So far, I've discussed characters as if they must be flesh-and-blood people. But inanimate things and even abstractions can serve as characters, so long as you make them the subjects of a series of sentences that tell a story. For instance, we might have solved the problem of the previous example by choosing *studies* as our character:

> ✓ To understand what causes psychiatric disorders, *studies* should look for more than one variable rather than adopt a strategy in which *they* test only one biological variable or assume that a single gene is responsible for a psychopathology.

Now the sentence is clear but also appropriately professional.

You can also tell stories whose main characters are abstractions, even nominalizations, so long as you make them subjects of a series of sentences and clauses. Here's a story about *freedom of speech*, a familiar abstraction made up of two nominalizations (subjects are underlined; verbs are capitalized):

> <u>No human right</u> is more basic than *freedom of speech*, <u>which</u> ENSURES individual expression and GUARANTEES the open flow of ideas in society. <u>It</u> AROSE as a pillar of modern political thought during the late eighteenth century, and in 1948, <u>it</u> WAS RECOGNIZED by the United Nations as a universal right. <u>It</u> protects not only unpopular political views but also other forms of controversial expression, including artistic expression. Nevertheless, <u>*freedom of speech*</u> IS not absolute: <u>it</u> IS BOUNDED by other rights and principles, including. . . .

Like *studies* in the last example, *freedom of speech* becomes a character because it (or an associated pronoun like *which* or *it*) appears as the subject of verbs that state specific actions: *ensures, guarantees, arose,* and so on. In this case, two passive verbs, *was recognized* and *is bounded,* keep the phrase in the subject position.

But when you use abstractions as characters, you can create a problem. A story about an abstraction as familiar as *freedom of speech* is clear enough, but if you surround an unfamiliar abstract character with a lot of other abstractions, readers may feel that your writing is unnecessarily dense.

For example, few of us are familiar with the terms *prospective intention* and *immediate intention,* so most of us are likely to struggle with a story about them, especially when they are surrounded by other abstractions (actions are boldfaced; human characters are italicized):

> The **argument** is this. The cognitive component of **intention** exhibits a high degree of **complexity**. **Intention** is temporally divisible into two: prospective **intention** and immediate **intention**. The cognitive function of prospective **intention** is the **representation** of a *subject's* similar past **actions**, *his* current situation, and *his* course of future **actions**. That is, the cognitive component of prospective **intention** is a **plan**. The cognitive function of immediate **intention** is the **monitoring** and **guidance** of ongoing bodily **movement**.
>
> —Myles Brand, *Intending and Acting: Toward a Naturalized Action Theory*

We can make that passage clearer if we tell its story from the point of view of flesh-and-blood characters (italicized; actions are boldfaced; verbs are capitalized):

> ✓ *I* ARGUE this about **intention**. It HAS a complex cognitive component of two temporal kinds: prospective and immediate. *We* USE prospective **intention** to REPRESENT how *we* HAVE ACTED in our past and present and how *we* WILL ACT in the future. That is, *we*

USE the cognitive component of prospective **intention** to HELP *us* PLAN. *We* USE immediate **intention** to MONITOR and GUIDE *our* bodies as *we* MOVE them.

But have I made this passage say something that the writer didn't mean? Some argue that any change in form changes meaning. In this case, the writer might offer an opinion, but only his readers could decide whether the two passages have different meanings, because at the end of the day, a passage means only what careful and competent readers think it does.

Here's the point: Most readers want the subjects of verbs to name flesh-and-blood characters. But often, you must write about abstractions. When you do, turn them into virtual characters by making them the subjects of verbs that tell a story. If readers are familiar with your abstractions, no problem. But when they are not, avoid using lots of other abstract nominalizations around them. When you revise an abstract passage, you may have a problem if the hidden characters are "people in general." Unfortunately, unlike many other languages, English offers no good way to name a generic "doer." Try a general term for whoever is doing the action, such as *researchers, social critics, one*, and so on. If that won't work, try *we*.

Exercise 4.1

Analyze and revise these sentences so that each has a specific character as the subject of a specific verb. To revise, you may have to invent characters. Use *we, I,* or any other word that seems appropriate. For the first four sentences, I suggest possible characters in brackets.

1. Contradictions among the data require an explanation. [we]
2. Having their research taken seriously by professionals in the field was hard work for the students. [student researchers]
3. In recent years, the appearance of new interpretations about the meaning of the discovery of America has led to a reassessment of Columbus's place in Western history. [historians]

4. Resistance has been growing against building mental health facilities in residential areas because of a belief that the few examples of improper management are typical. [residents]

5. A decision about forcibly administering medication in an emergency room setting despite the inability of an irrational patient to provide legal consent is usually an on-scene medical decision.

6. The performance of the play was marked by enthusiasm, but there was a lack of intelligent staging.

7. Despite the critical panning of the show's latest season the love of the loyal fans was not affected.

8. The rejection of the proposal was a disappointment but not a surprise because our expectation was that a political decision had been made.

CHARACTERS AND PASSIVE VERBS

More than any other advice, you probably remember *Write in the active voice, not the passive.* That's not bad advice, but it has exceptions.

When you write in the active voice, you typically put

- the AGENT or source of an action in the subject
- the GOAL or receiver of an action in a DIRECT OBJECT:

	subject	verb	object
Active:	I	lost	the money
	character/agent	action	goal

A verb is in the passive voice when its PAST PARTICIPLE is preceded by a form of *be* (as it is in this next example). The passive differs from the active in two ways:

- The subject names the goal of the action.
- The agent or source of the action is after the verb in a *by*-phrase or dropped entirely:

	subject	be + verb	prepositional phrase
Passive:	The money	was lost	[by me].
	goal	action	character/agent

The terms *active* and *passive* are ambiguous, however, because they can refer both to those two *grammatical constructions* and to how a sentence *makes you feel*. We call a sentence *passive* if it feels flat, even if its verb is not in the passive voice. Compare these two sentences:

> We can manage the problem if we control costs.
>
> Problem management requires cost control.

Grammatically, both sentences are in the active voice, but the second *feels* passive for three reasons:

- Neither of its actions—*management* and *control*—are verbs; both are nominalizations.
- The subject is *problem management*, an abstraction.
- The sentence lacks flesh-and-blood characters.

To understand why we respond to those two sentences as we do, we have to keep these meanings distinct. In what follows, I discuss grammatical passives.

Choosing Between Active and Passive

Some critics of style tell us to avoid the passive everywhere because it adds words and often deletes the character or agent, the "doer" of the action. But the passive is sometimes the better choice. To choose between active and passive, you have to answer three questions:

1. **Must your readers know who is responsible for the action?**
   Often, we don't say who does an action because we don't know or readers won't care. We naturally choose the passive in these sentences:

   ✓ The president **WAS RUMORED** to have considered resigning.

   ✓ Those who **ARE FOUND** guilty can **BE FINED**.

   ✓ Valuable records should always **BE KEPT** in a safe.

If we do not know who spreads rumors, we cannot say. And no one doubts who finds people guilty or fines them or who should keep records safe, so we don't have to say. So those passives are the right choice.

   Sometimes, of course, writers use the passive when they don't want readers to know who is responsible for an action, especially when the doer is the writer:

Because the test **WAS** not **COMPLETED**, the flaw **WAS UNCORRECTED**.

I will discuss the issue of intended impersonality in Lesson 12.

2. **Would the active or passive verb help your readers move more smoothly from one sentence to the next?** We depend on the beginning of a sentence to give us a context of what we know before we read what's new. A sentence confuses us when it opens with information that is new and unexpected. In this next passage, the subject of the second sentence gives us new and complex information (boldfaced) before we read more familiar information that we recall from the previous sentence (italicized):

> We must decide whether to improve education in the sciences alone or to raise the level of education across the whole curriculum. **The weight given to industrial competitiveness as opposed to the value we attach to the liberal arts** _{new information} WILL DETERMINE _{active verb} *our decision.* _{familiar information}

In the second sentence, the verb *determine* is in the active voice. But we could read the sentence more easily if it were passive, because the passive would put the short, familiar information (*our decision*) first and the newer, more complex information last, the order we prefer:

> ✓ We must decide whether to improve education in the sciences alone or raise the level of education across the whole curriculum. *Our decision* _{familiar information} WILL BE DETERMINED _{passive verb} **by the weight we give to industrial competiteness as opposed to the value we attach to the liberal arts.** _{new information}

I discuss where to put old and new information more extensively in Lesson 5.

3. **Would the active or passive give readers a more consistent and appropriate point of view?** The writer of this next passage reports the end of World War II in Europe from the point of view of the Allies. To do so, she uses active verbs to make the Allies a consistent sequence of subjects:

> ✓ By early 1945, *the Allies* HAD essentially DEFEATED _{active} Germany; all that remained was a bloody climax. *American, French, British,* and *Russian forces* HAD BREACHED _{active} its borders and WERE BOMBING _{active} it around the clock. But *they* HAD not yet so DEVASTATED _{active} Germany as to destroy its ability to resist.

Had she wanted to explain history from the German point of view, she would have used passive verbs to make Germany the subject/character:

> ✓ By early 1945, *Germany* HAD essentially BEEN DEFEATED; _{passive} all that remained was a bloody climax. *Its borders* HAD BEEN BREACHED, _{passive} and *it* WAS BEING BOMBED _{passive} around the clock. *It* HAD not BEEN SO DEVASTATED, _{passive} however, that *it* could not RESIST. _{active}

Here's the point: Many writers use the passive too often, but you will struggle to write clearly if you avoid it entirely. Use it in these contexts:

- You don't know who did an action, readers don't care, or you don't want them to know.
- You want to shift a long, unfamiliar, or complex bundle of information to the end of a sentence, especially when doing so lets you begin with a bundle that is shorter, more familiar, or simpler.
- You want to focus your readers' attention on a particular character.

Exercise 4.2

In the following, change all active verbs into passives, and all passives into actives. Which sentences improve? Which do not? (In the first two, active verbs that could be passive are italicized; verbs already passive are boldfaced.)

1. Independence is **gained** by young people when skills are **learned** that the marketplace *values*.
2. Different planes of the painting are **noticed**, because their colors are **set** against a background of shades of gray that are **laid** on in layers that cannot be **seen** unless the surface is **examined** closely.
3. In this article, it is argued that the Vietnam War was fought to extend influence in Southeast Asia and was not ended until it was made clear that the United States could not defeat North Vietnam unless atomic weapons were used.
4. Science education will not be improved in this nation to a level sufficient to ensure that American industry will be supplied with skilled workers and researchers until more money is provided to primary and secondary schools.

The "Objective" Passive vs. *I/We*

Some scholarly writers use the passive voice to avoid first-person subjects (*I* and *we*) and create an objective point of view:

> Based on the writers' verbal intelligence, prior knowledge, and essay scores, their essays WERE ANALYZED for structure and

evaluated for richness of concepts. The subjects WERE then DIVIDED into a high- or low-ability group. Half of each group WAS randomly ASSIGNED to a treatment group or to a placebo group.

The writer could have written this:

> Based on the writers' verbal intelligence, prior knowledge, and essay scores, *I* ANALYZED their essays for structure and EVALUATED them for richness of concepts. *I* then SEPARATED the subjects into high- and low-ability groups. *I* randomly ASSIGNED half of each group to a treatment group or to a placebo group.

Is that less objective? Opinions differ, but I don't think so. Nevertheless, the practice of using the passive voice to eliminate first-person subjects is common, especially in the natural and social sciences.

I would note, however, that this impersonal, "scientific" style is a modern development. In his "New Theory of Light and Colors" (1672), Sir Isaac Newton wrote this charming first-person account of an experiment:

> I procured a triangular glass prism, to try therewith the *celebrated phenomena* of colours. And in order thereto, having darkened my chamber, and made a small hole in my window-shuts, to let in a convenient quantity of the sun's light, I placed my prism at its entrance, that it might be thereby refracted to the opposite wall. It was at first a very pleasing divertisement to view the vivid and intense colours produced thereby...

Were Newton writing for a scientific journal today, he might have started, "A triangular glass prism was procured. . . ."

But even today, scholars, including scientists, don't use this dense, impersonal style all the time. In fact, they use the active voice and *I* and *we* regularly. These next passages come from articles in respected journals:

> ✓ This paper is concerned with two problems. Briefly: how can **we** best handle in a transformational grammar, (i) Restrictions on . . ., To illustrate, **we** may cite . . ., **we** shall show . . .
>
> —P.H. Matthews, "Problems of Selection in Transformational Grammar," *Journal of Linguistics*

> ✓ The survey assessed approximately fifty political–cultural variables, too many to examine in a single paper. As a first step, **we** have selected for discussion certain items which involve the cultural requisites for democracy. . . .
>
> —Andrew J. Nathan and Tianjian Shi, "Cultural Requisites for Democracy in China: Findings from a Survey," *Daedalus*

Here are the first few words of several consecutive sentences from an article in *Science*, a journal of great prestige:

> ✓ **We** examine . . ., **We** compare . . ., **We** have used . . ., Each has been weighted . . ., **We** merely take . . ., They are subject . . ., **We** use . . ., Efron and Morris describe . . ., **We** observed . . ., **We** might find . . .
>
> —John P. Gilbert, Bucknam McPeek, and Frederick Mosteller, "Statistics and Ethics in Surgery and Anesthesia," *Science*

It is not true that academic writers always avoid the first person. But they do tend to use it in certain places and in certain ways. Most commonly, the first person appears in what is called METADISCOURSE.

Metadiscourse

Look again at the passages above. The first, with its passive verbs, describes research procedures that anyone could do. The other passages, those that use active verbs and the first person, describe the writers' own writing and thinking. These passages are examples of *metadiscourse*, or language that refers not to a writer's subject matter but to the writer, the reader, or the writing itself (the Greek prefix "meta-" means "after" or, in this context, "about").

Metadiscourse can appear anywhere, but it is most common in introductions and conclusions, where writers explain what they are going to do or what they have done. While you should not use metadiscourse excessively (see Lesson 9), most writing contains some, and it can help your readers follow and understand you better. Here are some ways you can use metadiscourse:

- To explain your thinking or writing: *In this paper, we will argue/claim/show. . . .; I conclude from these data that. . . .*
- To trace logic or form of your argument: *First . . .; In addition . . .; Most important . . . ; Consequently. . . .*
- To address your readers: *As you recall . . .; Consider. . . .*
- To describe the organization of your document: *This paper is divided into three parts . . .; Our argument proceeds as follows. . . .*
- To refer to other parts of your document: *In the passage above . . .; As demonstrated by Figure 1. . . .*
- To express a stance or point of view: *Not unexpectedly . . .; We concur that . . .; It seems unlikely that. . . .*
- To hedge or intensify your argument: *usually, perhaps, seems, in some respects . . .; very, clearly, certainly . . . .* (I discuss hedges and intensifiers more in Lesson 9.)

Here's the point: Some writers and editors avoid the first person by using the passive everywhere, but deleting an *I* or *we* doesn't make a researcher's thinking more objective. We know that behind those impersonal sentences are still flesh-and-blood people doing, thinking, and writing. In fact, the first-person *I* and *we* are common in scholarly prose when used with verbs that name actions unique to the writer.

Exercise 4.3

The verbs in 1 through 4 below are passive, but two could be active because they are metadiscourse verbs that would take first-person subjects. Revise the passive verbs that should be changed into active verbs. Then go through each sentence again and revise nominalizations into verbs as needed.

1. It is believed that a lack of understanding about the risks of alcohol is a cause of student bingeing.
2. The model has been subjected to extensive statistical analysis.
3. Success in exporting more crude oil for hard currency is suggested here as the cause of the improvement of the Russian economy.
4. The creation of a database is being considered, but no estimate has been made in regard to the potential of its usefulness.

The verbs in 5 through 8 are active, but some of them should be passive because they are not metadiscourse verbs. Revise the active verbs that should be changed into passive verbs, and revise in other ways as needed.

5. In Section IV, I argue that the indigenous peoples engaged in overcultivation of the land, leading to its exhaustion as a food-producing area.
6. Our intention in this book is to help readers achieve an understanding not only of the differences in grammar between Arabic and English but also the differences in worldview as reflected by Arabic vocabulary.
7. To make an evaluation of changes in the flow rate, I made a comparison of the current rate with the original rate on the basis of figures I had compiled with figures that Jordan had collected.
8. We performed the tissue rejection study on the basis of methods developed with our discovery of increases in dermal sloughing as a result of cellular regeneration.

Noun + Noun + Noun

One more stylistic choice does not directly involve characters and actions, but I discuss it here because it can distort the match that readers expect between the form of an idea and the grammar of its expression. It is the long COMPOUND NOUN phrase:

> Early *childhood thought disorder misdiagnosis* often results from unfamiliarity with recent *research literature* describing such conditions. This paper is a review of seven recent studies in which are findings of particular relevance to *pre-adolescent hyperactivity diagnosis* and to *treatment modalities* involving *medication maintenance level evaluation procedures.*

It is fine to modify one noun with another, as common phrases such as *stone wall, student center, space shuttle,* and many others show.

But strings of nouns feel lumpy, so avoid them, especially ones you invent. Revise compound nouns of your own invention, especially when they include nominalizations. Just reverse the order of words and find prepositions to connect them:

1	2	3	4	5
early	childhood	thought	disorder	misdiagnosis
misdiagnose	disordered	thought	in early	childhood
5	4	3	1	2

Reassembled, it looks like this:

> Physicians misdiagnose[5] disordered[4] thought[3] in young[1] children[2] because they are unfamiliar with recent literature on the subject.

If, however, a long compound noun includes a technical term in your field, keep that part of the compound and unpack the rest:

> Physicians misdiagnose[5] **thought disorders**[3,4] in young[1] children[2] because they are unfamiliar with recent literature on the subject.

Exercise 4.4

Identify and revise the strings of nouns in these sentences:

1. Diabetic patient blood pressure reduction may be brought about by renal depressor application.
2. The goal of this article is to describe text comprehension processes and recall protocol production.

3. On the basis of these principles, we may now attempt to formulate narrative information extraction rules.

4. This paper is an investigation into information processing behavior involved in computer human cognition simulation.

5. Enforcement of guidelines for new automobile tire durability must be a Federal Trade Commission responsibility.

6. The Social Security program is a monthly income floor guarantee based on a lifelong contribution schedule.

CLARITY AND THE PROFESSIONAL VOICE

Every group expects its members to show that they accept its values by adopting its distinctive voice. The apprentice banker must learn not only to think and look like a banker but also to speak and write like one. Too often, though, aspiring professionals try to join the club by writing in its most complex technical language. When they do, they adopt an exclusionary style that erodes the trust a civil society depends on, especially in a world where information and expertise are the means to power and control.

It is true that some research can never be made clear to intelligent lay readers—but less often than many researchers think. Here is an excerpt from Talcott Parsons, a social scientist who was as revered for his influence on his field as he was ridiculed for the opacity of his prose.

Apart from theoretical conceptualization there would appear to be no method of selecting among the indefinite number of varying kinds of factual observation which can be made about a concrete phenomenon or field so that the various descriptive statements about it articulate into a coherent whole, which constitutes an "adequate," a "determinate" description. Adequacy in description is secured insofar as determinate and verifiable answers can be given to all the scientifically important questions involved. What questions are important is largely determined by the logical structure of the generalized conceptual scheme which, implicitly or explicitly, is employed.

We can make that clearer to moderately well-educated readers:

Without a theory, scientists have no way to select from everything they could say about a subject only that which they can fit into a coherent whole that would be an "adequate" or "determinate" description. Scientists describe something "adequately" only when they can verify answers to all the questions they think are important. They decide what questions are important based on their implicit or explicit theories.

And we could make it even more concise:

> Whatever you describe, you need a theory to fit its parts into a whole. You need a theory not only to verify answers but even to decide what questions to ask.

My versions lose the nuances of Parsons's passage, and the last one loses some of its content. But his excruciatingly dense style numbs all but his most masochistically dedicated readers. Most readers would accept the tradeoff.

Einstein said that everything should be made as simple as possible, but no simpler. Accordingly, your writing should be as complex as necessary, *but no more.*

IN YOUR OWN WORDS

Exercise 4.5

Go through a page of your own writing. Circle all of the nominalizations and label all of the verbs as active or passive. For each nominalization and for each passive verb, state the specific reason you used it. If you cannot give a reason, revise it.

Exercise 4.6

Select a passage from a major work in your field. With a partner, analyze its professional voice. What sorts of characters does it use? What is the balance between active and passive verbs? How are nominalizations used? How, and how extensively, does it use metadiscourse? Try to distinguish traits specific to this work from those that characterize the *field's* professional voice. Now, revise a passage of your own writing so that it imitates that voice. What did you have to change?

SUMMING UP

1. Readers judge prose to be clear when subjects of sentences name characters and verbs name actions.

| Fixed Positions | Subject | Verb | _____ | Grammar Level |
| Movable Elements | Character | Action | _____ | Story Level |

2. If you tell a story in which you make abstract nominalizations its main characters and subjects, use as few other nominalizations as you can:

> *A nominalization* is a **replacement** of a verb by a noun, often resulting in **displacement** of characters from subjects by nouns.
>
> ✓ When *a nominalization* REPLACES a verb with a noun, *it* often DISPLACES characters from subjects.

3. Use a passive if the agent of an action is self-evident:

> *The voters* REELECTED the president with 54% of the vote.
>
> ✓ *The president* WAS REELECTED with 54% of the vote.

4. Use a passive if it lets you replace a long subject with a short one:

> Research demonstrating the soundness of our reasoning and the need for action SUPPORTED *this decision.*
>
> ✓ *This decision* WAS SUPPORTED BY research demonstrating the soundness of our reasoning and the need for action.

5. Use a passive if it gives your readers a coherent sequence of subjects:

> ✓ By early 1945, *the Axis nations* had BEEN essentially DEFEATED; all that remained was a bloody climax. *The German borders* had BEEN BREACHED, and both *Germany and Japan* were being bombed around the clock. *Neither country,* though, had BEEN so DEVASTATED that *it* could not RESIST.

6. Use an active verb if it is a metadiscourse verb:

> The terms of the analysis must BE DEFINED.
>
> ✓ We must DEFINE the terms of the analysis.

7. When possible, rewrite long compound noun phrases:

> We discussed the **board**[1] **candidate**[2] **review**[3] **meeting**[4] **schedule**[5].
>
> ✓ We discussed the **schedule**[5] of **meetings**[4] to **review**[3] **candidates**[2] for the **board**[1].

Cohesion and Coherence

*It is a common Fault in Writers, to allow their Readers too much
knowledge: They begin with that which should be the Middle, and
skipping backwards and forwards, 'tis impossible for any one but he
who is perfect in the Subject before, to understand their Work, and
such an one has no Occasion to read it.*
—BENJAMIN FRANKLIN

*The two capital secrets in the art of prose composition are these:
first, the philosophy of transition and connection; or the art by
which one step in an evolution of thought is made to arise out
of another: all fluent and effective composition depends on the
connections; secondly, the way in which sentences are made
to modify each other; for the most powerful effects in written
eloquence arise out of this reverberation, as it were, from each
other in a rapid succession of sentences.*
—THOMAS DE QUINCEY

UNDERSTANDING HOW SENTENCES CONNECT

So far, I have focused mainly on individual sentences, and I have treated clarity as if we could achieve it just by mapping characters and actions onto subjects and verbs. But readers need more than individually clear sentences before they feel a passage "hangs together." These two passages, for example, say much the same thing but feel very different:

> 1a. The safeguard of democracy everywhere—an educated citizenry—is being threatened by college costs that have been rising fast for the last several years. Increases in family income have been significantly outpaced by increases in tuition at colleges and universities during that period. Only the children of the wealthiest families in our society will be able to afford a college education if this trend continues. Knowledge and intellectual skills, in addition to wealth, will divide us as a people, when that happens. Equal opportunity and the egalitarian basis of our democratic society could be eroded by such a divide.

> ✓ 1b. In the last several years, college costs have been rising so fast that they are now threatening the safeguard of democracy everywhere: an educated citizenry. During that period, tuition has significantly outpaced increases in family income. If this trend continues, a college education will soon be affordable only by the children of the wealthiest families in our society. When that happens, we will be divided as a people not only by wealth, but by knowledge and intellectual skills. Such a divide will erode equal opportunity and the egalitarian basis of our democratic society.

The first seems choppy, even disorganized; the second seems more connected.

But like the word *clear*, the words *choppy, disorganized,* and *connected* refer not to the words on the page but to how they make us *feel.* What is it about the *arrangement* of words in (1a) that makes us feel we are moving through it in fits and starts? Why does (1b) seem to flow more easily? We base those judgments on two aspects of word order:

- We judge a sequence of sentences to be *cohesive* based on how each sentence ends and the next begins.

- We judge a whole passage to be *coherent* based on how all the sentences in it cumulatively begin.

In this lesson, I discuss the cohesion and coherence of passages; in Lessons 7 and 8, I discuss the coherence of whole documents.

COHESION

The Sense of Flow

In Lesson 4, we devoted a few pages to that familiar advice, *Avoid passives*. If we always did, we would choose the active verb in sentence (2a) over the passive in (2b):

> 2a. The collapse of a dead star into a point perhaps no larger than a marble CREATES $_{active}$ a black hole.

> 2b. A black hole IS CREATED $_{passive}$ by the collapse of a dead star into a point perhaps no larger than a marble.

But we might choose otherwise in context. Consider:

> [1]Some astonishing questions about the nature of the universe have been raised by scientists studying black holes in space. **[2a]The collapse of a dead star into a point perhaps no larger than a marble creates a black hole.** [3]So much matter compressed into so little volume changes the fabric of space around it in puzzling ways.

> [1]Some astonishing questions about the nature of the universe have been raised by scientists studying black holes in space. **[2b]A black hole is created by the collapse of a dead star into a point perhaps no larger than a marble.** [3]So much matter compressed into so little volume changes the fabric of space around it in puzzling ways.

In this context, our sense of "flow" calls not for (2a), the sentence with the active verb, but for (2b), the one with the passive.

The reason is clear: the last four words of sentence (1) introduce an important character—*black holes in space*. But with sentence (2a), the next concepts we hit are *collapsed stars* and *marbles*, information that seems to come out of nowhere:

> [1]Some astonishing questions about the nature of the universe have been raised by scientists studying <u>black holes in space.</u> [2a]<u>The collapse of a dead star into a point perhaps no larger than a marble</u> creates. . . .

If, however, we follow sentence (1) with (2b), the sentence with the passive verb, we feel those sentences connect more smoothly, because now the first words in (2b) repeat what we just read at the end of (1):

> [1]. . . by scientists studying <u>black holes in space.</u> [2b]<u>A black hole</u> is created by. . . .

Note too that the passive lets us put at the *end* of sentence (2b) words that connect it to the *beginning* of sentence (3):

> [1]. . . <u>black holes in space.</u> [2b]<u>A black hole</u> is created by the collapse of a dead star into **a point perhaps no larger than a marble.**

[3]**So much matter compressed into so little volume** changes the fabric of space around it in puzzling ways.

> *Here's the point:* Sentences are *cohesive* when the last few words of one sentence set up information that appears in the first few words of the next. That's what gives us our experience of flow. And in fact, that's the main function of the passive in the language: to let us arrange sentences so that they flow easily from one to the next.

Managing Information: Old Before New

We learn by connecting new information to what we already know. In sentences, therefore, readers prefer to encounter information that is old or familiar *to them* before they encounter information that is new or unfamiliar. So:

1. **Begin sentences with information familiar to your readers.** Readers get that familiar information in two ways. First, they remember words from the sentences they just read. That's why in our example about black holes, the beginning of (2b) coheres with the end of (1) and why the beginning of (3) coheres with the end of (2b). Second, readers bring to a sentence a general knowledge of its subject. We would not be surprised, for example, to find the next sentence (4) begin like this:

    . . . changes the fabric of space around it in puzzling ways. [4]**Astronomers have reported** that . . . .

The word *Astronomers* did not appear in the preceding sentences, but since we are reading about space, we wouldn't be surprised to find it beginning a sentence in the passage.

2. **End sentences with information that readers cannot anticipate.** Your sentences have to tell your readers something new, but readers always prefer to receive this new information after they have read something familiar.

3. **Begin sentences with information that readers will find simple; end with information they will find complex.** This guideline follows from the others. What's familiar to your readers will seem simple to them; what's unfamiliar will seem complex.

You can more easily see when others fail to observe this old-before-new principle than when you do, because after you've worked on your own ideas for a while, they all seem familiar—to you. But hard as it is to distinguish old from new in your own writing, you have to try, because readers expect sentences to begin with information that is familiar to *them* and to end with information that is new. Thwart this expectation too often and your readers won't understand you (or at least think they don't).

In every sequence of sentences you write, you have to balance principles that make individual sentences clear and principles that make the whole passage cohesive. *But in that tradeoff, give priority to helping readers create a sense of cohesive flow.* Fortunately, the principle of old before new cooperates with the principle of characters as subjects. Once you mention your main characters, readers recognize them as familiar. So when characters are up front, so is familiar information.

Here's the point: So far, we have identified three main principles of clarity. Two are about sentences:

- Make main characters the subjects of sentences.
- Make important actions verbs.

The third is about sentences as well, but it also explains how sentences flow together:

- Put old information before new information.

These principles usually complement one another, but if you have to choose among them, favor the third. The way you organize old and new information determines how cohesive readers will find your writing. And for readers, a passage's overall *cohesion* trumps the *clarity* of individual sentences.

QUICK TIP   Writers often refer to something in a previous sentence with words such as *this*, *these*, *that*, *those*, *another*, *such*, *second*, or *more*. When you use any of those signals, try to put them at or close to the beginning of a sentence:

> How to calculate credits for classes taken in a community college is **another** issue that we must consider.

> ✓ **Another** issue that we must consider is how to calculate credits for classes taken in a community college.

Exercise 5.1

Revise these two passages to improve their flow by putting old information first in each sentence. In (1), I have boldfaced the words that I feel are old information.

1. Two aims—the recovery of the American economy and the modernization of America into a military power—were **in the president's mind when he assumed office.** The drop in unemployment figures and inflation, and the increase in the GDP testifies to **his success in the first.** But America's increased involvement in international conflict without any clear set of political goals indicates **less success with the second.** Nevertheless, increases in the military budget and a good deal of saber rattling **pleased the American voter.**

2. The components of Abco's profitability, particularly growth in Asian markets, will be highlighted in our report to demonstrate its advantages versus competitors. Revenue returns along several dimensions—product type, end-use, distribution channels, etc.— will provide a basis for this analysis. Likely growth prospects of Abco's newest product lines will depend most on the development of distribution channels in China, according to our projections. A range of innovative strategies will be needed to support the introduction of new products.

COHERENCE

A Sense of the Whole

When you create cohesive flow, you take the first step toward helping readers feel that your prose hangs together. But they will judge you to be a competent writer only when they also feel that your writing has *coherence,* a quality different from *cohesion.* It's easy to confuse these words because they sound alike.

- *Cohesion* is when pairs of sentences fit together the way two pieces of a jigsaw puzzle do (recall the black hole example).

- *Coherence* is when all the sentences in a piece of writing add up to a larger whole, the way all the pieces in a puzzle add up to the picture on the box.

This next passage has good cohesive flow because we move from one sentence to the next without a hitch:

Sayner, Wisconsin, is the snowmobile capital of the world. The buzzing of snowmobile engines fills the air, and their tank-like tracks crisscross the snow. The snow reminds me of Mom's mashed potatoes, covered with furrows I would draw with my fork. Her mashed potatoes usually make me sick—that's why I play with them. I like to make a hole in the middle of the potatoes and fill it with melted butter. This behavior has been the subject of long chats between my analyst and me.

Though its individual sentences are cohesive, that passage as a whole is incoherent. (It was created by six different writers, one of whom wrote the first sentence, with the other five sequentially adding one sentence, knowing only the immediately preceding one.) It is incoherent for three reasons:

1. The subjects of the sentences are entirely unrelated.
2. The sentences share no common themes or ideas.
3. The paragraph has no one sentence that states what the whole passage is about.

I will discuss that second point in Lesson 6 and the third one in Lesson 8. The rest of this lesson focuses on the first point, shared subjects.

Subjects and Topics

For 500 years, English teachers have defined *subject* in two ways:

1. The "doer" of the action
2. What a sentence is "about" or "comments" on, its TOPIC

In Lessons 3 and 4, we saw why that first definition doesn't work: the subjects of many sentences are not doers. Here, for example, the subject is an action: *The **explosion** was loud.* Here it is a quality: ***Correctness** is not writing's highest virtue.* Here it is just a grammatical placeholder: *It was a dark and stormy night.*

But also flawed is that second definition: *A subject is what a sentence is about.* It is flawed because, often, a sentence's topic is stated elsewhere than in the grammatical subject.

For example, none of the MAIN SUBJECTS in these sentences names their topics.

- The main subject of this sentence is *it*, but its topic is *your claim*, the object of the preposition *for*:

  It is impossible for **your claim** to be proved.

- The subject of this sentence is *I*, but its topic is *this question*, the object of *to*:

  In regard to **this question,** *I* believe more research is needed.

- The subject of this sentence is *it*, but its topic is *our proposal*, the subject of a verb in a subordinate clause:

    It is likely that **our proposal** will be accepted.

- The subject of this sentence is *no one*, but its topic is *such results*, a direct object shifted to the front for emphasis:

    Such results *no one* could have predicted.

Topics and Coherence

A sentence's topic does not have to be its grammatical subject, although in writing that is clear and coherent, it often is. *Topic* is not a grammatical term but a psychological one: it refers to the idea that readers expect the sentence to be "about" or "comment" on. Readers expect to find this idea stated toward the beginning of the sentence.

Readers consider a passage coherent to the degree that they can quickly and easily see two things:

- the topics of individual sentences and clauses
- how the topics in the passage make up a related set of concepts

How does this passage strike you?

> Consistent ideas toward the beginnings of sentences, especially in their subjects, help readers understand what a passage is generally about. A sense of coherence arises when a sequence of topics comprises a narrow set of related ideas. But the context of each sentence is lost by seemingly random shifts of topics. Unfocused paragraphs result when that happens.

The passage seems choppy and disorganized because the topics of its sentences are inconsistent and diffuse. They do not focus our attention on a limited set of related ideas:

> <u>Consistent ideas toward the beginnings of sentences</u>, especially in their subjects, help readers understand what a passage is generally about. <u>A sense of coherence</u> arises when <u>a sequence of topics</u> comprises a narrow set of related ideas. But <u>the context of each sentence</u> is lost by seemingly random shifts of topics. <u>Unfocused, even disorganized paragraphs</u> result when that happens.

Now compare that passage to this revision, with the new topics boldfaced:

> **Readers** understand what a passage is generally about when **they** see consistent ideas toward the beginnings of sentences, especially

in their subjects. **They** feel a passage is coherent when **they** read a sequence of topics that focuses on a narrow set of related ideas. But when **topics** seem to shift randomly, **readers** lose the context of each sentence. When **that** happens, **they** feel they are reading paragraphs that are unfocused and even disorganized.

The subjects of sentences and clauses focus our attention on just two concepts—*readers* and *topics*—and form a strong TOPIC STRING: *readers, they, they, they, topics, readers, that, they [readers]*. That is why this passage seems more coherent.

How to Revise: Topics

Here is how to analyze and revise your writing so it is coherent.

1. **Analyze**
   a. Underline the first seven or eight words of every sentence in a passage, stopping when you hit a verb.
   b. If you can, underline the first five or six words of every clause in those sentences.
2. **Assess**
   a. Do the underlined words constitute a relatively small set of related ideas? Even if you see how they are related, will your readers? If you answer *no*, you should revise.
   b. Do the underlined words name the most important characters, real or abstract? Again, if you answer *no*, you should revise.
   c. Imagine giving the passage a title. The words in it are likely to name important topics.
3. **Rewrite**
   a. In most of your sentences, although not necessarily all, use subjects to name topics.
   b. Put these subjects/topics close to the beginnings of your sentences.
   c. Be sure that those topics are, in context, familiar to your readers.

QUICK TIP   When you start to draft a new section of your paper, list the topics and characters you intend to write about. Include not just flesh-and-blood characters, but important concepts as well. As you draft, try to put those characters into the subjects of most of your sentences. If you do not mention one of those characters for several sentences, you may have gotten off track.

Likewise, when you must read a passage you expect to be difficult, first skim it quickly to find its main topics and characters. Think about them for a moment. The more sharply you have them in mind, the more easily you will understand the passage.

BEGINNING SENTENCES WELL

It is hard to begin a sentence well. Readers want to get to a subject/topic quickly, but too often we begin sentences in ways that keep readers from doing that. It's called *throat-clearing*. Throat-clearing typically begins with metadiscourse (review pp. 58–59) that connects a sentence to the previous one, with transitions such as *and*, *but*, *therefore*:

> And therefore . . . .

We then add a second kind of metadiscourse that expresses our attitude toward what is coming, words such as *fortunately, perhaps, allegedly, it is important to note, for the most part*, or *in a manner of speaking*:

> And therefore, it is important to note . . . .

Then we indicate time, place, or manner:

> And therefore, it is important to note that, in Eastern states since 1980 . . . .

Only then do we get to the subject/topic:

> And therefore, it is important to note that, in Eastern states since 1980, **acid rain** has become a serious problem.

When you open several sentences like that, your readers have a hard time seeing not just what each sentence is about, but the focus of the whole passage. When you find a sentence with lots of words before its subject/topic, revise:

> ✓ Since 1980, therefore, **acid rain** has become a serious problem in the Eastern states.

Here's the point: Before you begin writing, name the things you are writing about. Those are your *topics.* They should be short, concrete, familiar words, and more often than not, they should name the main characters in your story. Most of your subjects should be topics. And be consistent: do not vary your subjects for the sake of variety. Together, your subjects should name the topics that tell your readers what a passage as a whole is "about."

Exercise 5.2

Revise these passages to give them more consistent topic strings. Identify words that name what the passages "comment" on and use those words as subjects of most of the sentences. In (1), words that could be consistent subjects/topics are boldfaced.

1. **Vegetation** covers the earth, except for those areas continuously covered with ice or utterly scorched by continual heat. Richly fertilized plains and river valleys are places where **plants** grow most richly, but also at the edge of perpetual snow in high mountains. The ocean and its edges as well as in and around lakes and swamps are **densely vegetated.** The cracks of busy city sidewalks have **plants** in them as well as in seemingly barren cliffs. Before humans existed, the earth was covered with **vegetation,** and the earth will have **vegetation** long after evolutionary history swallows us up.

2. The power to create and communicate a new message to fit a new experience is not a competence animals have in their natural states. Their genetic code limits the number and kind of messages that they can communicate. Information about distance, direction, source, and richness of pollen in flowers constitutes the only information that can be communicated by bees, for example. A limited repertoire of messages delivered in the same way, for generation after generation, is characteristic of animals of the same species, in all significant respects.

Two Qualifications

Alleged Monotony

A common piece of advice is, *Vary how you begin your sentences.* That's a bad idea, especially when you change subjects just to make them different. When you see the same topic in several sentences *in your own prose* you might think a passage is monotonous. But your readers may be grateful for the repetition, because it will help them focus on your ideas.

On the other hand, you might revise if you find you have used exactly the same words for the same topics in exactly the same positions. This passage goes over the top in that kind of consistency:

> **"Moral climate"** is created when an objectivized moral standard for treating people is accepted by others. **Moral climate** results from norms of behavior that are accepted by society whereby if people conform they are socially approved of, or if they don't they are shunned. In this light, **moral climate** acts as a reason to refrain from saying or doing things that the community does not support. **A moral climate** encourages individuals to conform to a moral standard and apply that standard to their own circumstances.

In such passages, you can vary a few of the words that refer to a repeated topic:

> **"Moral climate"** is created. . . . **This climate** results. . . . In this light, **morality** acts. . . . **A moral climate** encourages. . . .

Be cautious, though: most writers change topics too often.

Faked Coherence

Some writers try to fake coherence by lacing their prose with conjunctions like *thus, therefore, however*, and so on, regardless of whether they signal real logical connections. An example:

> Because the press is the major medium of interaction between the president and the people, how it portrays him influences his popularity. **Therefore,** it should report on the president objectively. Both reporters and the president are human, **however,** subject to error and favoritism. **Also,** people act differently in public than they do in private. **Hence,** to understand a person, it is important to know the whole person, his environment, upbringing, and education. **Indeed,** from the correspondence with his family, we can learn much about Harry S. Truman, our thirty-third president.

Experienced writers use these connecting devices, but they depend more on the logical flow of their ideas. They are especially careful not to overuse words like *and, also, moreover, another*, and so on, words that say simply *Here's one more thing.* You need a *but* or *however* when you contradict or qualify what you just said, and you can use a *therefore* or *consequently* to wind up a line of reasoning. But avoid using words like these more than a few times a page. Your readers don't need them when your sentences are cohesive and the passage they make up is coherent.

In Your Own Words

Exercise 5.3

Writers often violate the principle that old information should come before new information because they know their own writing too well: to them, everything can seem like old information. So work with a reader to analyze the flow of old and new information in a passage of your writing. Have a reader go through a passage of your writing and underline every piece of new information. If the beginnings of sentences are underlined, you need to revise. Do so.

Exercise 5.4

In Lesson 4 (p. 55), I noted that you could change the point of view of a passage by changing the characters/topics that appear as subjects in its sentences:

By early 1945, *the Allies* had essentially defeated *Germany* . . . .

By early 1945, *Germany* had essentially been defeated by *the Allies* . . . .

The first version is written from the point of view of the Allies, the second from that of Germany.

Experiment with the point of view of a passage of your own writing. First, circle words that name characters/topics, wherever they appear. Then underline the subject of every clause. You should see that some characters/topics appear most often as subjects, while others appear most often in other parts of your sentences (likely after the verb). Revise the passage by using those other characters/topics as subjects and by moving characters/topics used as subjects after the verb. What changes do you notice in the feel or even meaning of the passage?

Exercise 5.5

Writers use conjunctions and transitions like *also, furthermore, moreover, another, but, however, although, nevertheless,* and *consequently* to help readers see the connections among their ideas. But such words can also be used to bluff, to fake connections that aren't really there. Writers are most likely to fake connections when they are struggling to figure out or to express their ideas. Select a piece of writing you are struggling with, and have a reader call your bluffs. Ask your reader to circle words that assert logical connections that don't seem to be there. Then revise as necessary. Work to refine not only your writing but also your ideas and thinking.

SUMMING UP

I noted in Lessons 3 and 4 that to understand a sentence, readers have to integrate two levels of sentence structure: the grammar level and the story level. I now add a third level, the information level. Writers can put familiar information and unfamiliar information anywhere in a sentence, but readers prefer to find these kinds of information in particular places. Just as readers prefer characters to align with subjects and actions with verbs, so they expect to find old, familiar information toward the beginning of a sentence, aligned with its topic, and new, unfamiliar information toward the end. We can graphically integrate these principles with our others. (I'll fill in the empty box in Lesson 6):

Fixed Positions	Topic			
Movable Elements	Old/Familiar	New/Unfamiliar		Information Level
Fixed Positions	Subject	Verb	_____	Grammar Level
Movable Elements	Character	Action	_____	Story Level

The principles from this lesson are these:

1. Begin sentences with subjects or, sometimes, short introductory phrases that communicate old information, information that your readers are familiar with (boldfaced); give new, unfamiliar information (italicized) toward the ends of sentences:

   > The *number of dead in the Civil War* exceeded **all other wars in American history** combined. A reason for *the lingering animosity between North and South* today is **the memory of this terrible carnage**.

   > ✓ Of **all the wars in American history**, none has exceeded the Civil War in *the number of dead*. **The memory of this terrible carnage** is one reason for the *lingering animosity between North and South today*.

2. Through a series of sentences, keep your topics short and reasonably consistent:

> **Competition between Asian and American companies in the Pacific** is the first phase of this study. **Labor costs and the ability to introduce new products quickly in particular** are examined. **A plan that will show American industry how to restructure its facilities** will be developed from this study.

> ✓ In the first phase of this study, **we** examine how **Asian and American companies** compete in the Pacific region. **We** examine in particular their labor costs and ability to introduce new products quickly. **We** develop from this study a **plan** that will show **American industry** how to restructure its facilities.

Lesson

6

Emphasis

In my end is my beginning.
—T. S. ELIOT

All's well that ends well.
—WILLIAM SHAKESPEARE

UNDERSTANDING HOW SENTENCES END

If you consistently write sentences whose subjects name a few central characters and topics, and you join them to strong verbs, you'll likely get the rest of the sentence right and, in the process, create a passage that is both cohesive and coherent. But if the first few words of a sentence are worth special attention, so are the last few. How you end your sentences affects how readers judge not only the clarity and strength of individual sentences, but also their collective cohesion and coherence.

When readers build up momentum in the first nine or ten words of a sentence, they more easily get through complicated material that follows. Compare:

1a. A sociometric and actuarial analysis of Social Security revenues and disbursements for the last six decades to determine changes in projecting deficits is the subject of this study.

✓ 1b. In this study, we analyze Social Security's revenues and disbursements for the last six decades, using sociometric and actuarial criteria to determine changes in projecting deficits.

As we start (1a), we struggle to understand its technical terms at the same time we are hacking through a subject twenty-two words long. In (1b), we go through just five words to get past a subject and verb and eleven more before we hit a term—sociometric—that might slow us down. By that point we have enough momentum to carry us through the complexity to the sentence's end.

Complex Grammar

Which of these two sentences do you prefer?

> 2a. Lincoln's claim that the Civil War was God's punishment of both North and South for slavery appears in the last part of the speech.

> 2b. In the last part of his speech, Lincoln claims that God gave the Civil War to both North and South as a punishment for slavery.

Most readers prefer (2b), because it begins simply with a short introductory phrase followed by a one-word subject and a specific verb, and then moves toward grammatical complexity. We discussed that issue in Lesson 5.

Complex Meaning

Another kind of complexity is in the meanings of words, especially technical terms. Compare these two passages:

> 3a. The role of calcium blockers in the control of cardiac irregularity can be seen through an understanding of the role of calcium in the activation of muscle cells. The regulatory proteins actin, myosin, tropomyosin, and troponin make up the sarcomere, the basic unit of muscle contraction. The energy-producing, or ATPase, protein myosin makes up its thick filament, while actin, tropomyosin, and troponin make up its thin filament. Interaction of myosin and actin triggers muscle contraction.

> ✓ 3b. When a muscle contracts, it uses calcium. We must therefore understand how calcium affects muscle cells to understand how cardiac irregularity is controlled by drugs called calcium blockers. The basic unit of muscle contraction is the sarcomere. It has two filaments, one thin and one thick. Those filaments consist of four proteins that regulate contraction: actin, tropomyosin, and troponin in the thin filament and myosin in the thick one. Muscles contract when the protein actin in the thin filament interacts with myosin, an energy-producing or ATPase protein in the thick filament.

Both passages use the same technical terms, but (3b) is clearer to those who know nothing about the chemistry of muscles.

Those passages differ in two ways. First, information that is only implicit in (3a) is stated explicitly in (3b). More important, almost all the technical terms in (3a) are toward the beginnings of sentences and clauses, increasing the passage's feeling of complexity:

> 3a. The role of **calcium blockers** in the control of **cardiac irregularity** can be seen through an understanding of the role of calcium in the activation of muscle cells.
>
> The **regulatory proteins actin, myosin, tropomyosin, and troponin** make up the **sarcomere**, the basic unit of muscle contraction.
>
> The **energy-producing, or ATPase, protein myosin** makes up its thick filament, while **actin, tropomyosin, and troponin** make up its thin filament.
>
> **Interaction of myosin and actin** triggers muscle contraction.

In (3b), those technical terms appear toward the ends of sentences:

> . . . uses **calcium**.
>
> . . . is controlled by drugs called **calcium blockers**.
>
> . . . is the **sarcomere**.
>
> . . . four proteins that regulate contraction: **actin, tropomyosin, and troponin** in the thin filament and **myosin** in the thick one.
>
> . . . **myosin**, an **energy-producing or ATPase protein** in the thick filament.

This way of introducing unfamiliar terms works even for prose intended for professional readers. In this next passage, from the *New England Journal of Medicine,* the writer deliberately uses metadiscourse just to put the new technical term at the end:

> The incubation of peripheral-blood lymphocytes with a lymphokine, interleukin-2, generates lymphoid cells that can lyse fresh, noncultured, natural-killer-cell-resistant tumor cells but not normal cells. *We term these cells* **lymphokine-activated killer (LAK) cells.**

Here's the point: Your readers want you to organize your sentences to help them manage two kinds of difficulty:

- long and complex phrases and clauses
- new information, particularly unfamiliar technical terms

In general, your sentences should begin with elements that are relatively short: a short introductory phrase or clause, followed by a short, concrete subject, followed by a verb expressing a specific action. After the verb, the sentence can go on for several lines, if it is well constructed (see Lessons 10 and 11). The general principle is to carry the reader not from complexity to simplicity but from simplicity to complexity.

EMPHASIS AND STRESS

In the last lesson, we said that the first few words of a sentence are important because they state its *topic,* what the sentence is "about" or "comments" on. The last few words of a sentence are also important, because they receive special emphasis. You can sense that when you hear your voice rise at the end of a sentence to emphasize one syllable more strongly than the others:

> . . . more strongly than the ó-thers.

We'll call this most emphatic part of a sentence its STRESS.

How you manage that stress position helps establish the voice readers hear in your prose, because if you end a sentence on words that carry little meaning, your sentence will seem to end weakly:

> Climate change could raise sea levels to a point where much of the world's low-lying coastal areas would disappear, **according to most atmospheric scientists.**

> ✓ According to most atmospheric scientists, climate change could raise sea levels to a point where much of the world's low-lying coastal areas **would disappear**.

In Lessons 4 and 5, we saw how different subjects/topics create different points of view (pp. 55–56, 71–73). You can also manage your endings to emphasize important themes.

Compare these passages. The first laments the way universities in the 1990s responded to a decline in the number of potential students—by becoming increasingly commercial:

> The universities were going to have to pursue students much **as businesses pursue customers.** They were going to have to treat their prospective students **as potential buyers.** And they were going to have to treat their existing students **as customers too,** for students **can always switch brands.**

> —Mark Edmundson, *Why Teach? In Defense of a Real Education*

Moving those references to businesses, customers, buyers, and brands out of the sentences' ends blunts the passage's edge:

> The universities were going to have to act like **businesses pursuing customers** to attract prospective students. And because **customers can always switch brands**, universities were going to have to take the same approach with their existing students too.

In some cases, changing a sentence's stress can even change its meaning. Which company would you invest in?

> Although the company's sales remain strong, **its stock price has slipped.**

> Although the company's stock price has slipped, **its sales remain strong.**

According to that first sentence, the company is in trouble; according to the second, it's a bargain.

Here's the point: Just as we look to the first few words of a sentence for point of view, so we look to the last few words for special emphasis. You can revise a sentence to emphasize particular words that you want readers to hear stressed and thereby note as particularly significant.

How To Revise: Stress

If you have managed your subjects and topics well, you will by default put the words you want to emphasize toward the ends of your sentences. To test this, read your sentence aloud and, as you reach the last three or four words, tap your finger hard as if emphasizing them in a speech. If you tap on words that do not deserve strong emphasis, look for words that do. Then put those words closer to the end. Here are some ways to do that.

Three Tactical Revisions

1. **Trim the end.**

> Sociobiologists claim that our genes control our social behavior **in the way we act in situations we are in every day.**

Since *social behavior* means *the way we act in situations . . . ,* we can drop everything after *behavior:*

> ✓ Sociobiologists claim that our genes **control our social behavior**.

2. **Shift peripheral ideas to the left.**

> The data offered to prove ESP are weak, **for the most part.**

> ✓ **For the most part**, the data offered to prove ESP are **weak.**

Particularly avoid ending with anticlimactic metadiscourse:

> Job opportunities in computer programming are getting scarcer, **it must be remembered.**

> ✓ **It must be remembered** that job opportunities in computer programming are getting scarcer.

3. **Shift new information to the right.** A more common way to manage stress is by moving new information to the end of a sentence:

> **Questions about the ethics of withdrawing intravenous feeding** are more difficult [than something just mentioned].

> ✓ More difficult [than something just mentioned] are **questions about the ethics of withdrawing intravenous feeding.**

Six Syntactic Devices to Emphasize the Right Words

There are a number of syntactic devices that let you manage where in a sentence you stress units of new information. (You just read one of them.)

1. ***There* shift** Some editors discourage all *there is/there are* constructions, but using them lets you shift a subject to the right to emphasize it. Compare:

> **Several syntactic devices** let you manage where in a sentence you locate units of new information.

> ✓ *There are* **several syntactic devices** that let you manage where in a sentence you locate units of new information.

Experienced writers commonly begin a paragraph with *there* to introduce new topics and concepts that they develop in sentences that follow.

2. **Passives (for the last time)** A passive verb lets you flip a subject and object to get old and new information in the right order. Compare these sentences:

> Some claim that **our genes** influence _{active} aspects of behavior that we think are learned. **Our genes,** for example, seem to determine. . . .

> ✓ Some claim that aspects of behavior that we think are learned are in fact influenced _{passive} **by our genes. Our genes,** for example, seem to determine. . . .

3. *What* **shift** This is another device that shifts a part of the sentence to the right, thereby emphasizing it more:

> We need a monetary policy that would end fluctuations in money supply, unemployment, and inflation.

> ✓ **What** we need **is** a monetary policy that would end fluctuations in money supply, unemployment, and inflation.

4. *It* **shift** When you have a subject consisting of a long NOUN CLAUSE, you can move it to the end of the sentence and start with an *it*:

> **That oil prices would be set by OPEC** once seemed inevitable.

> ✓ *It* once seemed inevitable **that oil prices would be set by OPEC.**

5. *Not only X, but (also) Y (as well)* In this next pair, note how the *but* emphasizes the last element of the pair:

> We must clarify these issues and **develop trust.**

> ✓ We must *not only* clarify these issues *but also* **develop trust.**

Unless you have a reason to emphasize the negative, end with the positive:

> The point is to highlight our success, **not to emphasize our failures.**

> ✓ The point is not to emphasize our failures but **to highlight our success.**

6. **Pronoun substitution and ellipsis** This is a fine point: a sentence can end flatly when you repeat a word that you used just a few words before at the end of a sentence, because the voice we hear in our mind's ear drops off at the end. If you read aloud the preceding sentence, this one, and the next, you can hear that drop at the end of each sentence. To avoid that kind of flatness, rewrite or use a pronoun instead of repeating the word at the end of the sentence. For example:

> A sentence will seem to end flatly if at its end you use a word that you used just a few words before, because when you repeat that word, your voice **drops.** Instead of repeating the noun, use a **pronoun.** The reader will at least hear emphasis on the word just **before** *it*.

Occasionally, you can just delete words that repeat earlier ones:

> It is sometimes possible to represent a complex idea in a simple sentence, but more often you cannot.

One of the characteristics of especially elegant prose is how writers use a handful of devices to end their sentences. I will discuss those in Lesson 11.

QUICK TIP   You can easily check whether you have stressed the right words by reading your sentences aloud: as you speak the last few words, raise your voice and tap the table with your fingers. If you've stressed the wrong words, your voice and table thumping will feel wrong:

> It is sometimes possible to represent a complex idea in a simple sentence, but more often you cannot represent it in that kind of sentence.

If you've stressed the right words, your voice and table thumping will feel right:

> It is sometimes possible to represent a complex idea in a simple sentence, but MORE **OF**TEN YOU CAN**NOT**.

Exercise 6.1

Revise these sentences to emphasize the right words. In the first three, I boldfaced what I think should be stressed. Then eliminate wordiness, nominalizations, etc.

1. The President's tendency **to rewrite the Constitution** is the biggest danger to America, in my opinion, at least.

2. A new political philosophy that could affect our society **well into the twenty-first century** may emerge from these studies.

3. There are **limited** opportunities for faculty to work with individual students in large colleges and universities.

4. Building suburban housing developments in floodplains has led to the existence of extensive and widespread flooding and economic disaster in parts of our country in recent years, it is now clear.

5. The teacher who makes an assignment of a long final term paper at the end of the semester and who then gives only a grade and nothing else such as a critical comment is a common object of complaint among students at the college level.

6. Renting textbooks rather than buying them for basic required courses such as mathematics, foreign languages, and English, whose textbooks do not go through yearly changes, is feasible, however, economically speaking.

Exercise 6.2

Revise these passages so that their sentences begin with appropriate topics and end with appropriate emphasis.

1. Athens's catastrophic Sicilian Invasion is the most important event in Thucydides's *History of the Peloponnesian War*. Three-quarters of the history is devoted to setting up the invasion because of this. Through the step-by-step decline in Athenian society that Thucydides describes, we can see how he chose to anticipate the Sicilian Invasion. The inevitability that we associate with the tragic drama is the basic reason for the need to anticipate the invasion.

2. Whether the date an operation intends to close down might be part of management's "duty to disclose" during contract bargaining is the issue here, it would appear. The minimization of conflict is the central rationale for the duty that management has to bargain in good faith. In order to allow the union to put forth proposals on behalf of its members, companies are obligated to disclose major changes in an operation during bargaining, though the case law is scanty on this matter.

TOPICS, STRESS, THEMES, AND COHERENCE

There is one more function performed by the stress of certain sentences, one that helps readers think a whole passage is coherent. As we saw in the last lesson, readers take the clearest topic to be a short noun phrase that comes early in a sentence, usually as its subject. That's why most of us judge this next paragraph to be unfocused: its sentences seem to open randomly, from no consistent point of view:

1a. Great strides in the early and accurate diagnosis of Alzheimer's disease have been made in recent years. Not too long ago, senility in an older patient who seemed to be losing touch with reality was often confused with Alzheimer's. Genetic clues have become the basis of newer and more reliable tests in the last few years, however. The risk of human tragedy of another kind, though, has resulted from the increasing accuracy of these tests: predictions about susceptibility to Alzheimer's have become possible long before the appearance of any overt symptoms. At that point, an apparently healthy person could be devastated by such an early diagnosis.

If we revise that paragraph to make the topics more consistent, we also make it more coherent (topics are boldfaced):

✓ 1b. In recent years, **researchers** have made great strides in the early and accurate diagnosis of Alzheimer's disease. Not too long ago, when

a physician examined an older patient who seemed out of touch with reality, **she** had to guess whether the **person** was senile or had Alzheimer's. In the past few years, however, **physicians** have been able to use new and more reliable tests focusing on genetic clues. But in **the accuracy of these new tests** lies the risk of another kind of human tragedy: **physicians** may be able to predict Alzheimer's long before its overt appearance, but **such an early diagnosis** could psychologically devastate an apparently healthy person.

The paragraph now focuses on just two topics: researchers/ physicians and testing/diagnosis.

But there is one more revision that would make it more coherent still. Readers expect the opening sentence or two of a passage to announce its key concepts, and they look for those concepts in the last few words of those opening sentences, especially the first. Therefore, follow this principle:

> Put key words in the stress position of a passage's *first* sentence to emphasize the key concepts it will repeat and develop.

The first sentence of that revised paragraph stresses advances in diagnosis: . . . *the early and accurate diagnosis of Alzheimer's disease.* The passage, however, is not about diagnosis but its risks. That organizing concept, though, does not appear until more than halfway through the paragraph. Readers would grasp the point of the paragraph better if all of its key concepts appeared in the first sentence, *specifically toward its end, in its stress position.*

Here is a new first sentence for the paragraph that would help readers focus on the key concepts not just of *Alzheimer's* and *new diagnoses*, but of *new problem* and *informing those most at risk:*

> In recent years, researchers have made great strides in the early and accurate diagnosis of Alzheimer's disease, but those **diagnoses** have raised **a new problem** about **informing those most at risk who show no symptoms of it.**

We can call those key concepts that run through a passage its THEMES.

Look at the highlighted words in the passage below one more time:

- The boldfaced words are about testing.
- The italicized words are about mental states.
- The capitalized words are about a new problem.

Each of those concepts is announced toward the end of the new opening sentence, especially the theme of the new problem.

✓ 1c. In recent years, researchers have made great strides in the early and accurate **diagnosis** of *Alzheimer's disease*, but those **diagnoses** have raised A NEW PROBLEM about INFORMING THOSE *MOST AT RISK* WHO SHOW *NO SYMPTOMS OF IT*. Not too long ago, when a physician examined an older patient who seemed *out of touch with reality*, she had to **guess** whether that person had *Alzheimer's* or was *only senile*. In the past few years, however, physicians have been able to use **new and more reliable tests** focusing on genetic clues. But in the accuracy of these **new tests** lies the RISK OF ANOTHER KIND OF HUMAN TRAGEDY: physicians may be able to **predict** *Alzheimer's* long before its overt appearance, but such an early **diagnosis** could PSYCHOLOGICALLY DEVASTATE AN APPARENTLY HEALTHY PERSON.

That passage now coheres, or "hangs together," for three reasons:

- Its topics consistently focus on physicians and diagnosis.
- Running through it are strings of words that focus on the themes of (1) tests, (2) mental conditions, and (3) a new problem.
- And no less important, the opening sentence helps us notice those themes by emphasizing them at its end.

Again, signal a passage's key concepts in the stress positions of its opening sentences, especially the first. This principle applies to fairly long paragraphs (short, introductory, or transitional paragraphs follow different patterns). It also applies to longer passages, even whole documents.

Here's the point: We depend on concepts running through a passage to create a sense of its coherence. You help readers identify those concepts in two ways:

- Repeat those that name characters as topics of sentences, usually as subjects.
- Repeat others as themes elsewhere in a passage, in nouns, verbs, and adjectives.

Readers are more likely to notice those themes if you emphasize them at the end of the sentence that introduces the passage.

QUICK TIP   For a paragraph more than five or six sentences long, underline the sentence that you think best introduces or frames the rest of the paragraph. If you can't do that quickly, your paragraph probably has a problem. If you can, circle the important words in the sentence. Those words should sound like a title for the paragraph. If they do not, your paragraph may confuse your readers. We will return to this matter in Lesson 8.

IN YOUR OWN WORDS

Exercise 6.3

Read a page of your own writing aloud, raising your voice and tapping your fingers at the ends of your sentences (as suggested in the Quick Tip on page 86). What do you notice? How often do you seem to be stressing the wrong words, and how often the right ones? Can you detect any patterns? How does your meaning change when you inadvertently stress the wrong words?

Exercise 6.4

Have a reader use the Three Tactical Revisions on pages 83–84 ("trim the end," "shift peripheral ideas to the left," or "shift new information to the right") to revise at least 4–5 sentences of your writing.

- In trimming the ends of sentences, did your reader cut material that you thought was necessary?
- Did your reader treat as peripheral ideas that you thought were important?
- Are you surprised by what your reader classified as "new information"?

Which revisions improved your writing, and which did not? Why?

SUMMING UP

Like subject and verb positions, the topic and stress positions of a sentence are relatively fixed. And just as readers want characters to align with subjects and actions to align with verbs, so they expect to find old, familiar information at the beginning of a sentence along with its topic, and new, unfamiliar information toward the end, where it receives stress or emphasis. We can graphically integrate the principles from this lesson with our others, adding a fourth level to our sentence diagram. I call this fourth level the *attention level* because it concerns not just how easily readers understand a sentence but what they *focus on* or *attend to* in it.

Fixed Positions	Topic	Stress	Attention Level
Movable Elements	Short, simple, old	Long, complex, new	Information Level
Fixed Positions	Subject	Verb	———	Grammar Level
Movable Elements	Character	Action	———	Story Level

1. Use the end of a sentence to introduce long, complex, or otherwise difficult-to-process material, particularly unfamiliar technical terms and new information.

> **A determination of involvement of lipid-linked saccharides in the assembly of oligosaccharide chains of ovalbumin *in vivo*** was the principal aim of this study. *In vitro* **and *in vivo* studies utilizing oviduct membrane preparations and oviduct slices and the antibiotic tunicamycin** were undertaken to accomplish this.

> ✓ The principal aim of this study was to determine how **lipid-linked saccharides are involved in the assembly of oligosaccharide chains of ovalbumin *in vivo*.** To accomplish this, studies were undertaken *in vitro* and *in vivo*, **utilizing the antibiotic tunicamycin on preparations of oviduct membrane and on oviduct slices.**

2. Use the stress position at the very end to emphasize words that you want your readers to hear emphasized in their mind's ear:

> The universities were going to have to act like businesses pursuing customers **to attract prospective students.**

> ✓ The universities were going to have to pursue students much **as businesses pursue customers.**

> —Mark Edmundson

3. Use the stress of a sentence that introduces a passage to announce the key themes that the rest of the passage will develop:

> In recent years, researchers have made great strides in the early and accurate **diagnosis** of *Alzheimer's disease*, but those **diagnoses** have raised A NEW PROBLEM about INFORMING THOSE *MOST AT RISK* WHO SHOW *NO SYMPTOMS OF IT*. Not too long ago, when a physician examined an older patient who seemed *out of touch with reality*, she had to **guess** whether that person had *Alzheimer's* or was *only senile*. In the past few years, however, physicians have been able to use **new and more reliable tests** focusing on genetic clues. But in the accuracy of these **new tests** lies the RISK OF ANOTHER KIND OF HUMAN TRAGEDY: physicians may be able to **predict** *Alzheimer's*. long before its overt appearance, but such an early **diagnosis** could PSYCHOLOGICALLY DEVASTATE AN APPARENTLY HEALTHY PERSON.

PART THREE

Clarity of Form

Well begun is half done.
—ANONYMOUS

The beginning is half of the whole.
—PLATO

Lesson

7

Motivation

A problem well-put is half solved.
—JOHN DEWEY

*Looking back, I think it was more difficult to see what the
problems were than to solve them.*
—CHARLES DARWIN

*The formulation of a problem is often more essential than its
solution, which may be merely a matter of mathematical or
experimental skill. To raise new questions, new possibilities,
to regard old questions from a new angle, requires creative
imagination and marks real advance in science.*
—ALBERT EINSTEIN

ACADEMIC AND PROFESSIONAL WRITING

The principles I discussed in Part Two apply to sentences and
short passages in all kinds of writing. I now turn in Part Three
to principles that apply to longer units of discourse, to sections
and whole texts. While these principles are relevant to most kinds
of expository and argumentative writing, I focus on how they
apply to kinds of writing people do in college, as scholars and
researchers, and on the job.

Of course, the various GENRES of academic and professional writing—critical essays, research reports, legal briefs, business proposals, even op-eds—differ from one another in many ways. But they also share features in common, features readers rely on to help them follow and make sense of what they read. This lesson addresses two of the most important of these: introductions and conclusions. Lesson 8 explains things you can do throughout your text to lead readers to experience it as organized and coherent. In both lessons, I take my examples mainly from academic genres, but the advice and principles apply to professional genres as well.

UNDERSTANDING MOTIVATION

Writers working in academic and professional contexts generally want to inform or persuade readers who know less than they do, which means they are vulnerable to thinking their writing is clear when their readers won't. Also, they can't assume their readers are already deeply invested in what they have to say. Accordingly, when you write in these contexts, you face a double challenge:

- to let readers know what to expect so that they can read more knowledgeably
- to motivate readers so that they want to read carefully

You do these things best when you write not just about a *topic* that interests you but about a *problem* that is important to your readers.

Stating Problems in Introductions

From the moment you begin to plan a writing project, think of your task not just as passing on information that interests *you*, but as posing a problem that will interest *your readers*. If they don't yet care—or even know—about that problem, you have to show them why they should. Such readers will ask, *So what?* That's a fair question, and you get one shot at answering it: in your introduction. That's where you must motivate readers to see your problem as their own.

For example, read this introduction (all these examples are much shorter than typical ones):

1a. When college students go out to relax on the weekend, many now "binge," downing several alcoholic drinks quickly until they are drunk or even pass out. It is a behavior that has been spreading through colleges and universities across the country, especially at large state universities. It once was done mostly by men, but now even women binge. It has drawn the attention of parents, college administrators, and researchers.

That introduction offers only a topic: it does not motivate us to care about it. Unless a reader is already interested in the issue, she may shrug and ask, *So what? Who cares that college students drink a lot?*

Contrast that introduction with this one: it tells us why bingeing is not just an interesting topic but a problem worth our attention:

> 1b. Alcohol has been a big part of college life for hundreds of years. From football weekends to fraternity parties, college students drink and often drink hard. But a new kind of drinking known as "binge" drinking is spreading through our colleges and universities. Bingers drink quickly not to be sociable but to get drunk or even to pass out. Bingeing is far from the harmless fun long associated with college life. In the last six months, it has been cited in at least six deaths, many injuries, and considerable destruction of property. It crosses the line from fun to reckless behavior that kills and injures not just drinkers but those around them. We may not be able to stop bingeing entirely, but we must try to control its worst costs by educating students in how to manage its risks.

As short as that is, (1b) has the three parts that appear in most introductions. Each part has a role in motivating a reader to read on. The parts are these:

> **Shared Context—Problem—Solution/Main Point/Claim**
>
> Alcohol has been a big part of college life . . . drink hard. _{shared context} But a new kind of drinking known as "binge" drinking is spreading . . . kills and injures not just drinkers but those around them. _{problem} We may not be able to stop bingeing entirely, but we must try to control its worst costs by educating students in how to manage its risks. _{solution/main point/claim}

Part 1: Establishing a Shared Context

Most pieces of writing open with a shared context, as does (1b):

> Alcohol has been a big part of college life for hundreds of years. From football weekends to fraternity parties, college students drink and often drink hard. _{shared context} But a new kind of drinking known as "binge" . . .

That shared context offers historical background, but it might have been a recent event, a common belief, or anything else that reminds readers of what they know, have experienced, or readily accept.

Event: A recent State U survey showed that 80% of first-year students engaged in underage drinking in their first month on campus, a fact that should surprise no one. _{shared context} But what is worrisome is the spread among first-year students of a new kind of drinking known as "binge" . . .

Belief: Most students believe that college is a safe place to drink for those who live on or near campus. And for the most part they are right. _{shared context} But for those students who get caught up in the new trend of "binge" drinking, . . .

These forms of shared context play a special role in motivating readers to read on. In (1b), I wanted you to accept that context as a seemingly unproblematic base for thinking about binge drinking *just so that I could then challenge it.* I set you up so that I could say, in effect, *you may think you know the whole story, but you don't.* That *but* signals the coming qualification:

. . . drink and often drink hard. _{shared context} **BUT a new kind of drinking known as "binge" drinking is spreading** . . .

In other words, college drinking seems unproblematic, *but it turns out not to be.* I wanted that small surprise to motivate you to go on reading.

No opening move is more common among experienced writers: open with a seeming truth, then qualify or even reject it. You can find countless examples in newspapers, magazines, and especially professional journals. This opening context can be a sentence or two, as here; in a journal, it can be paragraphs long, where it is called a *literature review,* a survey of what researchers have said that the writer will qualify or correct.

Part 2: Stating the Problem

Sometimes when writers address specialized readers, they might skip the shared context and jump directly to the second part of an introduction: the statement of a problem. More commonly, though, they open with a shared context to set up this problem statement, introducing it with a word such as *but* or *however:*

Alcohol has been a big part of college life for hundreds of years. From football weekends to fraternity parties, college students drink and often drink hard. _{shared context} **But** a new kind of drinking known as "binge" drinking is spreading through our colleges and universities. Bingers drink quickly not to be sociable but to get drunk or even to pass out. Bingeing is far from the harmless fun long associated with college life. In the last six months, it has been cited in at least

six deaths, many injuries, and considerable destruction of property.
It crosses the line from fun to reckless behavior that kills and injures
not just drinkers but those around them. _{problem} We may not be able
to . . .

The Two Parts of a Problem   For readers to think that something is a problem, it must have two parts:

- The first part is some *condition* or *situation:* terrorism, rising tuition, binge drinking, anything that has the potential to
cause trouble.

- The second part is the *intolerable consequence* of that condition, a *cost* that readers don't want to pay.

That cost is what motivates readers. They want to eliminate or at
least ameliorate it, because it makes them unhappy. To identify
the cost of a problem, imagine someone asking *So what?* after
you state its condition. Answer that question and you have found
the cost:

> But a new kind of drinking known as "binge" drinking is spreading
> through our colleges and universities. Bingers drink quickly not to
> be sociable but to get drunk or even to pass out. _{condition} *So what?*
> **Bingeing is far from the harmless fun long associated with col-
> lege life. In the last six months, it has been cited in at least six
> deaths, many injuries, and considerable destruction of property.
> It crosses the line from fun to reckless behavior that kills and
> injures not just drinkers but those around them.** _{cost of the condition}

The condition is binge drinking; the cost is death and injury.
Readers have to see the condition and cost *together* before they
recognize a problem.

Two Kinds of Problems: Practical and Conceptual   There are
two kinds of problems, and each motivates readers in a different
way. You have to write about them differently.

- A *practical* problem concerns a condition or situation in the
world and demands an *action* as its solution. That students
binge drink and harm themselves is a practical problem.

- A *conceptual* problem concerns what we think about something and demands a *change in understanding* as its solution. That we don't know why students binge is a conceptual
problem.

Writers outside the academic world most often address practical
problems; writers inside it most often address conceptual ones.

Practical Problems   We usually name a practical problem in a word or two: *cancer, unemployment, binge drinking.* But that's a shorthand. Those terms name only the condition: they say nothing about costs. Most conditions sound like trouble, but anything can be the condition of a problem if its palpable costs make you unhappy. If winning the lottery made you suffer the loss of friends and family, it would be a practical problem.

You may think that the costs of a problem like bingeing are too obvious to state, but you cannot count on readers to see the problem as you do. Some readers may see different costs. Where you see death and injury, a university publicist might see only bad press: *Those binge drinking students make us look like a party school, which hurts our image with parents.* More callous readers might see no costs at all: *So what if college students injure or kill themselves? What's that to me?* If so, you have to figure out how to make such readers see that those costs affect them. If you can't describe the costs you see so that they matter *to your readers,* they won't care about what you've written.

Conceptual Problems   A conceptual problem has the same two parts as a practical one: a condition and its costs. But beyond that, the two sorts of problem are very different.

The condition of a conceptual problem is always something that we do not know or understand. We can express this condition as a question: *How much does the universe weigh? Why does the hair on your head keep growing, but the hair on your legs doesn't?*

The cost of a conceptual problem is not the palpable unhappiness we feel from pain, suffering, and loss; it is the dissatisfaction we feel because we don't understand something important to us. We can express this cost as something *more important* that readers don't know, as *another, larger question:*

Cosmologists do not know how much the universe weighs. condition *So what?* Well, if they knew, they might figure out something more important: Will time and space go on forever, or will they end? And if they do, when and how? cost/larger question

Biologists don't know why some hair keeps growing and other hair stops. condition *So what?* If they knew, they might understand something more important: What turns growth on and off? cost/larger question

Administrators do not know why students underestimate the risks of binge drinking. condition *So what?* If they knew, they might figure out something more important: Would better information at orientation help students make safer decisions about drinking? cost/larger question

Sometimes, as in the last example, the larger question is about something readers do not know how to do. But that is still a conceptual problem, because it concerns our ignorance and because its solution is not an action but information.

Think of it like this: for a conceptual problem, you answer a small question so that your answer contributes to answering a larger, more important one. Readers are motivated because your small question inherits its importance from that larger one.

> *Here's the point:* Like your readers, you will usually be more motivated by large questions. But limited resources— time, funding, knowledge, skill, pages—may keep you from addressing a large question satisfactorily. So you have to find a question you *can* answer. When you plan your paper, look for a question that is small enough to answer but is also connected to another question large enough for you *and your readers* to care about.

Part 3: Stating the Solution

The solution is your main point or claim. We solve practical problems with action: readers (or someone) must *change what they do*. We solve conceptual problems with information: readers (or someone) must *change what they think*. Your answer to a small question then helps readers understand a larger one.

Practical Problems: What We Should Do   To solve a practical problem, you must propose that the reader (or someone) *do* something to change a condition in the world:

> . . . behavior that crosses the line from fun to recklessness that kills and injures not just drinkers but those around them. _{problem} **We may not be able to stop bingeing entirely, but we must try to control its worst costs by educating students in how to manage its risks.** _{solution/point}

Conceptual Problems: What We Should Think   To solve a conceptual problem, you must state something you want readers to *understand* or *believe*:

> . . . we can better understand not only the causes of this dangerous behavior but also the nature of risk-taking behavior in general. _{problem} **This study reports on our analysis of the beliefs of 300 first-year**

college students. **We found that students were more likely to binge if they knew more stories of other students bingeing, so that they believed that bingeing is far more common than it actually is.** solution/point

As Darwin and Einstein said, nothing is more difficult than finding a good question, because without one, you don't have an answer worth supporting.

Here's the point: Some writers, especially student writers, believe the impact of their ideas depends on how forcefully they state them. But a strong main point, claim, or thesis alone will not make a paper persuasive. Readers will find your claims most meaningful if you present them as solutions to problems, practical or conceptual, that your readers care about.

QUICK TIP   When you read an academic book or article, look first for the implied question in its problem statement and then for its main claim, which answers that question. They will help focus your reading. If you don't find a question in the introduction, look for one in the conclusion. If that fails, find the main claim and ask yourself, *What question does this answer?* The more you understand *why* a writer is telling you something, the better you will understand what she writes.

Another Part: Prelude

What best motivates readers is a problem in need of a solution, but a catchy opening can vividly introduce themes central to your problem. To name this device, we can use a musical term: *prelude.* Writers in the natural and social sciences rarely use preludes. They are more common in the humanities and most common in writing for the general public.

Here are three preludes that could establish key themes in a paper about binge drinking.

1. A Quotation

"If you're old enough to fight for your country, you're old enough to drink to it."

2. A Startling Fact

A recent study reports that at most colleges three out of four students "binged" at least once in the previous thirty days, consuming more than five drinks at a sitting. Almost half binge once a week, and those who binge most are not just members of fraternities but their officers.

3. An Illustrative Anecdote

When Jim S., president of Omega Alpha, accepted a dare from his fraternity brothers to down a pint of whiskey in one long swallow, he didn't plan to become this year's eighth college fatality from alcohol poisoning.

We can combine all three:

It is often said that "if you're old enough to fight for your country, you're old enough to drink to it." quotation Tragically, Jim S., president of Omega Alpha, no longer has a chance to do either. When he accepted a dare from his fraternity brothers to down a pint of whiskey in one long swallow, he didn't expect to become this year's eighth college fatality from alcohol poisoning. anecdote According to a recent study, at most colleges, three out of four students have, like Jim, drunk five drinks at a sitting in the last thirty days. And those who drink the most are not just members of fraternities but—like Jim S. —officers. striking fact

Drinking, of course, has been a part of American college life since the first college opened . . . shared context But in recent years . . . problem

Here, then, is a general plan for your introductions:

Prelude
Shared Context
Problem [Condition + Cost]
Solution / Main Point / Claim

Not every introduction must follow that plan exactly. Preludes are relatively uncommon. In special circumstances, writers omit or rearrange other parts as well. Here are four common variations:

- When readers know a subject well, writers sometimes skip the shared context and open with the problem.
- When readers know a problem well, writers sometimes state the cost before the condition.

- When readers can be counted on to recognize the costs, writers sometimes skip them and just state the condition.

- When readers are willing to wait (which is rare), writers sometimes save their solution/main point/claim for the conclusion, ending the introduction with a promise that a solution will come.

Although many successful introductions use these variations, your best option is to follow the general pattern until you have lots of experience with it.

HOW TO REVISE: INTRODUCTIONS

To analyze, assess, and revise your introduction, do this:

1. **Determine whether you are posing a practical or conceptual problem.** Do you want readers to *do* something or to *think* something?

2. **Draw a line after your introduction.** If you cannot quickly locate the end of your introduction, neither will your readers, who might then miss both your problem and its solution, the main point of your paper.

3. **Divide the introduction into its three parts: shared context + problem + solution/main point/claim.** If you cannot quickly make those divisions, your introduction is likely to seem unfocused.

4. **Make sure the first word of the first sentence after the shared context is *but, however,* or some other word indicating that you will challenge that shared context.** If you don't explicitly signal the contrast between the shared context and the problem, readers may miss it.

5. **Divide the problem into two parts: condition and cost.**

   5a. **Is the condition the right kind for the problem?**
   - For a practical problem, the condition must be something that exacts a palpable cost.
   - For a conceptual problem, the condition must be something not known or understood. This should be stated not as a direct question, *What causes bingeing?*, but as a statement of what we do not know: *But we do not know why bingers ignore known risks.*

5b. **Does the cost appropriately answer *So what*?**
- For a practical problem, the answer to *So what?* must state some palpable consequence of the condition that causes unhappiness.
- For a conceptual problem, the answer to *So what?* must state some more significant issue that is not known or understood.

6. **Underline your solution/main point/claim.** This should appear at the end of the introduction in its stress position, and should state the key themes that the rest of your paper will develop (more on that in Lesson 8).

CONCLUSIONS

A good introduction motivates your readers, introduces your key themes, and states your main point, the solution to your motivating problem. Get your introduction straight, and readers can read the rest more quickly and understand it better.

A good conclusion serves a different end: as the last thing your reader reads, it should bring together your point, its significance, and its implications for thinking further about your problem. Conclusions vary more than introductions, but in a pinch, you can map the parts of your introduction onto your conclusion. Just reverse their order:

1. **Open your conclusion by stating (or restating) the gist of your point, the main claim of your paper, the solution to your problem:**

   Though we can come at the problem of bingeing from several directions, the most important is education, especially in the first week of a student's college life. But that means each university must devote time and resources to it.

2. **Explain its significance by answering *So what?* Answer in a new way, if you can; if you can't, restate what you offered in the introduction, now as a benefit:**

   If we do not start to control bingeing soon, many more students will die.

   If we start to control bingeing now, we will save many lives.

3. **Suggest a further question or problem to be resolved, something still not known. Answer *Now what?*:**

   Of course, even if we can control bingeing, the larger issue of risk-taking in general will remain a serious problem.

4. **End with an anecdote, quotation, or fact that echoes your prelude.** We'll call this by another musical term, your *coda* (again, used most often in popular writing, rarely in the natural and social sciences):

> We should not underestimate how deeply entrenched bingeing is: We might have hoped that after Jim S.'s death from alcohol poisoning, his university would have taken steps to prevent more such tragedies. Sad to say, it reported another death from bingeing this month.

There are other ways to conclude, but this one works when nothing better comes to mind.

In Your Own Words

Exercise 7.1

For this exercise, you can use pieces of writing that are finished or still in progress. For each, draw a line between the problem and the solution. Underline the condition and bracket the cost. Classify the problem of each as conceptual or practical. Then rewrite the conceptual problems as practical ones and the practical problems as conceptual ones. What did you have to change? Were some problems easier to rewrite in this way than others? Why?

Exercise 7.2

Writers, especially in academic contexts, can struggle more with problem statements than with other parts of their introductions. It makes sense that writers would have this struggle. To state a problem, writers need to understand not only their own ideas but also the motives of their readers. This exercise will help you do that. For a project you are just beginning, do the following:

1. In a sentence, state your *topic:* In this paper I am writing about _____ (e.g., science in Tennyson's *In Memoriam,* the effects of Citizens United v. Federal Election Commission on election financing, the space shuttle *Columbia* accident).

2. In a sentence, state why *you* selected this particular topic out of the many you could have chosen: I care about my topic because _____. (If you cannot complete this sentence, you need to do more thinking about your topic or choose another. You cannot expect your readers to care if you can't say why you do.)

3. In a sentence, state your *main point* or *claim:* The point I want to make about [topic] is that _____.

4. In a paragraph, describe one person (real or imagined) who would care deeply about your ideas. What does she (or he) look like? What does she do for a living? What are her personal interests? What books has she read in the past two months?

5. Now write a short letter to the person you have described, explaining to her why she should care about your paper.

You will probably find phrases and ideas in this letter that you can use in your problem statement.

Exercise 7.3

Analyze introductions from three readings in your area of study or expertise using the procedure on pp. 103–104:

1. Determine whether the problem is practical or conceptual.

2. Draw a line at the introduction's end.

3. Divide the introduction into its three parts: shared context, problem, and solution/main point/claim. Do these three parts appear? Are they in the right order?

4. Circle the word or phrase (usually *but* or *however*) that indicates a challenge to the shared context.

5. Divide the problem into its two parts: condition and cost. Does the cost answer the question *So what?*

6. Underline the solution/main point/claim.

What patterns did you notice? Now do the same with an introduction of your own.

SUMMING UP

You best motivate readers with an introduction that states a problem readers want to see solved.

For a practical problem the key is to state its costs so clearly that readers will ask not *So what?* but *What do we do?* Here is a plan for introducing a practical problem:

> Alcohol has been a part of college life for hundreds of years. From football weekends to fraternity parties, college students drink and often drink hard. shared context

Open the introduction with *shared context,* a brief statement of what you will go on to qualify or even contradict.

But a new kind of drinking known as "binge" drinking is spreading through our colleges and universities. Bingers drink quickly not to be sociable but to get drunk or even to pass out. _{condition} *So what?*

Follow that with a statement of the condition of the problem. Introduce it with a *but, however, on the other hand,* etc. Imagine a *So what?* after it.

Bingeing is far from harmless. In the last six months, it has been cited in six deaths, many injuries, and considerable destruction of property. It crosses the line from fun to reckless behavior that kills and injures not just drinkers but those around them. _{costs}

Answer that imagined *So what?* with a statement of the consequences of that condition, its costs *to your readers* that they do not want to pay.

We may not be able to stop bingeing entirely, but we must try to control its worst costs by educating students in how to manage its risks. _{solution}

Conclude with a statement of the solution to the problem, an *action* that will eliminate or at least ameliorate the costs.

For conceptual problems, the key is to state a small question worth answering because it helps to answer a larger, more significant one. Here is a plan for introducing conceptual problems:

Colleges are reporting that binge drinking is increasing. We know its practical risks. We also know that bingers ignore those risks, even after they have learned about them. _{shared context}

Open the introduction with *shared context,* a brief statement of what you will go on to qualify or even contradict.

But we don't know what causes bingers to ignore the known risks: social influences, a personality attracted to risk, or a failure to understand the nature of the risks. condition/first, small question *So what?*

Follow that with a statement of the condition of the problem. Introduce it with a *but, however, on the other hand,* etc. State something that is not known or well understood. Imagine a *So what?* after it.

If we can determine why bingers ignore known risks of their actions, we can better understand not only the causes of this dangerous behavior but also the nature of risk-taking behavior in general. cost/second, larger question

Answer that imagined *So what?* with the cost of the condition, a larger and more important issue that is not known or understood but that might be answered if we know the answer to the first question.

In this study, we analyzed the beliefs of 300 first-year college students to determine . . . We found that . . . solution

Conclude your introduction with a statement of the solution to the problem, an answer to the first question that helps answer the second one as well.

Lesson

8

Global Coherence

*One of the most difficult things [to write] is the first paragraph.
I have spent many months on a first paragraph, and once I get it,
the rest just comes out very easily. In the first paragraph you solve
most of the problems with your book. The theme is defined, the
style, the tone.*
—GABRIEL GARCÍA MÁRQUEZ

UNDERSTANDING GLOBAL COHERENCE

In the last lesson, I explained how to create an introduction that does two things:

- Motivates your readers by stating a problem that they care about.
- Frames the rest of your document by stating the point and key concepts that you will develop in what follows.

In this lesson, I explain how that second point applies to all the parts of your document—its sections, subsections, and even paragraphs. Like the term *clear*, the term *coherent* doesn't refer to anything we find on the page. Coherence is an experience we create for ourselves as we make sense out of what we read.

What we look for on the page are signals that help us integrate what we are reading with the knowledge we already have. Your readers will understand your writing better and more easily when you build those signals into it deliberately. This lesson explains how to do that.

FORECASTING THEMES TO CREATE COHERENCE

In Lessons 5 and 6, we looked at those features that help readers create *local* coherence in short passages, but readers need more to grasp the *global* coherence of a whole document. To help them, you can use a by-now-familiar principle: begin each section or subsection of a document with a short, easily grasped segment that states its point and introduces the themes that organize the longer segment that follows, the body. Then in that body, support, develop, or explain that point and those themes.

To help readers grasp the coherence of a document and its sections, follow these six principles:

For the document:

1. Readers must know where the introduction ends and the body begins, as well as where each section ends and the next begins. Identify the start of each new section with a heading that includes the key themes for that section (see 5 below). If your field does not use headings, delete them for the final draft.

2. At the end of the introduction, readers look for the document's main point, claim, or solution to its problem, which should state the main themes developed in the rest. If you have good reason to save your main point for the conclusion, end your introduction with a sentence that promises the point to come *and* states the main themes.

3. In the body, readers look for the concepts announced as themes at the end of the introduction, using them to organize their understanding of the whole. Be sure that you repeat those themes regularly.

For each section and subsection:

4. Readers look for a short segment that introduces the section or subsection.

5. At the end of that introductory segment, readers look for a sentence that states both the point of the section and the specific concepts you will develop as distinctive themes for that section.

6. In the body of the section, readers look for the concepts announced as themes at the end of the introductory segment, using them to organize their understanding of that section. Be sure that you repeat them regularly.

QUICK TIP You can use these six principles to prepare yourself to read a difficult document. First, highlight the question in the problem statement and the main claim that answers it (see pp. 96–101). Next, for each section, highlight its introduction, point, and key concepts. If you don't find them in the introduction to a section, look for them at the end of the section. Finally, read through just the parts that you highlighted. When you then begin reading in detail, you will have in mind an overview that will help you better understand and remember the rest.

In the limited space we have here, I can't illustrate these principles with entire documents or even long sections. So I will use paragraphs and ask you to relate their structure to that of a whole section of a document.

For example, read this:

> 1a. Thirty sixth-grade students wrote essays that were analyzed to determine the effectiveness of eight weeks of training to distinguish fact from opinion. That ability is an important aspect of making sound arguments of any kind. In an essay written before instruction began, the writers failed almost completely to distinguish fact from opinion. In an essay written after four weeks of instruction, the students visibly attempted to distinguish fact from opinion, but did so inconsistently. In three more essays, they distinguished fact from opinion more consistently, but never achieved the predicted level of performance. In a final essay written six months after instruction ended, they did no better than they did in their pre-instruction essays. Their training had some effect on their writing during the instruction period, but it was inconsistent, and six months after instruction it had no measurable effect.

The first few sentences introduce the rest, but we don't see in them the key concepts that follow: *inconsistently, never achieved, no better, no measurable effect.* Those terms are crucial to the *point* of the whole passage. Worse, the passage doesn't give us that point until the very end: training had no long-term effect. And so as we read, the passage seems to ramble, until the end, when we learn what we need to know to make sense of it retrospectively. But that takes more effort than we should have to expend.

Compare this version:

> 1b. In this study, thirty sixth-grade students were taught to distinguish fact from opinion. They did so successfully during the instruction period, but the effect was inconsistent and less than predicted, and six

months after instruction ended, the instruction had no measurable effect. In an essay written before instruction began, the writers failed almost completely to distinguish fact from opinion. In an essay written after four weeks of instruction, the students visibly attempted to distinguish fact from opinion, but did so inconsistently. In three more essays, they distinguished fact from opinion more consistently, but never achieved the predicted level of performance. In a final essay written six months after instruction ended, they did no better than they did in their pre-instruction essay. We thus conclude that short-term training to distinguish fact from opinion has no consistent or long-term effect.

In (1b), we quickly grasp that the first two sentences introduce what follows. And in the second sentence, we see two things: both the point of the passage (underlined) and its key terms (boldfaced):

1b. In this study, thirty sixth-grade students were taught to distinguish fact from opinion. <u>They did so **successfully** during the instruction period, but the effect was **inconsistent** and **less than predicted**, and six months after instruction ended, the instruction had</u> **no measurable effect**.

Consequently, we feel the passage hangs together better, and we read it with more understanding.

Now imagine two documents: in one, the point of each section and of the whole appears at its *end* (as in 1a) and what openings there are do not introduce the key terms that follow; in the other, each point appears in an *introductory* segment to every paragraph, section, and of the whole (as in 1b). Which would be easier to read and understand? The second, of course.

Keep in mind this principle: put the point sentence at the end of the short opening segment; make it the *last* sentence that your reader reads before starting the longer, more complex segment that follows.

- In a paragraph, the introductory segment might be just a single sentence, so by default, it will be the last sentence readers read before they read what follows. If the paragraph has a *two*-sentence introduction (as did 1b), be sure that its point is the *second* sentence, still making it the last thing readers read before they read the rest.

- For sections, your introduction might be a paragraph or more. For a whole document, you might need several paragraphs. Even in those cases, put your point sentence at the end of that introductory segment, no matter how long it is. Make your point the last thing readers read before they begin reading the longer, more complex segments that follow.

Some inexperienced writers think that if they reveal their main point in their introduction, readers will be bored and not read on. Not true. If you motivate readers with an interesting problem, they will want to see how you address it.

> *Here's the point:*   To write a document that readers will think is coherent, open every unit—section, subsection, and the whole—with a short, easily grasped introductory segment. At the end of that opening segment, put a sentence that states both the point of the unit and the key concepts that follow. Such "point" sentences constitute the outline of your document, its logical structure. If readers miss them, they may judge your writing to be incoherent.

TWO MORE REQUIREMENTS FOR COHERENCE

We can make sense of almost anything we read if we know its points. But to make full sense of a passage, we must see two more things.

1. **Readers must see how everything in a section or whole is** *relevant* **to its point.** Consider this passage:

> We analyzed essays written by sixth-grade students to determine the effectiveness of training in distinguishing fact from opinion. In an essay written before training, the students failed almost completely to distinguish fact and opinion. These essays were also badly organized in several ways. In the first two essays after training began, the students attempted to distinguish fact from opinion, but did so inconsistently. They also produced fewer spelling and punctuation errors. In the essays four through seven, they distinguished fact from opinion more consistently, but in their final essay, written six months after completion of instruction, they did no better than they did in their first essay. Their last essay was significantly longer than their first one, however. Their training thus had some effect on their writing during the training period, but it was inconsistent and transient.

What are those sentences about spelling, organization, and length doing there? When readers can't see the relevance of sentences to a point, they are likely to judge what they read as being incoherent.

Unfortunately, I can't give you a simple rule of relevance, because it's so abstract a quality. I can only list its most important kinds. Sentences are relevant to a point when they offer these:

- background or context
- points of sections and the whole
- reasons supporting a point
- evidence, facts, or data supporting a reason
- an explanation of reasoning or methods
- consideration of other points of view

2. **Readers must see how the parts of your document are ordered.** Readers want to see not just how everything they read is relevant to a point, but what principle is behind the order of its parts. We look for three kinds of order: chronological, coordinate, and logical.

   - **Chronological** This is the simplest order, from earlier to later (or vice versa), as a narrative or as cause and effect. Signal time with *first, then, finally;* signal cause and effect with *as a result, because of that,* and so on. The passage about the essay research was chronologically organized.

   - **Coordinate** Two or more sections are coordinate when they are like pillars equally supporting a common roof. *There are three reasons why. . . .* Order those sections so that their sequence makes sense to your reader—by importance, complexity, and so on—then signal that order with words and phrases such as *first, second, . . .* or *also, another, more important, in addition,* and so on. That's how this section on order is organized.

   - **Logical** This is the most complex order: by example and generalization (or vice versa), premise and conclusion (or vice versa), or by assertion and contradiction. Signal logic with *for example, on the other hand, it follows that. . . .*

QUICK TIP Writers often order their documents chronologically because that is easiest for them. Once you have drafted a paper, read it through to see whether you have organized it simply as a narrative of your thinking. If you have, consider revising. Order your ideas not in the way that is easiest for you, but in the way that best helps your readers understand them.

On Paragraphs

In different kinds of writing, paragraphs follow different conventions. In newspaper articles, they are often only a sentence long. In this book, they are a bit longer. In academic papers and scholarly journal articles, they can run half a page or more. Here is some advice that will help you write coherent longer paragraphs:

- Begin with one or two short, easily grasped sentences that frame what follows.

- State the point of the paragraph (in traditional terms its *topic sentence*) in the last sentence of its introduction. If the introduction is just one sentence, it will be its point by default.

- Toward the end of that point sentence, name the key themes that thread through what follows.

Treat this advice as general guidance, not as a rigid template. Many longer paragraphs don't follow this tidy structure, and we get through them just fine. Even so, most begin with some kind of opening segment that frames what follows by introducing key themes and perhaps by stating the point. If the point doesn't appear at the beginning of a paragraph, it will usually come at the end.

Compare these two examples:

2a. The team obtained exact sequences of fossils—new lines of antelopes, giraffes, and elephants developing out of old and appearing in younger strata, then dying out as they were replaced by others in still later strata. The most specific sequences they reconstructed were several lines of pigs that had been common at the site and had developed rapidly. The team produced family trees that dated types of pigs so accurately that when they found pigs next to fossils of questionable age, they could use the pigs to date the fossils. By mapping every fossil precisely, the team was able to recreate exactly how and when the animals in a whole ecosystem evolved.

2b. By precisely mapping every fossil they found, the team was able to recreate exactly how and when the animals in a whole ecosystem evolved. They charted new lines of antelopes, giraffes, and elephants developing out of old and appearing in younger strata, then dying out as they were replaced by others in still later strata. The most exact sequences they reconstructed were several lines of pigs that had been common at the site and had developed rapidly. The team produced family trees that dated types of pigs so accurately that when they found pigs next to fossils of questionable age, they could use the pigs to date the fossils.

Paragraph (2a) makes its point in the last sentence; paragraph (2b) in its first sentence. Reading these paragraphs in isolation, you probably found (2b) slightly easier to understand. But in the context of an otherwise coherent text about fossil hunters and their work, (2a) probably wouldn't give you a problem.

If you have framed and organized your document and its sections well, your readers can make their way through a few paragraphs that are less than perfect. But if they don't know what your paragraphs are supposed to add up to, then no matter how well written they are individually, your readers may well feel lost.

A GENERAL PRINCIPLE OF CLARITY

This general principle implies many of our others. It applies to individual sentences, to longer paragraphs, to sections and subsections, and to whole documents:

> Readers are more likely to judge as clear any unit of writing that opens with a short segment that they can easily grasp and that frames the longer and more complex segment that follows.

Sentences: In a simple sentence, that short, easily grasped segment is a subject/topic. Compare these two:

> 1a. <u>Resistance in Nevada against its use as a waste disposal site</u> has been heated.

> 1b. <u>Nevada</u> has heatedly resisted its use as a waste disposal site.

In a complex sentence, that short, easily grasped segment is a main clause that expresses the point of its sentence. Compare these two:

> 2a. Greater knowledge of pre-Columbian civilizations and the effect of European colonization destroying their societies by inflicting on them devastating diseases has led to a historical reassessment of Columbus's role in world history.

> 2b. <u>Historians are reassessing Columbus's role in world history</u> because they know more about pre-Columbian civilizations and how European colonization destroyed their societies by inflicting on them devastating diseases.

The point of sentence (2a) is buried at its end. In (2b), the opening clause states the main point of the sentence, its most important claim: *Historians are reassessing Columbus's role in world history.* That claim is then supported by the longer and more complex clause that follows.

Paragraphs: In a paragraph, that short, easily grasped unit is an introductory sentence or two that both expresses the point of the paragraph and introduces its key concepts. Compare these two paragraphs:

3a. Thirty sixth-grade students wrote essays that were analyzed to determine the effectiveness of eight weeks of training to distinguish fact from opinion. That ability is an important aspect of making sound arguments of any kind. In an essay written before instruction began, the writers failed almost completely to distinguish fact from opinion. In an essay written after four weeks of instruction, the students visibly attempted to distinguish fact from opinion, but did so inconsistently. In three more essays, they distinguished fact from opinion more consistently, but never achieved the predicted level. In a final essay written six months after instruction ended, they did no better than they did in their pre-instruction essay. Their training had some effect on their writing during the instruction period, but it was inconsistent, and six months after instruction it had no measurable effect.

3b. <u>In this study, thirty sixth-grade students were taught to distinguish fact from opinion.</u> They did so **successfully** <u>during the instruction period, but the effect was **inconsistent** and **less than predicted**, and six months after instruction ended, the instruction had **no measurable effect.**</u>_{opening segment/point} In an essay written before instruction began, the writers failed almost completely to distinguish fact from opinion. In an essay written after four weeks of instruction, the students visibly attempted to distinguish fact from opinion, but did so inconsistently. In three more essays, they distinguished fact from opinion more consistently, but never achieved the predicted level. In a final essay written six months after instruction ended, they did no better than they did in their pre-instruction essay. We thus conclude that short-term training to distinguish fact from opinion has no consistent or long-term effect.

Paragraph (3a) has no clearly distinguished opening unit, and it does not announce the key themes of the paragraph. Paragraph (3b) has a clearly marked opening unit that states the point, and it clearly announces the key themes of the paragraph.

Sections: In a section or subsection, that short, easily grasped unit may be just a paragraph; in longer units, it will be proportionally longer. Even so, at its end it expresses the point of its unit and introduces the key concepts that follow. There is not enough space here to illustrate how that principle applies to a passage several paragraphs long, but it is easy to imagine.

Whole documents: In a whole document, that introductory unit might be one or more paragraphs long, perhaps even a few pages. Even so, it should be substantially shorter than the rest, and in a sentence at its end, it should state the point of the whole document and introduces its key concepts.

QUICK TIP   Budget your time for both drafting and revision so that you spend most of it on beginnings: the introduction to the whole, then the introductions to major sections, then introductions to subsections and long paragraphs, then the beginnings of sentences. Get beginnings straight, and the rest is likely to take care of itself.

The Costs and Benefits of Templated Writing

Some writers fear that patterns like these will inhibit their creativity and bore their readers. That's a reasonable concern, if you are writing a literary essay that explores your own thoughts as you have them, for readers who have the time and patience to follow the twists and turns of your thinking. If you are writing that kind of essay for that kind of reader, go to it. Don't tie yourself to what I've said here.

On most occasions, however, most of us read less for aesthetic pleasures than to understand what we need to know. You help readers toward this end when you follow the principles of clarity and coherence we've looked at in Parts Two and Three of this book.

Such writing may seem formulaic—to *you*, because *you* will be so conscious of the patterns you followed. But it earns the gratitude of readers who have too little time to read, understand, and remember everything they must and who will, in any event, focus more on understanding the substance of your writing than on critiquing its form.

In Your Own Words

Exercise 8.1

A basic principle of clarity is that any unit of discourse—a sentence, a paragraph, a section, a whole document—should begin with a short segment that introduces and frames the longer and more complex segment that follows. Go through a piece of your writing section by section. Draw a line after that short segment and circle words in that segment that signal key themes in what follows. If you cannot, revise.

Exercise 8.2

To feel a document (or a section of one) is coherent, a reader needs to understand how it is organized (review pp. 113–114). But writers, especially in early drafts, often organize their documents in the way that is easiest for them, not the way that is best for their readers. Specifically, writers often adopt a chronological or narrative structure by default. You can see why this is so. When getting ideas down on paper, it is easiest for writers simply to rehearse their thinking or research. But most often, readers do not want to hear a story of discovery but to understand a writer's points. Revising for global coherence, therefore, often involves translating a document from a chronological or narrative structure to a coordinate or logical one. A reader can help you do this.

Go through a document or section that you have organized chronologically. Highlight your points, paragraph by paragraph, and copy them onto index cards. Shuffle the cards and give them to a reader. Have a reader put the cards into what seems like their right order. Reorganize your document or section so that it follows that order. What did you have to change?

Summing Up

Plan your paragraphs, sections, and the whole on this model:

Researchers have made strides in the **early and accurate diagnosis** of *Alzheimer's,* [but <u>those diagnoses</u> have raised A NEW HUMAN PROBLEM about **informing** *those at risk* before they show any *symptoms of it.*]_{point}

Open each unit with a relatively short segment introducing it.

End that segment with a sentence stating the point of that unit.

Toward the end of that point sentence, use key themes that the rest of the unit develops.

Not too long ago, when <u>physicians</u> examined an older patient who seemed *out of touch with reality*, they had to **guess** whether that person had *Alzheimer's* or was *only senile*. In the past few years, however, they have been able to use **new and more reliable tests** focusing on genetic clues. But in <u>**the accuracy of these new tests**</u> lies the RISK OF ANOTHER KIND OF HUMAN TRAGEDY: physicians may be able to **predict** *Alzheimer's* long before its overt appearance, but such an <u>**early diagnosis**</u> could PSYCHOLOGICALLY DEVASTATE AN APPARENTLY HEALTHY PERSON.

In the longer segment that follows, use consistent topics (underlined).

Repeat key terms introduced toward the end of the opening segment (boldfaced, italicized, and capitalized).

Make every sentence follow the old-new principle.

Order sentences, paragraphs, and sections in a way that readers understand.

Make all sentences relevant to the point of the unit that they constitute.

PART FOUR

Grace

*There are two sorts of eloquence; the one indeed scarce
deserves the name of it, which consists chiefly in
laboured and polished periods, an over-curious and
artificial arrangement of figures, tinseled over with a
gaudy embellishment of words.... The other sort of
eloquence is quite the reverse to this, and which may be
said to be the true characteristic of the holy scriptures;
where the eloquence does not arise from a laboured and
farfetched elocution, but from a surprising mixture of
simplicity and majesty.*

—LAURENCE STERNE

Lesson

9

Concision

*Often I think writing is sheer paring away of oneself leaving
always something thinner, barer, more meager.*
—F. SCOTT FITZGERALD

*The ability to simplify means to eliminate the unnecessary
so that the necessary may speak.*
—HANS HOFMANN

UNDERSTANDING CONCISION

You write more clearly when you match your characters and
actions to your subjects and verbs, when you get the right characters into topics and the right words under stress, when you motivate readers with well-crafted introductions, and when you frame
your paragraphs, sections, and documents to help readers grasp
their global coherence. But readers may still think your prose a
long way from graceful if it's anything like this:

> In my personal opinion, it is necessary that we should not ignore the
> opportunity to think over each and every suggestion offered.

That sentence matches characters with subjects and actions
with verbs but in too many words: opinion is always personal, so
we don't need *personal*, and since this statement is opinion, we
don't need *in my opinion. Think over* and *not ignore* both mean

consider. Each and every is redundant. And suggestion is by definition offered. In fewer words:

✓ We should consider each suggestion.

Though not yet shapely or elegant, that sentence at least has the virtue of compactness or, as we'll call it, concision.

HOW TO REVISE: CONCISION

Readers think you write concisely when you use just enough words to say what you mean. Here are six principles that help you do that:

1. Delete words that mean little or nothing.
2. Delete words that repeat the meaning of other words.
3. Delete words implied by other words.
4. Replace a phrase with a word.
5. Change negatives to affirmatives.
6. Delete useless adjectives and ADVERBS.

Here they are again, in detail:

1. **Delete meaningless words.** Some words are verbal tics that we use as unconsciously as we clear our throats:

kind of	actually	particular	really	certain	various
virtually	individual	basically	generally	given	practically

Productivity **actually** depends on **certain** factors that **basically** involve psychology more than **any particular** technology.

✓ Productivity depends on psychology more than on technology.

2. **Delete doubled words.** Early in the history of English, writers got into the habit of pairing a French or Latin word with a native English one, because foreign words sounded more learned. Most paired words today are just redundant. Among the common ones:

full and complete	hope and trust	any and all
true and accurate	each and every	basic and fundamental
hope and desire	first and foremost	various and sundry

3. **Delete what readers can infer.** This redundancy is common but hard to identify, because it comes in so many forms.

   Redundant Modifiers Often, the meaning of a word implies others, especially its modifier (boldfaced):

   > Do not try to *predict* **future** events that **will completely** *revolutionize* society, because **past** *history* shows that it is the **final** *outcome* of minor events that **unexpectedly** *surprises* us more.

   ✓ Do not try to predict revolutionary events, because history shows that the outcome of minor events surprises us more.

   Some common redundancies:

terrible tragedy	various different	free gift
basic fundamentals	future plans	each individual
final outcome	true facts	consensus of opinion

   Redundant Categories Every word implies its general category, so you can usually cut a word that names it (boldfaced):

   > During that *period* **of time,** the *membrane* **area** became *pink* **in color** and *shiny* **in appearance.**

   ✓ During that *period,* the *membrane* became *pink* and *shiny*.

   In doing that, you may have to change an adjective into an adverb:

   > The holes must be aligned in an *accurate* **manner.**

   ✓ The holes must be aligned *accurately*.

   Sometimes you change an adjective into a noun:

   > The county manages the *educational* **system** and *public recreational* **activities.**

   ✓ The county manages *education* and *public recreation*.

   Here are some general nouns (boldfaced) often used redundantly:

large in **size**	round in **shape**	honest in **character**
unusual in **nature**	of a strange **type**	**area** of mathematics
of a bright **color**	at an early **time**	in a confused **state**

   General Implications This kind of wordiness is even harder to spot because it can be so diffuse:

   > Imagine trying to learn the rules for playing the game of chess.

   Learn implies *trying, rules* implies *playing the game, chess* is a *game*. So more concisely,

   ✓ Imagine learning the rules of chess.

4. **Replace a phrase with a word.** This redundancy is especially difficult to fix, because you need a big vocabulary and the wit to use it. For example:

> As you carefully go over what you have written to improve wording and catch errors of spelling and punctuation, the thing to do before anything else is to see whether you could use sequences of subjects and verbs instead of the same ideas expressed in nouns.

That is,

✓ As you edit, first replace nominalizations with clauses.

I compressed five phrases into five words:

carefully go over what you have written to improve wording and catch errors of spelling and punctuation	→	edit
the thing to do before anything else	→	first
use X instead of Y	→	replace
sequences of subjects and verbs	→	clauses
the same ideas expressed in nouns	→	nominalizations

I can't tell you when to replace a phrase with a word, much less give you the word. I can point out only that you should be alert for opportunities to do so, which is to say, try.

Here are some common phrases (boldfaced) to watch for. Note that some of these let you turn a nominalization into a verb (both italicized):

We must explain **the reason for** the *delay* in the meeting.

✓ We must explain **why** the meeting is *delayed*.

Despite the fact that the data were checked, errors occurred.

✓ **Even though** the data were checked, errors occurred.

In the event that you finish early, contact this office.

✓ **If** you finish early, contact this office.

In a situation where a class closes, you may petition to get in.

✓ **When** a class closes, you may petition to get in.

I want to say a few words **concerning the matter of** money.

✓ I want to say a few words **about** money.

There is a need for more careful *inspection* of all welds.

✓ You **must** *inspect* all welds more carefully.

We **are in a position** to make you an offer.

✓ We **can** make you an offer.

It is possible that nothing will come of this.

✓ Nothing **may** come of this.

Prior to the *end* of the training, apply for your license.

✓ **Before** training *ends*, apply for your license.

We have noted a **decrease/increase in the number of** errors.

✓ We have noted **fewer/more** errors.

5. **Change negatives to affirmatives.** When you express an idea in a negative form, not only must you use an extra word—*same → not different*—but you also force readers to do a kind of algebraic calculation. These two sentences mean much the same thing, but the affirmative is more direct:

Do not write in the negative.   →   Write in the affirmative.

You can rewrite most negatives:

not careful	→ careless	not many	→	few
not the same	→ different	not often	→	rarely
not allow	→ prevent	not stop	→	continue
not notice	→ overlook	not include	→	omit

Do not translate a negative into an affirmative if you want to emphasize the negative. (Is that such a sentence? I could have written, *Keep a negative sentence when…*)

Some verbs, prepositions, and conjunctions are implicitly negative:

Verbs	*preclude, prevent, lack, fail, doubt, reject, avoid, deny, refuse, exclude, contradict, prohibit, bar*
Prepositions	*without, against, lacking, but for, except*
Conjunctions	*unless, except when*

You can baffle readers if you combine *not* with these negative words. Compare these:

Except when you have **failed** to submit applications **without** documentation, benefits will **not** be **denied**.

✓ You will receive benefits only if you submit your documents.

✓ To receive benefits, submit your documents.

And you baffle readers completely when you combine negative words with passive verbs and nominalizations:

> There should be **no** submission of payments **without** notification of this office, **unless** the payment does **not** exceed $100.

To revise, first replace the nominalizations with verbs:

> Do not **submit** payments if you have not **notified** this office, unless you are **paying** less than $100.

Then change the negatives into affirmatives:

✓ If you pay more than $100, notify this office first.

6. **Delete adjectives and adverbs.** Many writers can't resist adding useless adjectives and adverbs. Try deleting every adverb and every adjective before a noun, and then restore *only* those that readers need to understand the passage. In this passage, which ones should be restored?

> At the heart of the argument culture is our habit of seeing issues and ideas as ~~absolute and irreconcilable~~ principles ~~continually~~ at war. To move beyond this ~~static and limiting~~ view, we can remember the ~~Chinese~~ approach to yin and yang. They are two principles, yes, but they are conceived not as ~~irreconcilable polar~~ opposites but as elements that coexist and should be brought into balance ~~as much as possible~~. As sociolinguist Suzanne Wong Scollon notes, "Yin is always present in and changing into yang and vice versa." How can we translate this ~~abstract~~ idea into ~~daily~~ practice?
>
> —Deborah Tannen, *The Argument Culture:*
> *Stopping America's War of Words*

Exercise 9.1

Prune the redundancy from these sentences.

1. Critics cannot avoid employing complex and abstract technical terms if they are to successfully analyze literary texts and discuss them in a meaningful way.

2. Scientific research generally depends on fully accurate data if it is to offer theories that will allow us to predict the future in a plausible way.

3. Most likely, a majority of all patients who appear at a public medical clinical facility do not expect special medical attention or treatment, because their particular health problems and concerns are often not major and for the most part can usually be adequately treated without much time, effort, and attention.

4. Notwithstanding the fact that all legal restrictions on the use of firearms are the subject of heated debate and argument, it is necessary that the general public not stop carrying on discussions pro and con in regard to them.

Where appropriate, change the following negatives to affirmatives, and do any more editing you think useful.

5. There is no possibility in regard to a reduction in the size of the federal deficit if reductions in federal spending are not introduced.
6. Do not discontinue medication unless symptoms of dizziness and nausea are not present for six hours.

Exercise 9.2

Here are sentences from two "free" offers.

You will not be charged your first monthly fee unless you don't cancel within the first thirty days.

To avoid being charged your first monthly fee, cancel your membership within the first thirty days.

Which is less clear? Why might it have been written like that? Revise it.

REDUNDANT METADISCOURSE

Lesson 4 described metadiscourse as language that refers to the following:

- the writer's intentions: *to sum up, candidly, I believe*
- directions to the reader: *note that, consider now, as you see*
- the structure of the text: *first, finally, in this section*

Almost everything you write needs some metadiscourse, but too much buries your ideas:

The last point I would like to make is that in regard to men-women relationships, it is important to keep in mind that the greatest changes have occurred in how they work together.

Only nine of those thirty-four words address men-women relationships:

men-women relationships...greatest changes...how they work together.

The rest is metadiscourse. When we prune it, we tighten the sentence:

> The greatest changes in men-women relationships have occurred in how they work together.

Now that we see what the sentence says, we can make it still more direct:

> ✓ Men and women have changed their relationships most in how they work together.

How writers use metadiscourse varies by field, but you can usually cut these two types:

1. **Metadiscourse That Attributes Your Ideas to a Source** Don't announce that something has been *observed, noticed, noted,* and so on; just state the fact:

   > High divorce rates **have been observed** to occur in areas that **have been determined to have** low population density.

   > ✓ High divorce rates occur in areas with low population density.

2. **Metadiscourse That Announces Your Topic** The boldfaced phrases tell your reader that you are about to state what your sentence is "about":

   > **This section introduces another** problem, that of noise pollution. **The first thing to say about it is** that noise pollution exists not only...

   Readers catch the topic more easily if you reduce the metadiscourse:

   > ✓ **Another** problem is noise pollution. **First**, it exists not only...

HEDGES AND INTENSIFIERS

Another kind of metadiscourse reflects the writer's certainty about what she is claiming. *Hedges* qualify your certainty; *intensifiers* increase it. Both can be redundant when used excessively. But they can also be useful, because they signal how well you balance caution and confidence and therefore influence how readers judge your character.

Hedges

These are common hedges:

Adverbs	*usually, often, sometimes, almost, virtually, possibly, allegedly, arguably, perhaps, apparently,*

	in some ways, to a certain extent, somewhat, in some/certain respects
Adjectives	*most, many, some, a certain number of*
Verbs	*may, might, can, could, seem, tend, appear, suggest, indicate*

Too much hedging sounds mealy-mouthed, like this:

> There **seems to be some** evidence to **suggest** that **certain** differences between Japanese and Western rhetoric **could** derive from historical influences **possibly** traceable to Japan's cultural isolation and Europe's history of cross-cultural contacts.

On the other hand, only a fool or someone with massive historical evidence would make an assertion as flatly certain as this:

> This evidence **proves** that Japanese and Western rhetorics differ because of Japan's cultural isolation and Europe's history of cross-cultural contacts.

In most academic writing, we more often state claims closer to this (note my own hedging):

> ✓ This evidence **suggests** that **aspects** of Japanese and Western rhetoric differ because of Japan's cultural isolation and Europe's history of cross-cultural contacts.

The verbs *suggest* and *indicate* let you state a claim about which you are less than 100-percent certain, but confident enough to propose:

> ✓ The evidence **indicates** that some of these questions remain unresolved.
> ✓ These data **suggest** that further studies are necessary.

Even confident scientists hedge. This next paragraph introduced the most significant breakthrough in the history of genetics, the discovery of the double helix of DNA. If anyone was entitled to be assertive, it was Crick and Watson. But they chose to be diffident (note, too, the first person *we;* hedges are boldfaced):

> We **wish to suggest a** [not *the*] structure for the salt of deoxyribose nucleic acid (D.N.A.).... A structure for nucleic acid has already been proposed by Pauling and Corey.... **In our opinion,** this structure is unsatisfactory for two reasons: (1) **We believe** that the material which gives the X-ray diagrams is the salt, not the free acid.... (2) **Some** of the van der Waals distances **appear** to be too small.

> —J. D. Watson and F. H. C. Crick, "Molecular Structure of Nucleic Acids"

Intensifiers

These are common intensifiers:

Adverbs	*very, pretty, quite, rather, clearly, obviously, undoubtedly, certainly, of course, indeed, inevitably, invariably, always, literally*
Adjectives	*key, central, crucial, basic, fundamental, major, principal, essential*
Verbs	*show, prove, establish, as you/we/everyone knows/can see, it is clear/obvious that*

The most common intensifier, however, is the absence of a hedge. Without the hedges, Crick and Watson's claim would be more concise but more aggressive. Compare this. I boldface the stronger words, but most of the aggressive tone comes from the *absence* of hedges:

> We ~~wish to suggest~~ **state here** ~~a~~ **the** structure for the salt of deoxyribose nucleic acid (D.N.A.)....A structure for nucleic acid has already been proposed by Pauling and Corey.... ~~In our opinion,~~ [T]his structure is unsatisfactory for two reasons: (1) ~~We believe that~~ [T]he material which gives the X-ray diagrams is the salt, not the free acid....(2) ~~Some of~~ [T]he van der Waals distances ~~appear to be~~ **are** too small.

Confident writers use intensifiers less often than they use hedges because they want to avoid sounding as assertive as this:

> For a century now, **all** liberals have argued against **any** censorship of art, and **every** court has found their arguments so **completely** persuasive that **not** a person **any** longer remembers how they were countered. As a result, today, censorship is **totally** a thing of the past.

Some writers think that kind of aggressive style is persuasive. Quite the opposite. If you state a claim moderately, readers are more likely to consider it thoughtfully:

> For **about** a century now, **many** liberals have argued against censorship of art, and **most** courts have found their arguments persuasive **enough** that **few** people remember **exactly** how they were countered. As a result, today, censorship is **virtually** a thing of the past.

QUICK TIP When most readers read a sentence that begins with something like *obviously, undoubtedly, it is clear that, there is no question that,* and so on, they reflexively think the opposite.

Exercise 9.3

Edit these for both unnecessary metadiscourse and redundancy.

1. But, on the other hand, we can perhaps point out that there may always be TV programming to appeal to our most prurient and, therefore, lowest interests.

2. In this particular section, I intend to discuss my position about the possible need to dispense with the standard approach to plea bargaining. I believe this for two reasons. The first reason is that there is the possibility of letting hardened criminals avoid receiving their just punishment. The second reason is the following: plea bargaining seems to encourage a growing lack of respect for the judicial system.

3. Depending on the particular position that one takes on this question, the educational system has taken on a degree of importance that may be equal to or perhaps even exceed the family as a major source of transmission of social values.

4. It is my belief that in regard to terrestrial-type snakes, an assumption can be made that there are probably none in unmapped areas of the world surpassing the size of those we already have knowledge of.

CONCISE, NOT TERSE

Having stressed concision so strongly, I must now step back. Readers don't like flab, but neither do they like a style so terse that it's all gristle and bone. Here is some amiable advice from the most widely read book on style, Strunk and White's *The Elements of Style:*

> Revising is part of writing. Few writers are so expert that they can produce what they are after on the first try. Quite often you will discover, on examining the completed work, that there are serious flaws in the arrangement of the material, calling for transpositions. When this is the case, a word processor can save you time and labor as you rearrange the manuscript. You can select material on the screen and move it to a more appropriate spot, or, if you cannot find the right spot, you can move the material to the end of the manuscript until you decide whether to delete it. Some writers find that working with a printed copy of the manuscript helps them to visualize the process of change; others prefer to revise entirely on screen. Above all, do not be afraid to experiment with what you have written. Save both the original and the revised versions; you can always use the computer to restore the

manuscript to its original condition, should that course seem best. Remember, it is no sign of weakness or defeat that your manuscript ends up in need of major surgery. This is a common occurrence in all writing, and among the best writers. (205 words)

We can shorten that paragraph just by erasing its redundancy:

Revising is part of writing. Few writers ~~are so expert that they can~~ produce what they are after on the first try. ~~Quite~~ Often you will discover ~~on examining the completed work, that there are serious~~ flaws in the arrangement of the material. ~~calling for transpositions.~~ When this is the case, a word processor can save you time and labor as you rearrange the manuscript. You can ~~select material on the screen and~~ move [material] to a more appropriate spot, or, if you cannot find the right spot, you can move the material to the end of the manuscript until you decide whether to delete it. Some writers find that working with a printed ~~copy of the~~ manuscript helps them to visualize the process of change; others prefer to revise ~~entirely~~ on screen. Above all, ~~do not be afraid to~~ experiment ~~with what you have written.~~ Save both the original and the revised versions; you can always ~~use the computer to~~ restore the manuscript to its original condition, ~~should that course seem best. Remember,~~ It is no sign of weakness or defeat that your manuscript ~~ends up in~~ need[s] ~~of major~~ surgery. This is ~~a~~ common ~~occurrence~~ in all writing, and among the best writers. (149 words)

With some rewording, we can cut that version by another third (revisions are italicized):

Revising is part of writing, *because* few writers ~~produce what they are after on the first try~~ *write perfect first drafts*. *If you use a word processor and find* ~~Often you will discover~~ flaws in *your* arrangement, ~~of the material. When this is the case, a word processor can save you time and labor as you rearrange the manuscript.~~ you can move material to a more appropriate spot, or, if you cannot find *one*, ~~the right spot, you can move the material~~ to the end ~~of the manuscript~~ until you decide whether to delete it. Some writers find ~~that working with~~ a printed manuscript helps them ~~to~~ visualize ~~the process of~~ change; others ~~prefer to~~ revise on screen. Above all, experiment. Save ~~both~~ the original ~~and the revised~~ version; you can always *go back to it* ~~restore the manuscript to its original condition.~~ It is no sign of weakness ~~or defeat~~ that your manuscript needs surgery. This is common in all writing, and among the best writers. (99 words)

And if we cut to the bone, we can reduce that in half:

Most writers revise because few write a perfect first draft. If you work on a computer, you can rearrange the parts by moving them around. If you save the original, you can always go back to it. Even great writers revise, so if your manuscript needs surgery, it signals no weakness. (51 words)

But in reducing that paragraph to a quarter of its original length, I've also stripped away its garrulous charm, a tradeoff that many readers would reject.

I can't tell you when you've written so concisely that your readers think you are terse, even abrupt. That's why you should listen to what readers say about your writing. They know what you never can: how it feels to be your reader.

IN YOUR OWN WORDS

Exercise 9.4

Revise a passage from a reading as I did the passage from Strunk and White's *The Elements of Style* (pp. 132–133). Pick a long paragraph or section (about 200 words). Now, shorten it to about 150 words, 100 words, 50 words. What does that passage gain or lose with each of these revisions?

Now do the same with a passage from your own writing.

Exercise 9.5

Every piece of writing needs some metadiscourse, but too much buries your ideas. Have a reader go through several pages of your writing and highlight all the metadiscourse. With your reader, address the following questions: Which instances of metadiscourse are useful, and which are unnecessary? Are there places without metadiscourse where some would be helpful? Revise as necessary.

SUMMING UP

You need more than concision to guarantee grace, but when you clear away deadwood, you can see the shape of a sentence more clearly.

1. Meaningless words

> Some polling sites reported various technical problems, but these did not really affect the election's actual result.

> ✓ Some polling sites reported technical problems, but these did not affect the election's result.

2. Redundant pairs

   If and when we can define our final aims and goals, each and every member of our group will be ready and willing to offer aid and assistance.

   ✓ If we define our goals, we will all be ready to help.

3. Redundant modifiers

   In the business world of today, official governmental red tape seriously destroys initiative among individual businesses.

   ✓ Government red tape destroys business initiative.

4. Redundant categories

   In the area of education, tight financial conditions are forcing school boards to cut nonessential expenses.

   ✓ Tight finances are forcing school boards to cut nonessentials.

5. Obvious implications

   Energy used to power industries and homes will in years to come cost more money.

   ✓ Energy will eventually cost more.

6. A phrase for a word

   A sail-powered craft that has turned on its side or completely over must remain buoyant enough so that it will bear the weight of those individuals who were aboard.

   ✓ A capsized sailboat must support those on it.

7. Indirect negatives

   There is no reason not to believe that engineering malfunctions in nuclear energy systems cannot be anticipated.

   ✓ Malfunctions in nuclear energy systems will surprise us.

8. Excessive metadiscourse

   It is almost certainly the case that totalitarian systems cannot allow a society to have what we would define as stable social relationships.

   ✓ Totalitarianism prevents stable social relationships.

9. Hedges and intensifiers

   The only principle here is the Goldilocks rule: not too much, not too little, but just right. This is a matter where you have to develop and then trust your ear.

Too certain: In my research, **I prove** that people with guns in their homes use them to kill themselves or family members instead of to protect themselves from intruders.

Too uncertain: **Some** of my recent research **seems** to **imply** that there **may** be a **risk** that certain people with guns in their homes **could** be **more prone** to use them to kill themselves or family members than to protect themselves from **possible** intruders.

Just right?   My research indicates that people with guns in their homes are more likely to use them to kill themselves or family members than they are to protect themselves from intruders.

Lesson

10

Shape

The structure of every sentence is a lesson in logic.
—JOHN STUART MILL

A long complicated sentence should force itself upon you, make you know yourself knowing it.
—GERTRUDE STEIN

You never know what is enough until you know what is more than enough.
—WILLIAM BLAKE

UNDERSTANDING THE SHAPE OF SENTENCES

If you can write clear and concise sentences, you have achieved much. But a writer who can't write a clear sentence longer than twenty words or so is like a composer who can write only jingles. Some advise against long sentences, but you cannot communicate every complex idea in a short one: you have to know how to write a sentence that is both long and clear.

Consider this sentence:

> In addition to the continual disagreements between Democrats and Republicans on the issues of the day, an explanation of why they so deeply distrust one another must include the divergent values and principles that give them their motivation, the support that arises from their distinct constituencies, and an acceleration of the history of conflict between them.

137

Even if that idea needs all those fifty-six words (it doesn't), they could be arranged into a more shapely sentence.

We can start revising by editing the abstractions into characters/subjects and actions/verbs and then breaking the sentence into shorter ones:

> We want to explain why Democrats and Republicans have come to so deeply distrust one another. One reason is their continual disagreements on the issues of the day. We must also consider the divergent values and principles that motivate them, the distinct constituencies that support them, and the accelerating history of conflict between them.

But that passage feels choppy. We prefer something like this:

> ✓ To explain why Democrats and Republicans have come to so deeply distrust one another, we must consider not only their continual disagreements on the issues of the day but also the divergent values and principles that motivate them, the distinct constituencies that support them, and the accelerating history of conflict between them.

That sentence is only four words shorter than the first, but it is not ungainly. So it can't be length alone that makes a long sentence difficult. In this lesson, I focus on how to write longer sentences that are also clear and shapely.

Readers get a sense of shapeless length from four things:

- They don't find a sentence's point near its beginning.
- They have to wait too long to get to the verb in the main clause.
- After the verb, they have to slog through a series of tacked-on phrases and subordinate clauses.
- They are stopped by one interruption after another.

STARTING WITH YOUR POINT

Compare these two sentences:

> High-deductible health plans and Health Saving Accounts into which workers and their employers make tax-deductible deposits result in workers taking more responsibility for their health care.

> ✓ Workers take more responsibility for their health care when they adopt high-deductible insurance plans and Health Saving Accounts into which they and their employers deposit tax-deductible contributions.

Unlike that lumbering first sentence, the second begins not with a long, abstract subject but with a short, concrete one familiar to

readers, directly followed by a verb stating a specific action: *Workers take....*
But it differs in another way too. That first sentence feels backward. We have to read more than twenty words before we see their relevance to its key claim, to its most important point: that workers take responsibility for their health care.

[High-deductible health plans and Health Saving Accounts into which workers and their employers make tax-deductible deposits]_{explanation/} _{support} [result in workers taking more responsibility for their health care.]_{point}

In contrast, the second sentence opens with an eight-word main clause stating its most important point clearly and concisely:

✓ [Workers take more responsibility for their health care]_{point} [when they adopt high-deductible insurance plans and Health Saving Accounts into which they and their employers make tax-deductible deposits.]_{explanation/support}

When we read its point first, we can anticipate the relevance of the next nineteen words *even before we read them.*

Here is a very general principle about how we read: we can best manage complexity when we begin with something short and direct that frames the more complex information that follows. We have seen how that principle applies to individual subjects and verbs. But it also applies to the *logical* elements of a long sentence, to its point and to its explanation or supporting information. When a point is dribbled out or delayed, we have to reconstruct it, then mentally reassemble the sentence into its logical parts. A point clearly stated up front gives us a context to understand the complexity that follows.

In fact, this principle of simple-before-complex applies to even larger units:

- Begin a paragraph with a sentence (or two) expressing its point so that readers can understand what follows (see pp. 115–116).

- Begin a section of a document with a paragraph or two stating its point (see pp. 110–113).

- Do the same for a whole document: begin with an introduction that states its point and frames the rest (see pp. 95–103).

Sentence, paragraph, section, or whole—how quickly, concisely, and *helpfully* you begin determines how easily your readers understand what follows.

How to Revise: Long Openings

Readers like to find a sentence's point near its beginning, but they won't if a sentence takes forever to get started:

> Since most undergraduate students change their fields of study at least once during their college careers, many more than once, first-year students who are not certain about their program of studies should not load up their schedules to meet requirements for a particular program.

That sentence takes thirty-one words to get to its main verb, *should . . . load up*. Here are two rules of thumb about beginning a sentence: (1) Get to the subject of the main clause quickly. (2) Get to the verb and object quickly.

Rule of Thumb 1: Get to the Subject Quickly

We have a problem with sentences that open with long introductory phrases and clauses, because as we read them, we have to keep in mind that the subject and verb of a main clause are still to come, and that load on our memory hinders easy understanding.

Compare these two versions. In (1a) we have to read and understand seventeen words before reading the main subject (underlined) and verb (capitalized). In (1b), we get past the main subject and verb in just six words:

> 1a. **Since most undergraduate students change their major fields of study at least once during their college careers,** <u>first-year students</u> who are not certain about the program of studies they want to pursue SHOULD not LOAD UP their schedules to meet requirements for a particular program.

> ✓ 1b. <u>First-year students</u> SHOULD not LOAD UP their schedules with requirements for a particular program if they are not certain about the program of studies they want to pursue, because **most change their major fields of study at least once during their college careers.**

When you find a sentence with a very long introductory clause, try moving that clause to the end. If it doesn't fit there, try turning it into a sentence of its own.

However, clauses beginning with *if, since, when,* and *although* usually refer to ideas already known and tend therefore to appear early in a sentence. If you choose to begin with such a clause, keep it short.

An exception is the style called "periodic" or "suspended," in which writers deliberately pile up introductory subordinate clauses (subordinating conjunctions boldfaced) to delay and thereby heighten the impact of a concluding main clause (italicized):

> **When** a society spends more on its pets than it does on its homeless, **when** it rewards those who hit a ball the farthest more highly than those who care most deeply for its neediest, **when** it takes more interest in the juvenile behavior of its richest children than in the deficient education of its poorest, *it has lost its moral center.*

Used sparingly, this kind of sentence can have a dramatic impact, especially when the last few words of the last clause are appropriately stressed. I discuss this matter again in Lesson 11.

Rule of Thumb 2: Get to the Verb and Object Quickly

Readers also want to get past the main subject to its verb and object. Therefore,

- Avoid long, abstract subjects.
- Avoid interrupting the subject-verb connection.
- Avoid interrupting the verb-object connection.

Avoid long, abstract subjects. Revise long subjects into short ones. Start by underlining whole subjects. If you find a subject longer than seven or eight words that includes a nominalization, especially as the simple subject, try turning the nominalization into a verb and using a character as its subject:

> **The company's <u>understanding</u> of the drivers of its profitability in the Asian market for small electronics** helped it pursue opportunities in Africa.

> ✓ **The <u>company</u>** was able to pursue opportunities in Africa because it UNDERSTOOD what drove profitability in the Asian market for small electronics.

A subject can also be long if it includes a long relative clause:

> A company **that focuses on hiring the best personnel and then trains them not just for the work they are hired to do but for higher-level jobs** is likely to earn the loyalty of its employees.

Try turning the relative clause into an introductory subordinate clause beginning with *when* or *if:*

> ✓ **When a company focuses on hiring the best personnel and then trains them not just for the work they are hired to do but for higher-level jobs,** it is likely to earn the loyalty of its employees.

But if the introductory clause turns out to be as long as that one, try moving it to the end of its sentence, especially if (1) the main clause is short and expresses the point of the sentence and (2) the moveable clause expresses newer and more complex information that supports or elaborates on the main clause.

> ✓ A company is likely to earn the loyalty of its employees **when it focuses on hiring the best personnel and then trains them not just for the work they are hired to do but for higher-level jobs.**

Or better yet, perhaps, turn it into a sentence of its own:

> ✓ Some companies focus on hiring the best personnel and then train them not just for the work they are hired to do but for higher-level jobs later. **Such companies are likely to earn the loyalty of their employees.**

Avoid interrupting the subject-verb connection.   You frustrate readers when you interrupt the connection between a subject and verb, like this:

> Some scientists, **because they write in a style that is impersonal and abstract,** do not easily communicate with laypeople.

That *because* clause after the subject forces us to hold our mental breath until we reach the verb, *do . . . communicate.* Move the interruption to the beginning or end of the sentence, depending on whether it connects more closely to what precedes or follows it (note the *since* instead of *because*).

> ✓ Since some scientists write in a style that is impersonal and abstract, they do **not easily communicate with laypeople. This lack of communication** damages...

> ✓ Some scientists do not easily communicate with laypeople because they write in **a style that is impersonal and abstract. It is a kind of style** filled with passives and...

We mind short interruptions less:

> ✓ Some scientists **deliberately** write in a style that is impersonal and abstract.

Avoid interrupting the verb-object connection.   We also like to get quickly past the verb to its object. This sentence doesn't let us do that:

> We must develop, **if we are to become competitive with other companies in our region,** a core of knowledge regarding the state of the art in effective industrial organizations.

Move the interrupting element to the beginning or end of the sentence, depending on what comes next:

✓ **If we are to compete with other companies in our region,** we must develop a core of knowledge about the state of the art in **effective industrial organizations. Such organizations provide...**

✓ We must develop a core of knowledge about the state of the art in effective industrial organizations **if we are to compete with other companies in our region. Increasing competition...**

When a prepositional phrase you can move is shorter than a long object, you can also try putting the phrase between the verb and object:

In a long sentence, put the newest and most important information that you want your reader to remember **at its end.**

✓ In a long sentence, put **at its end** the newest and most important information that you want your reader to remember.

Here's the point: Readers read most easily when you quickly get them to the subject of your main clause and then past that subject to its verb and object. Avoid long introductory phrases and clauses, long subjects, and interruptions between subjects and verbs and between verbs and objects.

Exercise 10.1

These sentences have long subjects. Revise.

1. Explaining why Shakespeare decided to have Lady Macbeth die off stage rather than letting the audience see her die has to do with understanding the audience's reactions to Macbeth's death.

2. An agreement by the film industry and by television producers on limiting characters using cigarettes, even if carried out, would do little to discourage young people from smoking.

3. A student's right to have access to his or her own records, including medical records, academic reports, and confidential comments by advisers, will generally take precedence over an institution's desire to keep records private, except when limitations of those rights under specified circumstances are agreed to by students during registration.

These sentences are ungainly because of interruptions. First, eliminate wordiness. Then correct the interruption.

4. TV "reality" shows, because they have an appeal to our fascination with real-life conflict because of our voyeuristic impulses, are about the most popular shows that are regularly scheduled to appear on TV.

5. Insistence that there is no proof by scientific means of a causal link between tobacco consumption and various disease entities such as cardiac heart diseases and malignant growth, despite the fact that there is a strong statistical correlation between smoking behavior and such diseases, is no longer the officially stated position of cigarette companies.

6. The continued and unabated emission of carbon dioxide gas into the atmosphere, unless there is a marked reduction, will eventually result in serious changes in the climate of the world as we know it today.

These sentences have long introductory phrases and clauses. Revise. Try to open your revised sentence with its point.

7. While grade inflation has been a subject of debate by teachers and administrators and even in newspapers, employers looking for people with high levels of technical and analytical skills have not had difficulty identifying desirable candidates.

8. Although one way to prevent foreign piracy of DVDs is for criminal justice systems of foreign countries to move cases faster through their systems and for stiffer penalties to be imposed, no improvement in the level of expertise of judges who hear these cases is expected any time in the immediate future.

9. Since school officials responsible for setting policy about school security have said that local principals may require students to pass through metal detectors before entering a school building, the need to educate parents and students about the seriousness of bringing onto school property anything that looks like a weapon must be made a part of the total package of school security.

HOW TO REVISE: SPRAWLING ENDINGS

This next sentence starts well but then sprawls through a string of four explanatory subordinate clauses:

No scientific advance is more exciting than genetic engineering,$_{point}$ which is a new way of manipulating the elemental structural units of life itself, which are the genes and chromosomes that tell our cells how to reproduce to become the parts that constitute our bodies.$_{explanation}$

Graphically, it looks like this:

No scientific advance is more exciting than genetic engineering, *[point and main subject and verb]*

> **which** is a new way of manipulating the elemental structural units of life itself, *[tacked-on relative clause]*
>> **which** are the genes and chromosomes *[tacked-on relative clause]*
>>> **that** tell our cells how to reproduce to become the parts *[tacked-on relative clause]*
>>>> **that** constitute our bodies. *[final tacked-on relative clause]*

You can identify this problem by having someone read your writing aloud. If that reader hesitates, stumbles over words, or runs out of breath before getting to the end of a sentence, so will someone reading your writing silently. You can revise in four ways: cut, turn subordinate clauses into independent sentences, change clauses to modifying phrases, or coordinate.

1. Cut

Try reducing some of the relative clauses to phrases by deleting *who/that/which* + *is/was*, etc.:

✓ Of the many areas of science important to our future, few are more promising than genetic engineering, ~~which is~~ a new way of manipulating the elemental structural units of life itself, ~~which are~~ the genes and chromosomes that tell our cells how to reproduce to become the parts that constitute our bodies.

Occasionally, you have to turn the remaining verb into a PRESENT PARTICIPLE by adding *-ing*:

The day is coming when we will all have numbers **that will identify** our financial transactions so that the IRS can monitor all activities **that involve** economic activity.

✓ The day is coming when we will all have numbers ~~that will~~ **identifying** our financial transactions so that the IRS can monitor all activities ~~that~~ **involving** economic activity.

2. Turn Subordinate Clauses into Independent Sentences

✓ Many areas of science are important to our future, but few are more promising than genetic engineering. It is a new way of manipulating the elemental structural units of life itself, the genes and chromosomes that tell our cells how to reproduce to become the parts that constitute our bodies.

3. Change Clauses to Modifying Phrases

You can write a long sentence but still avoid sprawl if you change relative clauses to one of three kinds of APPOSITIVE: a *resumptive*, *summative*, or *free* modifier. You have probably never heard these terms before, but they name stylistic devices you have read many times and so should know how to use.

Resumptive Modifiers   These two examples contrast a relative clause and a resumptive modifier:

> Since mature writers often use resumptive modifiers to extend a line of thought, we need a word to name what I have not done in this sentence, **which I could have ended at that comma but extended to show you a relative clause attached to a noun.**

> ✓ Since mature writers often use resumptive modifiers to extend a line of thought, we need a word to name what I am about to do in this sentence, **a sentence that I could have ended at that comma but extended to show you how resumptive modifiers work.**

The boldfaced resumptive modifier repeats a key word, *sentence*, and rolls on.

To create a resumptive modifier, find the noun the tacked-on clause modifies, pause after it with a comma, repeat the noun, and continue with a restrictive relative clause beginning with *that:*

> Since mature writers often use resumptive modifiers to extend a line of thought, we need a word to name what I am about to do in **this sentence,**
>
> > **a sentence that I could have ended at that comma, but extended to show you how resumptive modifiers work.**

You can also resume with an adjective or verb. In that case, you don't add a relative clause; you just repeat the adjective or verb and continue:

> ✓ It was American writers who found a voice that was both **true** and **lyrical,**
>
> > **true** to the rhythms of the working man's speech and **lyrical** in its celebration of his labor.

> ✓ All who value independence should **resist** the trivialization of government regulation,
>
> > **resist** its obsession with administrative tidiness and compulsion to arrange things not for our convenience but for theirs.

Occasionally, you can create a resumptive modifier with the phrase *one that*:

✓ I now address a problem we have wholly ignored, **one that** has plagued societies that sell their natural resources to benefit a few today rather than using them to develop new resources that benefit everyone tomorrow.

Summative Modifiers   Here are two sentences that contrast relative clauses and summative modifiers. Notice how the *which* in the first one feels "tacked on":

Economic changes have reduced the region's population growth to less than zero, **which will have serious social implications.**

✓ Economic changes have reduced the region's population growth to less than zero, **a demographic event that will have serious social implications.**

To create a summative modifier, end a grammatically complete segment of a sentence with a comma, add a term that sums up the substance of the sentence so far, and continue with a restrictive relative clause beginning with *that:*

Economic changes have reduced the region's population growth to less than zero,

a *demographic event* that will have serious social implications.

A summative modifier has the same effect as a resumptive modifier: it lets you bring a clause to a sense of closure, then begin afresh.

Free Modifiers   Like the other modifiers, a free modifier can appear at the end of a clause, but instead of repeating a key word or summing up what went before, it comments on the subject of the closest verb:

✓ Free modifiers resemble resumptive and summative modifiers, *letting* you [i.e., the free modifier lets you] **extend the line of a sentence while avoiding a train of ungainly phrases and clauses.**

Free modifiers usually begin with a present participle, as that one did, but they can also begin with a past participle, like this:

✓ Leonardo da Vinci was a man of powerful intellect,

driven by [i.e., Leonardo was driven by] **an insatiable curiosity and** *haunted* by **a vision of artistic perfection.**

A free modifier can also begin with an adjective:

✓ In 1939, the U.S. began to assist the British against Germany, *aware* [i.e., the U.S. was aware] **that it faced another world war.**

We call these modifiers *free* because they can either begin or end a sentence:

✓ **Driven by an insatiable curiosity,** Leonardo da Vinci was…

✓ **Aware that it faced another world war,** the U.S. in 1939 began…

> *Here's the point:* When you have to write a long sentence, don't just string together phrases and clauses, willy-nilly. Particularly avoid tacking one relative clause onto another onto another. Try extending the line of a sentence with resumptive, summative, and free modifiers.

4. Coordinate

COORDINATION is the foundation of a gracefully shaped sentence. It's harder to create good coordination than good modifiers, but when done well, it's more graceful. Compare these. My version is first; the original is second:

> The aspiring artist may find that even a minor, unfinished work which was botched may be an instructive model for how things should be done, while for the amateur spectator, such works are the daily fare which may provide good, honest nourishment, which can lead to an appreciation of deeper pleasures that are also more refined.

> ✓ For the aspiring artist, the minor, the unfinished, or even the botched work, may be an instructive model for how things should—and should not be done. For the amateur spectator, such works are the daily fare which provide good, honest nourishment—and which can lead to appreciation of more refined, or deeper pleasures.
>
> —Eva Hoffman, "Minor Art Offers Special Pleasures"

My revision sprawls through a string of tacked-on clauses.

> The aspiring artist may find that even a minor, unfinished work
> **which** was botched may be an instructive model for
> **how** things should be done,
> **while** for the amateur spectator, such works are the daily fare

> **which** may provide good, honest nourishment,
> **which** can lead to an appreciation of deeper pleasures
> **that** are also more refined.

Hoffman's original gets its shape from its multiple coordinations. Structurally, it looks like this:

For the aspiring artist, { the minor, the unfinished, or even the botched } work may be

an instructive model for how things { should and should not } be done.

For the amateur spectator, such works are

the daily fare { which provide { good, honest } nourishment— and which can lead to appreciation of { more refined, or deeper } pleasures. }

That second sentence in particular shows how elaborate coordination can get.

A UNIFYING PRINCIPLE: SHORT TO LONG

We should note a feature that distinguishes well-formed coordination. You can hear it if you read this next sentence aloud:

> We should devote a few final words to a matter that reaches beyond the techniques of research to the connections between those subjective values that reflect our deepest ethical choices and objective research.

That sentence seems to end too abruptly with *objective research*. Structurally, it looks like this:

$$
\ldots \text{between} \left\{ \begin{array}{c} \text{those subjective values that reflect our} \\ \text{deepest ethical choices} \\ \text{and} \\ \text{objective research.} \end{array} \right\}
$$

This next revision moves from shorter to longer by reversing the two coordinate elements and by adding a PARALLELISM to the second one to make it longer still. Read this one aloud:

✓ We should devote a few final words to a matter that reaches beyond the techniques of research to the connections between objective research and those subjective values that reflect our deepest ethical choices and strongest intellectual commitments.

Structurally, it looks like this:

$$
✓\ldots \text{between} \left\{ \begin{array}{c} \text{objective research} \\ \text{and} \\ \text{those subjective} \\ \text{values that reflect our} \end{array} \left\{ \begin{array}{c} \text{deepest ethical choices} \\ \text{and} \\ \text{strongest intellectual} \\ \text{commitments.} \end{array} \right\} \right\}
$$

A characteristic of especially elegant prose is how its writers elaborate all these devices for extending the line of a sentence, especially balanced coordination. I will discuss those devices and their elaboration in Lesson 11.

This principle of short to long is, in fact, one of the unifying principles of a clear prose style:

- It applies to the subject-verb sequence of individual sentences: the shorter the better to introduce the longer, more complex elements that follow.
- It applies to the principle of old before new: old information is usually objectively shorter than new information, but it is "psychologically" shorter, as well.
- It applies to ordering the logical elements of a long sentence: begin with its short point, then add the longer and more complex information that explains or supports it.
- It applies again here in balanced coordination: put shorter elements before longer ones.

Here's the point: Coordination lets you extend the line of a sentence more gracefully than by tacking on one element to another. When you can coordinate, try to order the elements so that they go from shorter to longer, from simpler to more complex.

QUICK TIP You can emphasize a coordination with CORRELATIVE CONJUNCTIONS: *both X and Y, not only X but also Y, (n)either X (n)or Y.* Compare these:

✓ The Golden Gate Bridge is an engineering marvel and a construction of stunning beauty.

✓ The Golden Gate Bridge is **both** an engineering marvel **and** a construction of stunning beauty.

When you use one of these conjunctions, however, be sure to put the *and, but,* or *(n)or* before a word that is coordinate with what follows the *both, not only,* and *(n)either.* In the first sentence below, *not only* precedes the verb while the *but* precedes its subject:

When you punctuate carefully, you **not only** *help* readers understand a complex sentence more easily, **but** *you* enhance your own image as a good writer.

They should precede the same part of speech:

✓ When you punctuate carefully, you **not only** *help* readers understand a complex sentence more easily, **but** *enhance* your own image as a good writer.

Exercise 10.2

Edit these sentences to address redundancy, wordiness, nominalizations, and other problems. Then create resumptive, summative, and free modifiers. In the first two, start a resumptive modifier with the word in boldface. Then use the word in brackets to create another sentence with a summative modifier. For example:

Within ten years, we could meet our energy **needs** with solar power. [a possibility]

Resumptive:

✓ Within ten years, we could meet our energy **needs** with solar power, **needs** that will soar as our population grows.

Summative:

✓ Within ten years, we could meet our energy needs with solar power, **a possibility** that few anticipated ten years ago.

Free:

✓ Within ten years, we could meet our energy needs with solar power, **freeing** ourselves of dependence on foreign oil.

But before you begin adding modifiers, edit these sentences for redundancy, wordiness, nominalizations, and other problems.

1. Many different school systems are making a return back to traditional education in the **basics**. [a change]
2. Within the period of the last few years or so, automobile manufacturers have been trying to meet new and more stringent-type quality control **requirements**. [a challenge]
3. The reasons for the cause of aging are a puzzle that has perplexed humanity for millennia.
4. The majority of young people in the world of today cannot even begin to have an understanding of the insecurity that a large number of older people had experienced during the period of the Great Depression.

TROUBLESHOOTING LONG SENTENCES

Even when they begin well and don't sprawl, long sentences can still go wrong. Here are some common problems.

Faulty Grammatical Coordination

Ordinarily, we coordinate elements only of the same grammatical structure: clause and clause, prepositional phrase and prepositional phrase, and so on. When you coordinate different grammatical structures, readers may feel you have created an offensive lack of parallelism. Careful writers avoid this:

The committee recommends {
revising the curriculum to recognize trends in local employment
and
that the division be reorganized to reflect the new curriculum.
}

They would correct that to this:

$$✔ \ldots \text{recommends} \begin{cases} \textbf{that the curriculum be revised} \\ \text{to recognize} \ldots \\ \qquad \text{and} \\ \textbf{that the division be reorganized} \\ \text{to reflect.} \ldots \end{cases}$$

Or to this:

$$✔ \ldots \text{recommends} \begin{cases} \textbf{revising the curriculum} \\ \text{to recognize} \ldots \\ \qquad \text{and} \\ \textbf{reorganizing the division} \\ \text{to reflect.} \ldots \end{cases}$$

However, some nonparallel coordinations do occur in well-written prose. Careful writers coordinate a noun phrase with a *how* clause:

$$✔ \text{We will attempt to delineate} \begin{cases} \textbf{the problems} \text{ of education} \\ \text{in developing nations} \\ \qquad \text{and} \\ \textbf{how coordinated efforts} \\ \textbf{can address} \text{ them in} \\ \text{economical ways.} \end{cases}$$

They coordinate an adverb with a prepositional phrase:

$$✔ \begin{array}{c} \text{The proposal appears} \\ \text{to have been written} \end{array} \begin{cases} \textbf{quickly,} \\ \textbf{carefully,} \\ \qquad \text{and} \\ \textbf{with the help} \text{ of many.} \end{cases}$$

Careful readers do not blink at either.

Faulty Rhetorical Coordination

We respond to coordination best when the elements are coordinate not only in grammar but also in thought. Some inexperienced writers coordinate by just joining one element to another with *and:*

> Grade inflation is a problem at many universities, **and** it leads to a devaluation of good grades earned by hard work **and** will not be solved simply by grading harder.

Those *ands* obscure the relationships among those claims:

> ✓ Grade inflation is a problem at many universities, **because** it devalues good grades that were earned by hard work, **but** it will not be solved simply by grading harder.

Unfortunately, I can't tell you how to recognize when elements are not coordinate in thought, except to say, "Watch for it."

Unclear Connections

Readers are bothered by a coordination so long that they lose track of its internal connections and pronoun references:

> Teachers should remember that students are vulnerable and uncertain about those everyday ego-bruising moments that adults ignore and that they do not understand that one day they will become as confident and as secure as the adults that bruise them.

We sense a flicker of hesitation about where to connect:

> ... and that they do not understand that one day they...

To revise a sentence like that, shorten the first half of the coordination so that you can start the second half closer to the point where the coordination began:

> ✓ Teachers should remember that students are vulnerable to ego-bruising moments that adults ignore and that they do not understand that one day....

Or repeat a word that reminds the reader where the coordination began (thereby creating a resumptive modifier):

> ✓ Teachers should remember that students are vulnerable to ego-bruising moments that adults ignore, **to remember** that they do not understand that....

Or repeat a noun to avoid an ambiguous pronoun:

> ✓ Teachers should remember that **students** are vulnerable to ego-bruising moments that adults ignore and that **students** do not understand that one day....

Ambiguous Modifiers

Sometimes modifiers are positioned so that readers are unsure what they modify:

> Overtaxing oneself in physical activity too frequently results in injury.

What happens too frequently, overtaxing or injuries? We can make its meaning unambiguous by moving *too frequently:*

> ✓ Overtaxing oneself too frequently in physical activity results in injury.

> ✓ Overtaxing oneself in physical activity results too frequently in injury.

A modifier at the end of a clause can ambiguously modify either a neighboring or a more distant phrase:

> Scientists have learned that their observations are as subjective as those in any other field **in recent years.**

We can move the modifier to a less ambiguous position:

> ✓ **In recent years,** scientists have learned that....

> ✓ Scientists have learned that **in recent years.**...

Dangling Modifiers

Another problem with a long sentence can be a dangling modifier. A modifier dangles when its implied subject differs from the explicit subject of the main clause:

> To overcome chronic poverty and lagging economic development in sub-Saharan Africa,$_{\text{dangling modifier}}$ a commitment to health and education$_{\text{whole subject}}$ is necessary for there to be progress in raising standards of living.

The implied subject of *overcome* is some unnamed agent, but the explicit subject of the main clause is *commitment.* To undangle the modifier, we make its implicit subject explicit:

> ✓ If **developed countries** are to overcome chronic poverty and lagging economic development in sub-Saharan Africa, a commitment to health and education is necessary....

Or better, make the implicit subject of the modifier the explicit subject of the clause:

> ✓ To overcome chronic poverty and lagging economic development in sub-Saharan Africa, **developed countries** must commit themselves to....

IN YOUR OWN WORDS

> ### *Exercise 10.3*
>
> Two rules of thumb for beginning sentences are (1) get to the subject quickly and (2) get to the verb and object quickly (see pp. 140–143). Go through a page of your writing and underline the first seven or eight words of every sentence. Revise those in which you do not come to the subject and the verb in those opening words.
>
> ### *Exercise 10.4*
>
> It is difficult for writers to identify their bad habits, because they know their own writing too well. So have a reader help you identify yours:
>
> - Do you take too long to get to your subjects and verbs?
> - Are your subjects too long?
> - Do you interrupt the connection between subject and verb, or verb and object?
> - Do you take too long to make your point (in sentences and in passages)?
> - Do you add subordinate clause to subordinate clause to subordinate clause?
>
> Have a reader go through a few pages of your writing and draw a line beside any passages that seemed unclear or difficult to get through, naming the cause of the difficulty if she can. If she can't, analyze the rough passages together. (You can trust a reader's judgment that *something* is amiss, even if that reader can't say exactly *what*.) Then revise.

SUMMING UP

Here are the principles for giving sentences a coherent shape:

1. Get quickly to the subject, then to the verb and its object:

   a. Avoid long introductory phrases and clauses. Revise them into their own INDEPENDENT CLAUSES:

   > Since most undergraduate students change their major fields of study at least once during their college careers, many more than once, **first-year students** who are not certain about the

program of studies they want to pursue should not load up their schedules to meet requirements for a particular program.

✓ **Most undergraduate students** change their major fields of study at least once during their college careers, so **first-year students** should not load up their schedules with requirements for a particular program if they are not certain about the program of studies they want to pursue.

b. Avoid long subjects. Revise a long subject into an introductory subordinate clause:

> **A company that focuses on hiring the best personnel and then trains them not just for the work they are hired to do but for higher-level jobs** is likely to earn the loyalty of its employees.

✓ **When a company focuses on hiring the best personnel and then trains them not just for the work they are hired to do but for higher-level jobs later,** it is likely to earn the loyalty of its employees.

If the new introductory clause is long, shift it to the end of its sentence:

✓ A company is likely to earn the loyalty of its employees **when it focuses on hiring the best personnel.…**

Or just break it out in a sentence of its own:

✓ **Some companies focus on hiring the best personnel and then train them not just for the work they are hired to do but for higher-level jobs later.** Such companies are likely to earn the loyalty of their employees.

c. Avoid interrupting subjects and verbs and also verbs and objects. Move the interrupting element to either the beginning or end of the sentence, depending on what the next sentence is about:

> Some scientists, **because they write in a style that is impersonal and abstract,** do not easily communicate with laypeople.

✓ **Since some scientists write in a style that is impersonal and abstract,** they do *not easily communicate with laypeople. This lack of communication damages.…*

✓ Some scientists do not easily communicate with laypeople *because they write in a style that is impersonal and abstract. It is a kind of style filled with passives.…*

2. Open the sentence with its point in a short main clause stating the key claim that you want the sentence to make:

> A new sales initiative that has created a close integration between the garden and home products departments has made significant improvements to the customer services that Acme offers.

> ✓ Acme has significantly improved its customer services with a new sales initiative that closely integrates the garden and home products departments.

3. After the main clause, avoid adding one subordinate clause to another to another to another:

    a. Trim relative clauses and break the sentences into two:

    > Of the many areas of science **that** are important to our future, few are more promising than genetic engineering, **which** is a new way of manipulating the elemental structural units of life itself, **which** are the genes and chromosomes **that** tell our cells how to reproduce to become the parts **that** constitute our bodies.

    > ✓ Many areas of science are important to our future, but few are more promising than genetic engineering. It is a new way of manipulating the elemental structural units of life itself, **which** are the genes and chromosomes **that** tell our cells how to reproduce to become the parts that constitute our bodies.

    > ✓ Of the many areas of science ~~that are~~ important to our future, few are more promising than genetic engineering, ~~which is~~ a new way of manipulating the elemental structural units of life itself, ~~which are~~ the genes and chromosomes that tell our cells how to reproduce to become the parts ~~that~~ constituting our bodies.

    b. Extend a sentence with a resumptive, summative, or free modifier:

    > ✓ **Resumptive:** When we discovered the earth was not the center of the universe, it changed our understanding of who we are, **an understanding changed again by Darwin, again by Freud, and again by Einstein.**

    > ✓ **Summative:** American productivity has risen to new heights, **an achievement that only a decade ago was considered an impossible dream.**

    > ✓ **Free:** Global warming will become a central political issue of the twenty-first century, **raising questions whose answers will affect the standard of living in every Western nation.**

c. Coordinate elements that are parallel both in grammar and in sense:

> Besides the fact that no civilization has experienced such rapid alterations in their spiritual and mental lives, the material conditions of their daily existence have changed greatly too.

> ✓ No civilization has experienced such rapid alterations in their spiritual and mental lives and in the material conditions of daily existence.

A last note: to write a long complex sentence that is also clear, you may need punctuation to help your reader through it. See Appendix I.

Lesson

11

Elegance

Anything is better than not to write clearly. There is nothing to be said against lucidity, and against simplicity only the possibility of dryness. This is a risk well worth taking when you reflect how much better it is to be bald than to wear a curly wig.
—SOMERSET MAUGHAM

Read over your compositions, and wherever you meet with a passage which you think is particularly fine, strike it out.
—SAMUEL JOHNSON

In literature the ambition of the novice is to acquire the literary language; the struggle of the adept is to get rid of it.
—GEORGE BERNARD SHAW

UNDERSTANDING ELEGANCE

Anyone who can write clearly, concisely, and coherently should rejoice to have achieved so much. But while most readers prefer bald clarity to the density of institutional prose, relentless simplicity can be dry, even arid. It has the spartan virtue of unsalted meat and potatoes, but like such fare, it is rarely memorable. A flash of elegance, however, can both fix a thought in our minds and give us a flicker of pleasure every time we recall it. Unfortunately, I can't tell you how to write elegantly in the same

160

way I have told you how to write clearly and coherently. In fact, I incline toward those who think that the most elegant elegance is disarming simplicity.

What I can do is show you a few devices that can shape a thought in ways that are both elegant and clear. Just knowing them, however, won't let you write elegantly, any more than knowing an accomplished chef's techniques and recipes will let you cook her signature dish. Like great cooking, elegant writing is a matter not of rules but of technique, taste, and talent. But techniques can be learned and practiced, and taste and talent can be educated and exercised.

Balance and Symmetry

What most makes a sentence graceful is a balance and symmetry among its parts, one echoing another in sound, rhythm, structure, and meaning. A skilled writer can balance almost any parts of a sentence, but the most common balance is based on coordination.

Coordinated Balance Here is a balanced sentence from a newspaper editorial decrying a decision to strip a Chicago-area Little League team of its national championship (the team was the first composed entirely of African American players to win the national title; Little League International found that the local league had improperly recruited the team's players):

> Its 11- and 12-year-old players, some from struggling neighborhoods, not only cheered a city challenged by violence but charmed the country with their stellar play and outstanding sportsmanship.

—Editorial Board, *The Washington Post*

Notice how the second VERB PHRASE balances the first:

Its 11- and 12-year-old players, some from struggling neighborhoods,

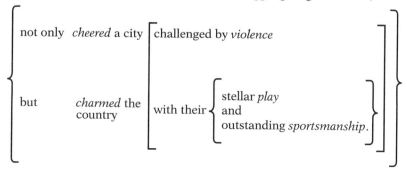

- The verb *charmed* echoes and amplifies the earlier *cheered*, with which it alliterates (or shares consonant sounds).
- The direct object *country* contrasts with *city*, an effect enhanced by the different articles that introduce these words.
- The participial phrase *challenged by violence*, which modifies *city*, is balanced by the prepositional phrase *with their stellar play and outstanding sportsmanship*, which modifies *country*. (This is an example of noncoordinated balance, in which different grammatical structures are balanced. Balanced coordination would have required another participial phrase: "but charmed a country *inspired by stellar play....*")
- This prepositional phrase not only contrasts the city's *violence* with the team's *play* and *sportsmanship*, but elegantly extends the line of the sentence with its compound object, itself composed of two alliterative and coordinated noun phrases. (To experience this effect, try swapping the verb phrases so the sentence reads "... not only charmed... but cheered..." and hear the difference.)

For those who notice and care, such sentences are impressive constructions.

Noncoordinated Balance   We can also balance structures that are not grammatically coordinate. In this example, the subject balances the object:

$$
\begin{bmatrix}
\textbf{Scientists} \text{ whose research} & \textit{creates revolutionary views of} \\
& \textit{the universe} \\
\text{invariably confuse} & \\
\textbf{those of us} \text{ who} & \textit{construe reality from our} \\
& \textit{common-sense experience of it.}
\end{bmatrix}
$$

Here, the PREDICATE of a relative clause in a subject balances the predicate of the sentence:

$$
\text{A government}
\begin{bmatrix}
\text{that is unwilling to } \textit{listen} \text{ to the} \\
\textit{moderate hopes} \text{ of } \textit{its citizenry} \\
\\
\text{must eventually } \textit{answer} \text{ to the } \textit{harsh} \\
\textit{justice} \text{ of } \textit{its revolutionaries.}
\end{bmatrix}
$$

Here a direct object balances the object of a preposition:

Those of us concerned with our school systems will not sacrifice

$$\begin{bmatrix} \text{the } \textit{intellectual growth} \text{ of} & \text{our } \textit{innocent children} \\ & \text{to} \\ \text{the } \textit{social engineering} \text{ of} & \textit{incompetent bureaucrats.} \end{bmatrix}$$

A more complicated balance:

Were I trading[1a]
$$\begin{bmatrix} \text{scholarly principles[2a]} \\ \text{for} \\ \text{financial security,[2b]} \end{bmatrix}$$

I would not be writing[1b]
$$\begin{bmatrix} \text{short books[3a]} \\ \text{on} \\ \text{minor subjects[3b]} \\ \text{for} \\ \text{small audiences.[3c]} \end{bmatrix}$$

In that sentence,

- a subordinate clause (1a), *Were I trading . . .*, balances the main clause (1b), *I would not be writing . . .*;
- the object of that subordinate clause (2a), *scholarly principles*, balances the object in the prepositional phrase (2b), *financial security*;
- the object in the main clause (3a), *short books*, balances objects in two prepositional phrases, (3b), *minor subjects*, and (3c), *small audiences* (with the balanced *short, minor,* and *small*).

Remember that you usually create the most rhythmical balance when each succeeding balanced element is a bit longer than the previous one (see pp. 149–150).

These patterns encourage you to think in ways that you otherwise might not. In that sense, they don't just shape your thinking; they generate it. Suppose you begin a sentence like this:

In his earliest years, Picasso was a master draftsman of the traditional human form.

Now try this:

In his earliest years, Picasso was **not only** a master draftsman of the traditional human form, **but also . . .**

To finish, you have to wonder what else he might—or might not—have been.

> *Here's the point:* The most striking feature of elegant prose is balanced sentence structure. You most easily balance one part of a sentence against another by coordinating them with *and, or, nor, but,* and *yet,* but you can also balance noncoordinated phrases and clauses. Used to excess, these patterns can seem merely clever, but used prudently, they can emphasize an important point or conclude a line of reasoning with a flourish that careful readers notice.

CLIMACTIC EMPHASIS

How you begin a sentence determines its clarity; how you end it determines its rhythm and grace. Here are five ways to end a sentence with special emphasis:

1. Weighty Words

When we get close to the end of a sentence, we expect words that deserve stress (pp. 82–83), so we may feel a sentence is anticlimactic if it ends on words of slight grammatical or semantic weight. At the end of a sentence, prepositions feel light—one reason we sometimes avoid leaving one there. The rhythm of a sentence should carry readers toward strength. Compare:

> Studies into intellectual differences among races are projects that only the most politically naive psychologist would be willing to give support to.

> ✓ Studies into intellectual differences among races are projects that only the most politically naive psychologist would be willing to support.

Adjectives and adverbs are heavier than prepositions, but lighter than nouns, the heaviest of which are nominalizations. Readers have problems with nominalizations in the subject of a sentence, but at the end they provide a satisfyingly climactic thump, particularly when two of them are in coordinate balance. Consider this excerpt from Winston Churchill's "Finest Hour" speech. Churchill ended it with a parallelism climaxing with a balanced pair of nouns:

> ... until in God's good time,
>
> the New World, with all its $\left\{ \begin{array}{c} \text{power} \\ \text{and} \\ \text{might} \end{array} \right\}$ steps forth to
>
> $\left\{ \begin{array}{c} \text{the } \textbf{rescue} \\ \text{and} \\ \text{the } \textbf{liberation} \end{array} \right\}$ of the old.

He could have written more simply, and more banally:

> ... until the New World rescues us.

2. *Of* + Weighty Word

This seems unlikely, but it's true. Look at how Churchill ends his sentence: the light *of* (followed by a lighter *a* or *the*) quickens the rhythm of a sentence just before the stress of the climactic monosyllable, *old:*

> ...the rescue and the liberation of the **old.**

We associate this pattern with self-conscious elegance, as in the first few sentences of Edward Gibbon's *History of the Decline and Fall of the Roman Empire* (contrast that title with *History of the Roman Empire's Decline and Fall*):

✓ In the second century of the Christian era, the Empire of Rome comprehended **the fairest part** *of* **the earth,** AND **the most civilized portion** *of* **mankind.** The frontiers of that extensive monarchy were guarded **by ancient renown** AND **disciplined valour.** The gentle but powerful influence of laws and manners had gradually cemented **the union** *of* **the provinces.** Their peaceful inhabitants **enjoyed and abused the advantages** *of* **wealth and luxury.** The image of a free constitution was preserved with decent **reverence:** the Roman senate appeared to possess the sovereign authority, and devolved on the emperors all **the executive powers** *of* **government.**

In contrast, this is flat:

> In the second century AD, the Roman Empire comprehended **the earth's fairest, most civilized part.** Ancient renown and disciplined valour guarded **its extensive frontiers.** The gentle but powerful influence of laws and manners had gradually **unified the provinces.**

Their peaceful inhabitants enjoyed and abused luxurious wealth while decently preserving what seemed to be **a free constitution.** Appearing to possess the sovereign authority, the Roman senate devolved on the emperors all **executive governmental powers.**

3. Echoing Salience

At the end of a sentence, readers hear special emphasis when a stressed word or phrase balances the sound or meaning of an earlier one. These examples are all from Peter Gay's *Style in History:*

✓ I have written these essays to anatomize this familiar yet really strange being, **style the centaur;** the book may be read as an extended critical commentary on Buffon's famous saying that **the style is the man.**

When we hear a stressed word echo an earlier one, these balances become even more emphatic:

✓ Apart from a few mechanical tricks of rhetoric, **manner** is indissolubly linked to **matter; style shapes,** and in turn is **shaped** by, **substance.**

✓ It seems frivolous, almost inappropriate, to be **stylish** about **style.**

Gay echoes both the sound and meaning of *manner* in *matter, style* in *substance, shapes* in *shaped by,* and *stylish* in *style.*

4. Chiasmus

The word *chiasmus* (pronounced kye-AZZ-muss) is from the Greek word for "crossing." A chiasmus balances elements in two parts of a sentence, but the second part reverses the order of the elements in the first part. For example, this next sentence would be both coordinate and parallel, but it does not end with a chiasmus, because the elements in the two parts are in the same order (1A1B : 2A2B):

✔ A concise style can improve both
$$\left\{ \begin{array}{c} \textbf{our own}^{1A} \ \textit{thinking}^{1B} \\ \text{and} \\ \textbf{our readers'}^{2A} \ \textit{understanding.}^{2B} \end{array} \right\}$$

Were we seeking a special effect, we could reverse the order of elements in the second part to mirror those in the first. Now the pattern is not 1A1B : 2A2B, but rather 1A1B : 2B2A:

✔ A concise style can improve not only
$$\left\{ \begin{array}{c} \textbf{our own}^{1A} \ \textit{thinking}^{1B} \\ \text{but} \\ \text{the } \textit{understanding}^{2B} \ \textbf{of our readers.}^{2A} \end{array} \right\}$$

The next example is more complex. The first two elements are parallel, but the last three mirror one another: AB CDE : AB EDC:

$$
\begin{bmatrix}
\text{You}^A & \text{reveal}^B & \textbf{your own}^C & \textit{highest rhetorical}^D & \text{\sc skill}^E \\
& & \text{by the way} \\
\text{you}^A & \text{respect}^B & \text{\sc the beliefs}^E & \textit{most deeply held}^D & \textbf{by your reader.}^C
\end{bmatrix}
$$

5. Suspension

Finally, you can wind up a sentence with a dramatic climax by ignoring some earlier advice. In Lesson 10, I advised you to open a sentence with its point. But self-consciously elegant writers often open a sentence with a series of parallel and coordinated phrases and clauses just so that they can delay and thereby heighten a sense of climax:

> If [journalists] held themselves as responsible for the rise of public cynicism as they hold "venal" politicians and the "selfish" public; if they considered that the license they have to criticize and defame comes with an implied responsibility to serve the public—if they did all or any of these things, they would make journalism more useful, public life stronger, and themselves far more worthy of esteem.

> —James Fallows. *Breaking the News*

That sentence (the last one in Fallows's book) opens with three *if* clauses and ends with a triple coordination. It ends on its longest member, one that itself ends with an *of* + nominalization (*worthy of esteem*). Like all such devices, however, the impact of a long suspension is inversely proportional to its frequency of use: the less it's used, the bigger its bang.

Here's the point: An elegant sentence should end on strength. You can create that strength in five ways:

1. End with a strong word, or better, a pair of them.
2. End with a prepositional phrase introduced by *of*.
3. End with an echoing salience.
4. Use a chiasmus.
5. Use a suspension to build up to the end.

EXTRAVAGANT ELEGANCE

When writers combine all these elements in a single sentence, we know they are aiming at something special, as in this next passage:

> Far from being locked inside our own skins, inside the "dungeons" of ourselves, we are now able to recognize that our minds belong, quite naturally, to a collective "mind," a mind in which we share everything that is mental, most obviously language itself, and that the old boundary of the skin is not boundary at all but a membrane connecting the inner and outer experience of existence. Our intelligence, our wit, our cleverness, our unique personalities—all are simultaneously "our own" possessions and the world's.
>
> —Joyce Carol Oates, "New Heaven and New Earth"

Here is the anatomy of that passage:

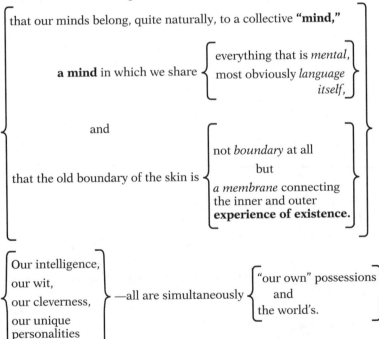

In addition to all the coordination, note the two resumptive modifiers:

> Far from being locked **inside** our own skins,
> > **inside** the "dungeons" of ourselves...
> our minds belong...to a collective **"mind,"**
> > **a mind** in which we share...

Note too the two nominalizations stressed at the end of the first sentence and the coordinate nominalizations at the end of the second:

> ...the inner and outer experience of existence.
> ..."our own" possessions and the world's.

Exercise 11.1

Here are some first halves of sentences to finish with balancing last halves. For example, suppose you are given this:
> Those who keep silent over the loss of small freedoms...
Then finish with something like this:
> ...will be silenced when they protest the loss of large ones.

1. Those who argue stridently over small matters...
2. While the strong are often afraid to admit weakness, the weak...
3. Some teachers mistake neat papers that rehash old ideas for...
4. When parents raise children who scorn hard work, the adults those children become will...

Exercise 11.2

These sentences end weakly. Edit them for clarity and concision, then revise them so that they end on more heavily stressed words, particularly with prepositional phrases beginning with *of*. For example:

> Our interest in paranormal phenomena testifies to the fact that we have **empty spirits and shallow minds.**
> ✓ Our interest in paranormal phenomena testifies to **the emptiness of our spirits and the shallowness of our minds.**

In the first three, I have boldfaced words you might nominalize.

1. If we invest our sweat in these projects, we must avoid appearing to work only because we are **interested** in ourselves.

2. The plan for the political campaign was concocted by those who were not sensitive to what we **needed** most critically.
3. Throughout history, science has made progress because dedicated scientists have ignored a **hostile** public that is uninformed.
4. Not one tendency in our governmental system has brought about more changes in American daily life than federal governmental agencies that are very powerful.

NUANCES OF LENGTH AND RHYTHM

Most writers don't plan the length of their sentences, but that's not a problem, unless every sentence is shorter than fifteen words or so, or much longer. Artful writers, however, do manage the lengths of their sentences purposefully.

Here, for example, Mary Wollstonecraft varies the length and form of her sentences to capture the sounds of a waterfall and the flood of thoughts and feelings it inspired:

> The impetuous dashing of the rebounding torrent from the dark cavities which mocked the exploring eye produced an equal activity in my mind. My thoughts darted from earth to heaven, and I asked myself why I was chained to life and its misery. Still the tumultuous emotions this sublime object excited were pleasurable; and, viewing it, my soul rose with renewed dignity above its cares. Grasping at immortality—it seemed as impossible to stop the current of my thoughts, as of the always varying, still the same, torrent before me; I stretched out my hand to eternity, bounding over the dark speck of life to come.
>
> We turned with regret from the cascade.
>
> —*Letters Written During a*
> *Short Residence in Sweden, Norway, and Denmark*

Her first sentence echoes the rush of the water by sprawling over two prepositional phrases and a relative clause before it reaches its verb. Her forty-one-word fourth sentence, with its erratic syntax and punctuation, similarly mirrors her rushing reflections. The very short sentence that begins the next paragraph contrasts starkly with those that precede it, announcing through its style as well as its sense the end of her reverie.

Exercise 11.3

Find three passages from your own reading in which writers vary the lengths of their sentences. What is the effect of this variation on the rhythm and meaning of the passages? Rewrite the passages so that their sentences are consistently fifteen to twenty-five words long. What is the effect of this change?

ELEGANCE AND CLARITY

We have seen how intricate elegant sentences and passages can become. But that fact shouldn't blind us to a more basic one: for a sentence or passage to be elegant, it must first be clear and coherent. Remember our five major principles:

- *Characters as subjects:* Use main characters in your "story" as the subjects of most of your sentences.

- *Actions as verbs:* Express the main actions performed by (or on) these characters as verbs, not nouns.

- *Old before new:* Begin sentences with familiar information, and end them with information readers cannot predict.

- *Short before long:* Begin with a short, easily grasped segment of information that frames the longer, more complex segments that follow. This principle applies not only to sentences but also to paragraphs, sections, and whole documents.

- *Topic then stress:* Begin sentences with what they are "about" or "comment on"; end with words that should receive special emphasis.

Now look again at the example with which we began this lesson, that sentence from *The Washington Post*:

> Its 11- and 12-year-old players, some from struggling neighborhoods, not only cheered a city challenged by violence but charmed the country with their stellar play and outstanding sportsmanship.

That sentence follows our principles straightforwardly:

- The subject *players* is a main character.
- The actions *cheered* and *charmed* are verbs.

- The sentence opens by repeating information from the preceding sentence, which mentions both the team and its players. It then tells us something new: that these players cheered the city and charmed the country.
- The sentence begins with a short segment (*Its 11- and 12-year-old players*) that announces its topic.
- The sentence ends by stressing those qualities that have endeared the players to the country: the quality of their play and sportsmanship.
- The second verb phrase is slightly longer than the first because of the compound object of the prepositional phrase.

Here is a more complicated example of elegant prose from the philosopher Michael J. Sandel. It follows our principles as well, but more subtly:

> When moral reflection turns political, when it asks what laws should govern our collective life, it needs some engagement with the tumult of the city, with the arguments and incidents that roil the public mind. Debates over bailouts and price gouging, income inequality and affirmative action, military service and same-sex marriage, are the stuff of political philosophy. They prompt us to articulate and justify our moral and political convictions, not only among family and friends but also in the demanding company of our fellow citizens.

> —*Justice: What's the Right Thing to Do?*

- The first sentence delays the subject with a pair of subordinate *when* clauses, but that's a stylistic choice. The sentence still announces the passage's main topic/character *moral reflection* at its beginning, and the first *when* clause is slightly shorter than the second, creating a sense of proportion. When we do get to the main clause, we find that main character as the subject—*its [moral reflection]*—and an action as the verb: *needs* (Sandel could have written *it is in need of…*). We also get quickly past the subject and verb to the direct object, *engagement*, which sets up the parallel *with* phrases that follow.
- Following the principle of old before new, the second sentence begins with a subject/topic—*Debates*—that names in a single word the concept introduced at the end of the first sentence. The sentence, with its sixteen-word whole subject *Debates…marriage* and short, five-word complement *the stuff of political philosophy* seems to depart from the principle of short before long. But that's a set-up: the concluding prepositional phrase *of moral philosophy* (*of* + weighty word) gives the

sentence's end a satisfying heft: the alternative *moral philosophy's stuff* sounds flat.

• The third sentence adheres to our principles more strictly. It repeats the subject/topic/character of the second sentence (characters as subjects, old before new) and gets quickly past the verb, which expresses the action performed by that character (actions as verbs), to the object. In fact, all of that happens in just three words, which gets us quickly to the lengthy infinitive phrase *to articulate...fellow citizens* that makes up the bulk of the sentence. And within that phrase, the two-syllable word *moral* is balanced by the longer four-syllable word *political*, and the four-word prepositional phrase *among family and friends* is balanced by the longer eight-word prepositional phrase *in the demanding company of our fellow citizens*. The principle of short before long organizes this sentence at every level: the whole, the phrase, and the word.

Again, I can't tell you directly how to write an elegant sentence. Instead, I have shown you some ways that adept writers apply and combine the basic principles of clear and coherent writing to achieve the effect of elegance. To write elegantly yourself, you must read those who write elegantly and, through that apprenticeship, develop an elegant style of your own. Only then can you look at your own writing and know when it is elegant or just inflated. To make that distinction, the only truly reliable rule is that *less is more*, for, in the words of the poet Marianne Moore, "compression is the first grace of style."

IN YOUR OWN WORDS

Exercise 11.4

You develop a knack for balance by imitating models—not word for word, just their general pattern. Pick some nicely balanced passages you admire, perhaps from sermons, political speeches, or dictionaries of quotations, and try imitating them. Choose a subject of your own, and follow your model's outline, as this writer did with this passage from the historian Frederick Jackson Turner:

> Survival in the wilderness requires the energy and wit to overcome the brute facts of an uncooperative Nature but rewards the person who acquires that power with the satisfaction of having done it once and with the confidence of being able to do it again.

> Life as a college student offers a few years of intellectual ex-
> citement but imposes a sense of anxiety on those who look
> ahead and know that its end is in sight.
>
> You can also imitate examples from this lesson.
>
> ## *Exercise 11.5*
>
> Congratulations! You have made it through eleven lessons on clar-
> ity and grace. This exercise is an opportunity for you to see how far
> you've come. Give a reader two 500-word passages of your writing,
> one completed before you started working through this book and
> another you have completed more recently. Can your reader tell
> which is which? What specific changes have you made in your writ-
> ing style? Use the principles from this book to describe the differ-
> ences between your old and new writing.

SUMMING UP

The qualities of elegance are too varied and subtle to capture in
a summary. Nevertheless, elegant passages typically have three
characteristics that may seem incompatible but are not:

- the simplicity of characters as subjects and actions as verbs
- the complexity of balanced syntax, meaning, sound, and
  rhythm
- the emphasis of artfully stressed endings

In short, the effect of elegance follows from the principles of
clarity and coherence, deftly applied and adapted.

PART FIVE

Ethics

*Ethics is in origin the art of recommending to others the
sacrifices required for cooperation with oneself.*
—BERTRAND RUSSELL

The Ethics of Style

Everything should be made as simple as possible, but not simpler.
—ALBERT EINSTEIN

*Simplicity is not a given. It is an achievement, a human invention,
a discovery, a beloved belief.*
—WILLIAM GASS

Style is the ultimate morality of mind.
—ALFRED NORTH WHITEHEAD

THE FIRST RULE OF ETHICAL WRITING

In the last eleven lessons, I have emphasized the responsibility writers owe readers to write clearly. But readers also have a responsibility to read carefully enough to understand ideas too difficult for Dick-and-Jane sentences. It would be impossible, for example, for an engineer to revise this into language clear to everyone:

> The drag force on a particle of diameter d moving with speed u relative to a fluid of density p and viscosity μ is usually modeled by $F=0.5C_Du^2A$, where A is the cross-sectional area of the particle at right angles to the motion.

Most of us do work hard to understand what we read—at least until we decide that a writer failed to work equally hard to help us understand or, worse, deliberately made our reading more difficult than it had to be. Once we decide that a writer is careless, lazy, or self-indulgent—well, our days are too few to spend them in such company.

In fact, our reactions as readers imply our responsibility as writers: if we don't want others to impose gratuitously difficult writing on us, then we ought not impose it on others. If we are socially responsible writers, we should strive for a style that is no simpler than our ideas require but also no more difficult than it has to be. Responsible writers follow a rule whose more general theme you probably recognize:

Write to others as you would have others write to you.

Few of us violate this rule deliberately, but we do underestimate its consequences. If our readers decide our writing is unnecessarily difficult, we risk losing more than their attention. We also risk losing what writers since Aristotle have called a reliable *ethos*—the character that readers infer from our writing. Do we seem sympathetic or callous? Trustworthy or deceitful? Amiably candid or impersonally aloof?

Over time, the *ethos* you project in individual pieces of writing hardens into your reputation. So writing clearly is not just altruistic. It is also pragmatic, because we tend to trust most a writer with a reputation for being thoughtful, responsible, and considerate of readers' needs.

But what is at stake here is more than even reputation: it is the ethical foundation of a literate society. We write ethically when, as a matter of principle, we would trade places with our intended readers and experience the consequences they do after they read our writing. Unfortunately, writers don't always live up to that standard. Sometimes they simply fall short, but they can also be intentionally deceptive. It is up to us as readers to judge which is which.

Unintended Obscurity

Those who write in ways that seem dense and convoluted rarely intend to do so. I do not believe, for example, that the writers of this next passage *knowingly* wrote it as unclearly as they did:

> A major condition affecting adult reliance on early communicative patterns is the extent to which the communication has been planned prior to its delivery. We find that adult speech behaviour takes on many of the characteristics of child language, where the communication is spontaneous and relatively unpredictable.
>
> —E. Ochs and B. Schieffelin, *Planned and Unplanned Discourse*

That means (I think):

> When we speak spontaneously, we rely on patterns of child language.

The authors might object that I have oversimplified their idea, but those eleven words express what I remember from their forty-seven. And what really counts, after all, is not what writers think they have put into a passage but what readers get out of it.

The ethical issue here is not those writers' willful indifference but their innocent ignorance. We can help such writers by reading carefully and charitably. And when given the opportunity, we can help them in another way as well, by telling them candidly how their writing affects us—and why. I know many of you think that right now you do not have the standing to do that. But one day, you will.

Intended Misdirection

The ethics of writing are clearer when writers knowingly work not to further their readers' interests but to disguise their own.

Example #1: Who Erred?   A major automotive repair company was once accused of overcharging its customers. It responded with this notice:

> With over two million automotive customers serviced last year in California alone, mistakes may have occurred. However, we want you to know that we would never intentionally violate the trust customers have shown in our company for more than 100 years.

In the first sentence, the writer avoided identifying the company as the party responsible for mistakes. The writer could have used a passive verb:

> ...mistakes **may have been made.**

But that would have encouraged us to wonder *By whom?* Instead, the writer found a verb that moved the company off stage by saying mistakes just "occurred," seemingly on their own.

In the second sentence, though, the writer used the first-person *we* to humanize the company, the responsible agent, and emphasize its good intentions:

> **we**...would never intentionally violate...

If we revise the first sentence to focus on the company and the second to hide it, we get a very different effect:

> When we serviced over two million automotive customers last year in California, we made mistakes. However, you should know that no intentional violation of more than 100 years of trust occurred.

That's a small point of stylistic manipulation, self-interested but innocent of any malign motives. This next one is more significant.

Example #2: Who Pays?   Consider this letter from a natural gas utility telling hundreds of thousands of customers that it was raising their rates. (The subject/topic in every clause, main or subordinate, is boldfaced.)

> **The State Utilities Commission** has authorized a restructuring of our rates together with an increase in Service Charge revenues effective at the start of the next calendar year. **This** is the first increase in our rates in over six years. **The restructuring of rates** is consistent with revised state policy that **rates for service to various classes of utility customers** be based upon the cost of providing that service. **The new rates** move revenues from every class of customer closer to the cost actually incurred to provide gas service.

That notice is a model of misdirection: after the first sentence, the writer never again begins a sentence with a human character, least of all the character whose interests are most at stake—the reader. The reader is mentioned only twice, in the third person, and never as a subject/topic/agent:

> …for service to various classes of utility **customers**

> …move revenues from every class of **customer**

The writer refers to the gas company only twice, in the phrase *our rates*, and never identifies the company as a responsible subject/topic/agent. Had the company wanted to make clear who the real "doer" was and who was being done to, the notice would have read more like this:

> According to the State Utilities Commission, **we** can now make **you** pay more for your gas service after the new year. **We** have not made **you** pay more in over six years, but under revised state policy, now **we** can.

We can reasonably charge this writer with breaching the First Rule of Ethical Writing: the deflection of responsibility seems deliberate, and the writer would surely not want that same kind of writing directed to him or her in a matter of personal interest.

Example #3: Who Dies?   Finally, here is a passage that raises an even greater ethical issue, one involving life and death. Some time ago, the Government Accounting Office investigated why more than half the car owners who got recall letters did not get their cars fixed. It found that car owners could not understand the letters or were not sufficiently alarmed by them to bring their cars back to the dealer for service.

Here is one such notice, which shows how writers can meet a legal obligation while evading an ethical one (I numbered the sentences):

> [1]A defect which involves the possible failure of a frame support plate may exist on your vehicle. [2]This plate (front suspension pivot bar support plate) connects a portion of the front suspension to the vehicle frame, and [3]its failure could affect vehicle directional control, particularly during heavy brake application. [4]In addition, your vehicle may require adjustment service to the hood secondary catch system. [5]The secondary catch may be misaligned so that the hood may not be adequately restrained to prevent hood fly-up in the event the primary latch is inadvertently left unengaged. [6]Sudden hood fly-up beyond the secondary catch while driving could impair driver visibility. [7]In certain circumstances, occurrence of either of the above conditions could result in vehicle crash without prior warning.

First, look at the subjects/topics of the sentences:

[1]a defect	[2]this plate	[3]its failure
[4]your vehicle	[5]the secondary catch	
[6]sudden hood fly-up	[7]occurrence of either condition	

The main character/topic of that story is not me, the driver, but my car and its parts. In fact, the writers—probably a team of lawyers—ignored me almost entirely (I am in *your vehicle* twice and *driver* once) and omitted all references to themselves. In sum, it says:

> There is a car that might have defective parts. Its plate could fail and its hood fly up. If they do, it could crash without warning.

The writers also nominalized important actions and made verbs passive when they referred to actions that might alarm me (n = nominalization, p = passive):

failure$_n$	vehicle directional control$_n$	heavy brake application$_n$
be misaligned$_p$	not be restrained$_p$	hood fly-up$_n$
is left unengaged$_p$	driver visibility$_n$	warning$_n$

If the writers intended to deflect my fear and maybe my anger, then they violated their ethical duty to write to me as they would have me write to them, for surely they would not swap places with a reader deliberately lulled into ignoring a dangerous, even life-threatening condition.

Of course, being candid has its costs. I would be naive to claim that everyone is free to write as he or she pleases, especially when a writer's job is to protect an employer's interests. Maybe the writers of that letter felt coerced into writing it as they did. But that doesn't mitigate the consequences. When we knowingly write in ways that we would not want others to write to us, we abrade the trust that sustains a civil society.

We should not, of course, confuse unethical indirectness with the human impulse to soften bad news. When a supervisor says *I'm afraid our new funding didn't come through,* we know it means *You have no job.* But that indirectness is motivated not by dishonesty but by kindness.

In short, our choice of subjects determines not just whether our writing is clear but also whether it is honest or deceptive.

Exercise 12.1

Revise the gas rate notice, using *you* as a subject/topic/agent. Then revise again, using *we*. For example:

> As the State Utilities Commission has authorized, *you* will have to pay us higher service charges after the start of the next calendar year/*we* can charge you more after...

Would the company resist sending either revision? Why? Was the original "good" writing? What do you mean by *good*?

Exercise 12.2

Revise the recall letter, making *you* the subject of as many verbs as you can and naming as many actions in verbs as you can. One of the sentences will read,

> If **you** BRAKE hard and the plate FAILS, **you** could...

Would the company be reluctant to send out that version? Is the original letter "good" writing? Which of the following, if either, is closer to the "truth"? Is that even the right question?

> If the plate fails, you could crash.

> If the plate fails, your car could crash.

RATIONALIZING OPACITY

Necessary Complexity

How should we respond to those who know they write in a complex style but claim they must because they are breaking new intellectual ground? Are they right, or is that a self-serving rationalization? This is a vexing question, not just because we can settle it only case by case but also because we may not be able to settle some cases at all, at least not to everyone's satisfaction.

Here, for example, is a sentence from a leading figure in contemporary literary theory:

> If, for a while, the ruse of desire is calculable for the uses of discipline soon the repetition of guilt, justification, pseudo-scientific theories, superstition, spurious authorities, and classifications can be seen as the desperate effort to "normalize" *formally* the disturbance of a discourse of splitting that violates the rational, enlightened claims of its enunciatory modality.
>
> —Homi K. Bhabha, "Of Mimicry and Man:
> The Ambivalence of Colonial Discourse"

Does that sentence express a thought so subtle and complex that its substance can be expressed only as written? Or is it academic babble? How do we decide whether in fact his nuances are, at least for ordinarily competent readers, just not accessible, given the time most of us have for figuring them out?

We owe our readers precise and nuanced prose, but we ought not to assume that they owe us an indefinite amount of their time to unpack it. If we deliberately write in ways that we know will make readers struggle—well, that's a gambit we choose to play. In the marketplace of ideas, truth is the prime value, but not the only one. Another is what it costs us to find it.

In the final analysis, I can suggest only that when writers claim their prose style must be difficult because their ideas are new, they are, as a matter of simple fact, more often wrong than right. The philosopher of language Ludwig Wittgenstein said:

> Whatever can be thought can be thought clearly; whatever can be written can be written clearly.

I'd add a nuance:

> ...and with just a bit more effort, more clearly still.

Salutary Complexity/Subversive Clarity

There are two more defenses of complexity: one claims that complexity is good for us, the other that clarity is bad.

As to the first claim, some argue that the harder we have to work to understand what we read, the more deeply we think and the better we understand. Everyone should be happy to know that no evidence supports so foolish a claim, and substantial evidence contradicts it.

As to the second claim, some argue that "clarity" is a device wielded by those in power to mislead us about who really controls our lives. By speaking and writing in deceptively simple ways, they say, those who control the facts dumb them down, rendering us unable to understand the full complexity of our political and social circumstances:

> It seems to us that those . . . who make a call for clear writing synonymous with an attack on critical educators have missed the role that the "language of clarity" plays in a dominant culture that cleverly and powerfully uses "clear" and "simplistic" language to systematically undermine and prevent the conditions from arising for a public culture to engage in rudimentary forms of complex and critical thinking.
>
> —Stanley Aronowitz, *Postmodern Education*

This writer makes one good point: language is deeply implicated in politics, ideology, and control. In our earliest history, the educated elite used writing itself to exclude the illiterate, then Latin and French to exclude those who knew only English. More recently, those in authority have relied on a vocabulary thick with Latinate nominalizations and on a Standard English that requires those Outs aspiring to join the Ins to submit to a decades-long education, during which time they are expected to acquire not only the language of the Ins but their values as well.

So is clarity an ideological value? Of course it is. How could it not be? But those who attack clarity as a conspiracy to oversimplify complicated social issues are as wrong as those who attack science because some use it for malign ends: it is not clarity that subverts, but the unethical use of it. Clarity is a value that is created by society and that society must work hard to maintain. We must simply insist that, in principle, those who manage our affairs have a duty to tell us the truth as clearly as they can. They probably won't, but that just shifts the burden to us to call them out on it.

> *Here's the point:*   Style depends on choices, and the ethical quality of those choices depends on the motives behind them. Only by knowing those motives can we know whether a writer would willingly subject herself to her own prose, to be influenced (or manipulated) by it as her readers are. We can't always pass ethical judgment on others, but we can certainly write ethically ourselves. Remember the First Rule of Ethical Writing: *Write to others as you would have others write to you.*

AN EXTENDED ANALYSIS

It is easy to condemn writers who seem to manipulate us to further their own interests. It is more difficult to pass judgment when we are manipulated by those whom we would never charge with deceit. But it is these instances that force us to think the hardest about matters of style and ethics. The Declaration of Independence, the founding document of the Unites States, is such a case. Here I examine how Thomas Jefferson, the Declaration's principal author, manages his prose style to influence how we respond to his argument.

The Declaration is celebrated for its logic. After a discussion of human rights and their origin, Jefferson lays out a simple syllogism:

Major premise:	When a long train of abuses by a government evinces a design to reduce a people under despotism, they must throw off such government.
Minor premise:	These colonies have been abused by a tyrant who evinces such a design.
Conclusion:	We therefore declare that these colonies are free and independent states.

His argument is as straightforward as the language expressing it is artful.

Jefferson begins with a preamble that asserts not the colonists' claim of independence but their obligation to justify it with good reasons:

> When, in the course of human events, it becomes necessary for one people to dissolve the political bonds which have connected them with another, and to assume among the powers of the earth, the

separate and equal station to which the laws of nature and of nature's God entitle them, a decent respect to the opinions of mankind requires that they should declare the causes which impel them to the separation.

He then organizes the Declaration into three parts. In the first, he offers his major premise, a philosophical justification for a people to throw off a tyranny and replace it with a government of their own:

We hold these truths to be self-evident, that all men are created equal, that they are endowed by their Creator with certain unalienable rights, that among these are life, liberty and the pursuit of happiness. That to secure these rights, governments are instituted among men, deriving their just powers from the consent of the governed. That whenever any form of government becomes destructive to these ends, it is the right of the people to alter or to abolish it, and to institute new government, laying its foundation on such principles and organizing its powers in such form, as to them shall seem most likely to effect their safety and happiness. Prudence, indeed, will dictate that governments long established should not be changed for light and transient causes; and accordingly all experience hath shown that mankind are more disposed to suffer, while evils are sufferable, than to right themselves by abolishing the forms to which they are accustomed. But when a long train of abuses and usurpations, pursuing invariably the same object evinces a design to reduce them under absolute despotism, it is their right, it is their duty, to throw off such government, and to provide new guards for their future security.

In Part 2, Jefferson applies these principles to the colonists' situation:

Such has been the patient sufferance of these colonies; and such is now the necessity which constrains them to alter their former systems of government. The history of the present King of Great Britain is a history of repeated injuries and usurpations, all having in direct object the establishment of an absolute tyranny over these states. To prove this, let facts be submitted to a candid world.

Those facts constitute a litany of King George's offenses against the colonies, evidence supporting Jefferson's minor premise that the king intended to establish "an absolute Tyranny over these States":

He has refused his assent to laws, the most wholesome and necessary for the public good.

He has forbidden his governors to pass laws of immediate and pressing importance,....

He has refused to pass other laws for the accommodation of large districts of people,....

He has called together legislative bodies at places unusual, uncomfortable, and distant....

Part 3 opens by reviewing the colonists' attempts to avoid separation:

In every stage of these oppressions we have petitioned for redress in the most humble terms: Our repeated petitions have been answered only by repeated injury. A prince, whose character is thus marked by every act which may define a tyrant, is unfit to be the ruler of a free people.

Nor have we been wanting in attention to our British brethren. We have warned them from time to time of attempts by their legislature to extend an unwarrantable jurisdiction over us. We have reminded them of the circumstances of our emigration and settlement here. We have appealed to their native justice and magnanimity, and we have conjured them by the ties of our common kindred to disavow these usurpations, which, would inevitably interrupt our connections and correspondence. We must, therefore, acquiesce in the necessity, which denounces our separation, and hold them, as we hold the rest of mankind, enemies in war, in peace friends.

Part 3 ends with the actual declaration of independence:

We, therefore, the representatives of the United States of America, in General Congress, assembled, appealing to the Supreme Judge of the world for the rectitude of our intentions, do, in the name, and by the authority of the good people of these colonies, solemnly publish and declare, that these united colonies are, and of right ought to be free and independent states; that they are absolved from all allegiance to the British Crown, and that all political connection between them and the state of Great Britain, is and ought to be totally dissolved; and that as free and independent states, they have full power to levy war, conclude peace, contract alliances, establish commerce, and to do all other acts and things which independent states may of right do. And for the support of this declaration, with a firm reliance on the protection of divine providence, we mutually pledge to each other our lives, our fortunes and our sacred honor.

Jefferson's argument is a model of cool logic, but his style inclines readers to accept that logic.

Parts 2 and 3 reflect the principles of clarity explained in Lessons 3–6. In Part 2, Jefferson made *He* (King George) the short, concrete subject/topic/agent of all the actions named:

He *has refused....*

He *has forbidden....*

He *has refused*. . . .

He *has called together*. . . .

He could have written this:

His assent to laws, the most wholesome and necessary for the public good, *has not been forthcoming*. . . .

Laws of immediate and pressing importance *have been forbidden*. . . .

Places unusual, uncomfortable, and distant from the depository of public records *have been required* as meeting places of legislative bodies. . .

Or he could have consistently focused on the colonists:

We *have been deprived* of Laws, the most wholesome and necessary. . . .

We *lack* Laws of immediate and pressing importance. . . .

We *have had to meet* at places usual, uncomfortable. . . .

In other words, Jefferson was not forced by the nature of things to make King George the active agent of every oppressive action. But that choice supported his argument that the king was a willfully abusive tyrant. Such a choice seems so natural, however, that we don't notice that it was a *choice.*

In Part 3, Jefferson also wrote in a style that reflects our principles of clarity: he again matched the characters in his story to the subjects/topics of his sentences. But here he switched characters to the colonists, named *we:*

Nor *have* **we** *been wanting* in attentions to our British brethren.

We *have warned* them from time to time. . . .

We *have reminded* them of the circumstances of our emigration. . . .

We *have appealed* to their native justice and magnanimity. . . .

. . .**we** *have conjured* them by the ties of our common kindred. . . .

They too *have been deaf* to the voice of justice and of consanguinity.

We *must,* therefore, *acquiesce* in the necessity. . . .

We. . .*do*. . .solemnly *publish and declare*. . . .

. . .**we** mutually *pledge* to each other our Lives. . . .

With only one exception, all the subjects/topics are *we.*

And again, Jefferson was not forced by the nature of things to do that. He could have made his British brethren subjects/topics:

Our British brethren *have heard* our requests....

They *have received* our warnings....

They *know* the circumstances of our emigration....

They *have ignored* our pleas....

But he chose to assign agency to the colonists to focus first on their attempts to negotiate, and only then on their action of declaring independence.

Again, his choices were not inevitable, but they seem natural, even unremarkable: *King George did all those bad things, so we must declare our independence.* What more is there to say about the style of Parts 2 and 3, other than that Jefferson made the obviously right choices?

Far more interesting are Jefferson's choices in Part 1, which has a quite different style. In fact, in Part 1, he wrote only two sentences that make real people the subjects of active verbs:

...**they** [the colonists] *should declare* the causes....

We *hold* these truths to be self-evident....

There are four other subject-verb sequences that have short, concrete subjects, but they are all in the passive voice:

...**all men** *are created* equal....

...**they** *are endowed* by their Creator with certain unalienable Rights....

...**governments** *are instituted* among **Men**....

...**governments long established** *should* not *be changed* for light and transient causes....

In the first two sentences, the agent is obviously God, but in the last two, the passives explicitly obscure the agency of people in general and the colonists in particular.

In the rest of Part 1, Jefferson chose a style that is *even more* impersonal, making abstractions the subjects/topics/agents of almost every important verb. In fact, most of his sentences would yield to the kind of revisions we described in Lessons 3–6:

When in the course of human events, **it** *becomes necessary* for one people to dissolve the political bands which have connected them with another....

✓ When in the course of human events, **we** *decide* **we** *must dissolve* the political bands which have....

...**a decent respect to the opinions of mankind** *requires* that they should declare **the causes** which *impel* them to the separation.

✓ If **we** decently *respect* the opinions of mankind, **we** *should declare* why **we** *have decided to separate.*

...**it** *is the right* of the people to alter or to abolish it, and to institute new Government....

✓ **We** *may alter or abolish* it, and *institute* new government....

Prudence, indeed, *will dictate* that governments long established should not be changed for light and transient causes....

✓ If **we** *are prudent,* **we** *will not change* governments long established for light and transient causes.

...**all experience** *hath shewn,* that **mankind** *are more disposed* to suffer, while evils are sufferable....

✓ **We** *know* from experience that **we** *choose* to suffer, while **we** *can suffer* evils....

...**a long train of abuses and usurpations**...*evinces* a design to reduce them under absolute Despotism.

✓ **We** *can see* a design in a long train of abuses and usurpations pursuing invariably the same Object—to reduce us under absolute Despotism.

Necessity...*constrains* them to alter their former Systems of government.

✓ **We** now *must alter* our former Systems of government.

Instead of writing as clearly and directly as he did in Parts 2 and 3, why in Part 1 did Jefferson *choose* to write in a style so indirect and impersonal? One ready answer is that Jefferson wanted to do more than justify the colonists' particular revolution. Rather, he wanted to establish a philosophical basis for just revolution in general. This idea, a profoundly destabilizing one in Western political thought, needed more justification than the colonists' mere desire to throw off a government they disliked.

What is most striking about the style of Part 1 is not its impersonal generality, but how relentlessly Jefferson uses that style to strip the colonists of any free will and to invest agency in higher forces that compel the colonists to act:

- **respect** for opinion *requires* that [the colonists] explain their action
- **causes** *impel* [the colonists] to separate
- **prudence** *dictates* that [the colonists] not change government lightly

- **experience** has *shown* [the colonists]
- **necessity** *constrains* [the colonists]

Even when abstractions do not explicitly compel the colonists, Jefferson implies that the colonists are not free agents:

- It [is] *necessary* to sever bonds.
- Mankind *are disposed* to suffer.
- It is their *duty* to throw off a tyrant.

In this light, even the assertion *We hold these truths to be self-evident* is a claim implying that the colonists did not discover those truths but that those truths revealed themselves to the colonists.

In short, in each part of the Declaration, Jefferson chose a style that suited its argument. In Parts 2 and 3, he chose a style so transparent and predictable that we don't even notice the choice. In Part 2, he made King George a freely acting agent of his actions by making him the subject/topic of every sentence; in Part 3, Jefferson made the colonists the agents of their own actions.

But to make the first part of his argument work, Jefferson had to make the colonists seem to be the coerced objects of higher powers. Since the only higher power named in the Declaration is a Creator, nature's God, that Creator is implicitly the coercive power that "constrains them to alter their former systems of government." Jefferson did not explicitly *say* that, much less defend it. Instead, he let the grammar of his sentences make that part of his argument for him.

The Declaration of Independence is a majestic document for reasons beyond its grammar and style. The same words that brought the United States into existence laid down fundamental values that justify the self-governance of all people everywhere.

But we ought not ignore Jefferson's rhetorical powers, in particular, the genius of his style. In crafting his argument, he also manipulated, managed, massaged—call it what you will—his language to support its logic in ways not apparent on a casual reading.

We might charge Jefferson with being mildly deceptive here, with using language instead of logic to establish the crucial premise of his argument: the colonists were not free to do other than what they did; they had no choice other than to revolt. But Jefferson had to use *some* style. Ultimately, it comes down to *ethos*, which is to say, ethics. We understand that skilled writers manage our responses not just explicitly through logical arguments but also implicitly through their prose style. But we expect such writers to have in mind not just their own interests but ours also. We don't trust the writer of that automobile recall letter, because the letter was almost certainly intended to deceive us: its style doesn't support its message but hides it. In contrast, we do trust Jefferson, because he manages his language not to mask his argument but to strengthen it.

In Your Own Words

Exercise 12.3

The First Principle of Ethical Writing is to write to others as you would have them write to you. Recall an occasion when you violated this principle or were tempted to. What was the situation? What did you do? Would you do anything differently now?

Exercise 12.4

We confront ethical issues in writing every day. For one week, pay attention to the writing you encounter in your everyday life: labels on products, the fine print on bills, bulk mail advertisements, spam in your email account, and so on. Select three of these texts that raise ethical issues you would like to talk about, and share them with a colleague or with your class. What ethical issues do your texts raise? Why do you imagine their writers wrote them as they did? How would your texts need to be revised to make them ethical?

Summing Up

How, finally, do we decide what counts as "good" writing? Is it clear, graceful, and candid, even if it fails to achieve its end? Or is it writing that does a job, regardless of its integrity and means? We have a problem so long as *good* can mean either ethically sound or pragmatically successful.

We resolve that dilemma by our First Principle of Ethical Writing:

> We are ethical writers when we would willingly put ourselves in the place of our readers and experience what they do as they read what we've written.

That puts the burden on us to imagine our readers and their feelings.

If you are even moderately advanced in your academic or professional career, you've experienced the consequences of unclear writing, especially when it's your own. If you are in your early years of college, though, you may wonder whether all this talk about clarity, ethics, and *ethos* is just so much finger-wagging. At the moment, you may be happy to find enough words to fill three pages, much less worry about their style. And you may be reading textbooks that have been heavily edited to make them clear to first-year students who know little or nothing about their content. So you may not yet have experienced much carelessly dense writing. But it's only a matter of time before you will.

Others wonder why they should struggle to learn to write clearly when bad writing seems so common and appears to cost its writers so little. What experienced readers know, and you eventually will, is that clear and graceful writers are so few that when we find them, we are desperately grateful. They do not go unrewarded.

I also know that for many writers crafting a good sentence or paragraph gives them pleasure enough. It is an ethical satisfaction some of us find not just in writing, but in everything we do: we find joy in doing good work, no matter the job, no matter who notices. It is a view expressed with clarity and grace by the philosopher Alfred North Whitehead, who identifies a "sense for style" in any art or endeavor as an aesthetic and, finally, moral appreciation for planned ends economically achieved:

> The administrator with a sense for style hates waste; the engineer with a sense for style economizes his material; the artisan with a sense for style prefers good work. Style is the ultimate morality of mind.
>
> —*The Aims of Education*

APPENDIX I
Punctuation

*There are some punctuations that are interesting
and there are some punctuations that are not.*
—GERTRUDE STEIN

UNDERSTANDING PUNCTUATION

Most writers think that punctuation must obey the same kind of
rules that govern grammar, and that managing commas and semicolons is like making verbs agree with subjects. In fact, you have
more options in how to punctuate than you might think, and if you
choose thoughtfully, you can help readers not only understand a
complex sentence more easily but create nuances of emphasis that
they will notice.

I will address punctuation as a functional problem: how do
we punctuate the end of a sentence, then its beginning, and finally
its middle? But first, we have to distinguish different kinds of
sentences.

Simple, Compound, and Complex Sentences

Sentences have traditionally been called *simple, compound,* and
complex. If a sentence has just one independent clause, it is
simple:

The greatest English dictionary is the *Oxford English Dictionary.*

If it has two or more independent clauses, it is *compound:*

[There are many good dictionaries][1],
[but the greatest is the *Oxford English Dictionary*][2].

If it has an independent clause and one or more subordinate clauses, it is *complex:*

[While there are many good dictionaries], subordinate clause
[the greatest is the *Oxford English Dictionary*]. independent clause

If it has at least two independent clauses, and at least one of them includes a subordinate clause, it is *compound-complex.*

These terms are potentially misleading, however, because they suggest that a grammatically simple sentence should also *feel* simpler than one that is grammatically complex. But that's not always true. For example, to most readers of the next two sentences, the grammatically simple one *feels* more complex than the grammatically complex one:

GRAMMATICALLY SIMPLE: Our review of the test led to our modification of it as a result of complaints by teachers.

GRAMMATICALLY COMPLEX: After we reviewed the test, we modified it because teachers complained.

We need another set of terms that more reliably indicate how readers are likely to respond to such sentences.

PUNCTUATED AND GRAMMATICAL SENTENCES

We can make a more useful distinction between what we will call *punctuated* sentences and *grammatical* sentences:

- A punctuated sentence begins with a capital letter and ends with a period, question mark, or exclamation point. It might be one word or more than a hundred.

- A grammatical sentence is a subject and verb in a main clause along with everything else depending on that clause.

We distinguish these two kinds of sentence because readers respond to them very differently: the paragraph you are now reading is one long punctuated sentence, but it is not as difficult to read as many paragraphs made up of shorter sentences with multiple subordinate clauses; I have chosen to punctuate as one long sentence what I might have punctuated as a series of shorter ones: that colon, those semicolons, and the comma before *but*, for example, could have been periods—and that dash could have been a period too.

Here is that long sentence you just read revised and repunctuated with virtually no change in its grammar, creating seven punctuated sentences:

> We distinguish these two kinds of sentence because readers respond to them very differently. The paragraph you are now reading is made up of short punctuated sentences. But it is not less difficult to read than many paragraphs made up of longer sentences with multiple independent clauses. I have chosen to punctuate as a series of separate sentences what I could have punctuated as one long one. The period before *but*, for example, could have been a comma. The last two periods could have been semicolons. And that period could have been a dash.

Though I changed little but the punctuation, those seven grammatical sentences feel different when punctuated as seven punctuated sentences. Like other aspects of style, punctuation is a matter less of following rules (although there are some) than of choosing among options: we create different effects through the choices we make.

PUNCTUATING THE ENDS OF SENTENCES

Above all else, you must know how to punctuate the end of a grammatical sentence. You can signal the end of a grammatical sentence in a number of ways, but signal it you must, because readers have to know where one grammatical sentence stops and the next begins. You can choose to separate pairs of grammatical sentences in ten ways. Three are common.

Three Common Forms of End Punctuation

1. **Period, Question Mark, or Exclamation Point Alone** The simplest, least noticeable way to signal the end of a grammatical sentence is with a period:

   ✓ In 1967, Congress passed civil rights laws to remedy problems of registration and **voting. These** had political consequences throughout the South.

   But if you create too many short punctuated sentences, your readers may feel your prose is choppy or simplistic. Experienced writers often revise very short grammatical sentences into subordinate clauses or even phrases, turning two or more grammatical sentences into one:

   ✓ **When Congress passed civil rights laws to remedy problems of registration and voting in 1967, they** had political consequences throughout the South.

✓ The civil rights laws **that Congress passed in 1967 to remedy problems of registration and voting** had political consequences throughout the South.

Be cautious, though: combine too many short grammatical sentences into one long one, and you may create a sentence that sprawls (see Lesson 10).

2. **Semicolon Alone** A semicolon is like a soft period; whatever is on either side of it should be a grammatical sentence (with an exception we'll discuss on p. 209). Use a semicolon instead of a period only when the first grammatical sentence has fewer than fifteen or so words and the content of the second grammatical sentence is closely linked to the first:

   ✓ In 1967, Congress passed civil rights laws that remedied problems of registration and **voting; those** laws had political consequences throughout the South.

   Many writers avoid semicolons because they find them mildly intimidating. So learning their use might be worth your time, especially if you want to be judged a sophisticated writer. Once every couple of pages is probably about right.

3. **Comma + Coordinating Conjunction** Readers are also ready to recognize the end of a grammatical sentence when they see a comma followed by two signals:

   • a coordinating conjunction: *and, but, yet, for, so, or, nor*
   • another subject and verb

      ✓ Technology companies need highly skilled workers**, so they recruit** aggressively at the best colleges and universities.

      ✓ The League of Nations was founded in 1920 to prevent another world war**, but its structural flaws kept** it from succeeding.

   Choose a period or semicolon if the two grammatical sentences are long and have their own internal punctuation.

   When readers encounter a coordinated series of three or more grammatical sentences, they accept just a comma between them, but only if they are short and have no internal punctuation:

      ✓ Baseball satisfies our admiration for **precision, basketball** speaks to our love of speed and **grace, and** football appeals to our lust for violence.

If any of the grammatical sentences have internal punctuation, separate them with semicolons:

✓ Baseball, the oldest indigenous American sport and essentially a rural one, satisfies our admiration for **precision; basketball,** our newest sport and now more urban than rural, speaks to our love of speed and **grace; and** football, a sport both rural and urban, appeals to our lust for violence.

Be careful not to overuse *and.* Readers want conjunctions to signal relationships among ideas, so too many grammatical sentences joined with *and* can feel simplistic.

Omit the comma, however, between a coordinated pair of short grammatical sentences if you introduce them with a modifier that applies to both of them:

✓ Once the financial crisis ended, the stock market **rebounded but unemployment** persisted.

A caution: even skilled writers sometimes use a comma incorrectly to punctuate the end of a grammatical sentence when they begin the next with *however.* Not this:

Taxpayers have supported public education, **however,** they now object because taxes have risen so steeply.

Because *however* is not a coordinating conjunction, that first sentence requires a period or semicolon (but keep the comma after *however):*

✓ Taxpayers have supported public education. **However,** they now object because taxes have risen so steeply.

✓ Taxpayers have supported public education; **however,** they now object because taxes have risen so steeply.

Four Less Common Forms of End Punctuation

Some readers have reservations about these next four ways of signaling the end of a grammatical sentence, but careful writers regularly use them.

4. **Period + Coordinating Conjunction** Some think it's wrong to begin a punctuated sentence with a coordinating conjunction such as *and* or *but* (review p. 13). But they are wrong. The second sentence here is entirely correct:

✓ Education cannot guarantee **freedom. And** when it is available to only a few, it becomes a tool of social repression.

Use this pattern no more than once or twice a page, especially with *and*.

5. **Semicolon + Coordinating Conjunction**   Writers occasionally end one grammatical sentence with a semicolon and begin the next with a coordinating conjunction.

    A comma is better if the two grammatical sentences are short, like these:

    ✓ Technology companies need highly skilled **workers, so** they recruit aggressively at the best colleges and universities.

But readers can be grateful for a semicolon if the two grammatical sentences are long and have their own internal commas:

    ✓ Problem solving, one of the most active areas of psychology, has made great strides in the last decade, particularly in understanding the problem-solving strategies of **experts; so** it is no surprise that educators have followed that research with interest.

Then again, readers would probably prefer a period there even more.

6. **Conjunction Alone**   Some writers signal a close link between short grammatical sentences with a coordinating conjunction alone, omitting the comma:

    ✓ Oscar Wilde violated a fundamental law of British **society and** we all know what happened to him.

But a warning: though writers of the best prose make this choice, some teachers consider it an error.

7. **Comma Alone**   Readers rarely expect to see just a comma used to separate two grammatical sentences, but they can manage if the sentences are short and closely linked in meaning, such as *cause-effect, first-second,* or *if-then:*

    ✓ Act in haste, repent at leisure.

Be sure, though, that neither has internal commas. Not this:

    Women, who have always been underpaid, no longer accept that discriminatory treatment, they are now doing something about it.

A semicolon would be clearer:

    ✓ Women, who have always been underpaid, no longer accept that discriminatory **treatment; they** are now doing something about it.

But the same warning: though writers of the best prose separate short grammatical sentences with just a comma, many teachers disapprove. That's because a comma alone is traditionally condemned as a "comma splice," in their view a grave error. So be sure of your readers before you experiment.

QUICK TIP When you begin a grammatical sentence with *but*, you can either put a comma at the end of the previous sentence or begin a new punctuated sentence by using a period and capitalizing *but*. Use a period + *But* if what follows is important and you intend to go on discussing it:

> ✓ The immediate consequence of higher gas prices was some curtailment of **driving. But** the long-term effect changed the car-buying habits of Americans, perhaps permanently, a change that the Big Three car manufacturers could not ignore. They . . .

Use a comma + *but* if what follows only qualifies what preceded.

> ✓ The immediate consequence of higher gas prices was some curtailment of **driving, but** that did not last long. The long-term effect was changes in the car-buying habits of Americans, a change that the Big Three car manufacturers could not ignore. They . . .

Three Special Cases: Colon, Dash, Parentheses

These last three ways of signaling the end of a grammatical sentence are a bit self-conscious, but might be interesting to those who want to distinguish themselves from most other writers.

8. **Colon** Discerning readers are likely to notice and appreciate when you end a sentence with an appropriate colon. They take it as shorthand for *to illustrate, for example, that is, therefore:*

> ✓ Dance is not widely **supported: no** company operates at a profit, and there are few outside major cities.

A colon can also signal more obviously than a comma or semicolon that you are balancing the structure, sound, and meaning of one clause against another:

> ✓ Civil disobedience is the public conscience of a democracy: mass enthusiasm is the public consensus of a tyranny.

If you follow the colon with a grammatical sentence, capitalize the first word or not, depending on how much you want to emphasize what follows (note: some handbooks claim that the first word after a colon should not be capitalized).

QUICK TIP   Avoid a colon if it breaks a clause into two pieces, neither of which is a grammatically complete sentence. Avoid this:

> **Genetic counseling requires: a** knowledge of statistical genetics, an awareness of choices open to parents, and the psychological competence to deal with emotional trauma.

Instead, put the colon only after a whole subject-verb-object structure:

> ✓ **Genetic counseling requires the following: a** knowledge of statistical genetics, an awareness of choices open to parents, and the psychological competence to deal with emotional trauma.

---

9. **Dash**   You can also signal balance more informally with a dash—it suggests a casual afterthought:

   ✓ Stonehenge is a **wonder—only** a genius could have conceived it.

   Contrast that with a more formal colon: it makes a difference.

10. **Parentheses**   You can use parentheses to insert a short grammatical sentence inside another one if what you put in the parentheses is like a short afterthought. Do not put a period after the sentence inside the parenthesis; put a single period outside:

   ✓ Stonehenge is a **wonder** (**only** a genius could have conceived it).

Though some ways of punctuating the end of a sentence are flat-out wrong, you can choose from among many that are right, and each has a different effect. If you look again at that passage by Mary Wollstonecraft about the waterfall (p. 170), you can see those choices in contrast.

Intended Sentence Fragments

A punctuated sentence that fails to include an independent main clause is wrong. At least in theory.

In fact, experienced writers often write fragments deliberately, as I just did. When intended, those fragments typically have two characteristics:

- They are relatively short, fewer than ten or so words.
- They are intended to reflect a mind at work, as if the writer were speaking to you, finishing a sentence, then immediately expanding and qualifying it. Almost as an afterthought, often ironically.

In this passage, Mark Twain uses sentence fragments (along with sentences beginning with conjunctions) to capture the element of chance in the circumstances that made him an author (fragments are boldfaced):

> For amusement I scribbled things for the Virginia City *Enterprise*. . . . One of my efforts attracted attention, and the *Enterprise* sent for me and put me on its staff.
>
> And so I became a journalist—**another link**. By and by Circumstance and the Sacramento *Union* sent me to the Sandwich Islands for five or six months, to write up sugar. I did it; **and threw in a good deal of extraneous matter that hadn't anything to do with sugar**. But it was this extraneous matter that helped me to another link.
>
> It made me notorious, and San Francisco invited me to lecture. **Which I did. And profitably**. I had long had a desire to travel and see the world, and now Circumstance had most kindly and unexpectedly hurled me upon the platform and furnished me the means. So I joined the "Quaker City Excursion."
>
> —"The Turning-Point of My Life"

You should know, however, that writers rarely use sentence fragments in academic prose. They are generally considered too casual. If you decide to experiment, be sure that your audience can see that you know what you're doing.

PUNCTUATING BEGINNINGS

You have no issues in punctuating the beginning of a sentence when you begin directly with its subject, as I did this one. However, as with this one, when a sentence forces a reader to plow through several introductory words, phrases, and clauses, especially when they have their own internal punctuation and readers might be confused by it all (as you may be right now), forget trying to get the punctuation right: just revise it.

There are a few rules that your readers expect you to follow, but more often you have to rely on judgment.

Five Reliable Rules

1. **Always separate an introductory element from the subject of a sentence with a comma if a reader might misunderstand the structure of the sentence, as in this one:**

   > When a lawyer concludes her argument has to be easily remembered by a jury.

   Do this:

   > ✓ When a lawyer **concludes, her** argument has to be easily remembered by a jury.

2. **Never end an introductory clause or phrase with a semicolon, no matter how it long is.** Readers take semicolons to signal the end of a grammatical sentence (but see p. 209 for an exception). Never this:

   > Although the museum possessed a formidable collection of Mesopotamian artifacts, some more than five thousand years **old; it** could display only a fraction of them.

   Use a comma there instead:

   > ✓ Although the museum possessed a formidable collection of Mesopotamian artifacts, some more than five thousand years **old, it** could display only a fraction of them.

3. **Never put a comma right after a subordinating conjunction if the next element of the clause is its subject.** Never this:

   > **Although, the art** of punctuation is simple, it is rarely mastered.

4. **Avoid putting a comma after the coordinating conjunctions** *and, but, yet, for, so, or,* **and** *nor* **if the next element is the subject.** Do not do this:

   > **But, we** cannot know whether life on other planets exists.

   Some writers who punctuate heavily put a comma after a coordinating or subordinating conjunction if an introductory word or phrase follows:

   > ✓ **Yet, during this period, prices** continued to rise.
   > ✓ **Although, during this period, prices** continued to rise, interest rates did not.

Punctuation that heavy can slow readers down, but it's your choice. These are also correct and for the reader, perhaps a bit brisker:

✓ Yet during this **period, prices** continued to rise.

✓ Yet during this **period prices** continued to rise.

5. **Put a comma after an introductory word or phrase if it comments on the whole of the following sentence or connects one sentence to another.** These include elements such as *fortunately, allegedly,* etc. and connecting adverbs like *however, nevertheless, otherwise,* etc. Readers hear a pause after such words.

✓ **Fortunately, we** proved our point.

But avoid starting many sentences with an introductory element and a comma. When we read a series of such sentences, the whole passage feels hesitant. However, we typically omit a comma after *now, thus,* and *hence:*

✓ **Now it** is clear that many will not support this position.

✓ **Thus the** only alternative is to choose some other action.

✓ Her computer crashed, and she had no backup. **Hence she** was forced to begin anew.

Two Reliable Principles

1. **Readers usually need no punctuation between a short introductory phrase and the subject:**

✓ **Once again we** find similar responses to such stimuli.

✓ **In 1066 William** the Conqueror landed on England's southern shore.

It is not wrong to put a comma there, but it slows readers down just as you may want them to be picking up speed.

2. **Readers usually need a comma between a long (four or five words or more) introductory phrase or clause and the subject:**

✓ When a lawyer begins her opening statement with a dry recital of the **law, the jury** is likely to nod off.

Punctuating Middles

This is where explanations get messy, because to punctuate inside a grammatical sentence—more specifically, inside a clause—you have to consider not only the grammar of that clause but also the nuances of rhythm, meaning, and emphasis that you want readers to hear in their mind's ear. There are, however, a few reliable rules you should follow.

Subject—Verb, Verb—Object

Do not put a comma between a subject and its verb, no matter how long the subject (nor between the verb and its object). Do not do this:

> A sentence that consists of many complex subordinate clauses and long phrases that all precede a **verb, may** seem to some students to demand a comma somewhere.

If you keep subjects short, you won't feel that you need a comma.

Occasionally, you cannot avoid a long subject, especially if it consists of a list of items with internal punctuation, like this:

> **The president, the vice president, the secretaries of the departments, senators, members of the House of Representatives, and Supreme Court justices take** an oath that pledges them to uphold the Constitution.

You can help readers sort it out with a summative subject:

- Insert a colon or a dash at the end of the list of subjects.

- Add a one-word subject that summarizes the preceding list:

> ✓ The president, the vice president, the secretaries of the departments, senators, members of the House of Representatives, and Supreme Court justices: **all** take an oath that pledges them to uphold the Constitution.

Choose a dash or a colon depending on how formal you want to seem. A dash is less formal.

Interruptions

When you interrupt a subject-verb or verb-object, you make it harder for readers to make the basic grammatical connections that create a sentence. So in general, avoid such interruptions, except for reasons of emphasis or nuance (see pp. 142–143).

If you must interrupt a subject and verb or verb and object with more than a few words, always put paired commas around the interruption.

> ✓ A sentence, **if it includes subordinate clauses,** may seem to need commas.

Generally speaking, do not use a comma when you tack on a subordinate clause at the end of an independent clause if that subordinate clause is necessary to understand the meaning of the sentence (this is analogous to a restrictive relative clause):

✓ No one should violate the **law just because** it seems unjust.

If the clause is not necessary, separate it from the main clause with a comma.

✓ No one should violate the **law, because** in the long run it will do more harm than good.

This distinction can be tricky at times.

You may locate ADVERBIAL PHRASES before, after, or in the middle of a clause, depending on the emphasis you want readers to hear. If in the middle, put a comma before and after. Compare the different emphases in these:

✓ **In recent years** modern poetry has become more relevant to the average reader.

✓ Modern poetry **has, in recent years, become** more relevant to the average reader.

✓ Modern poetry has **become, in recent years, more** relevant to the average reader.

✓ Modern poetry has become more relevant to the average reader **in recent years.**

Loose Commentary

"Loose commentary" differs from an interruption, because you can usually move an interruption elsewhere in a sentence. But loose commentary modifies what it stands next to, so it usually cannot be moved. It still needs to be set off with paired commas, parentheses, or dashes, unless it comes at the end of a sentence. In that case, replace the second comma or dash with a period.

It is difficult to explain exactly what counts as loose commentary because it depends on both grammar and meaning. One familiar distinction is between restrictive clauses and nonrestrictive clauses (see pp. 14–15), including appositives.

We use no commas with restrictive modifiers, modifiers that uniquely identify the noun they modify:

✓ The house **that I live in** is 100 years old.

But we always set off nonrestrictive modifiers with *paired* commas (unless the modifier ends the sentence):

✓ We had to reconstruct the **larynx, which is the source of voice,** with cartilage from the shoulder.

An appositive is just a truncated nonrestrictive clause:

✓ We had to rebuild the **larynx, ~~which is~~ the source of voice,** with cartilage from the shoulder.

You can achieve a more casual effect with a dash or parentheses:

✓ We had to rebuild the **larynx—the source of voice—with** cartilage from the shoulder.

✓ We had to rebuild the **larynx (the source of voice) with** cartilage from the shoulder.

A dash is useful when the loose commentary has internal commas. Readers are confused by the long subject in this sentence:

The nations of Central Europe, Poland, Hungary, Romania, Bulgaria, the Czech Republic, Slovakia, Bosnia, Serbia have for centuries been in the middle of an East-West tug-of-war.

They can understand that kind of structure more easily when they can see that loose modifier set off with dashes or parentheses:

✓ The nations of Central **Europe—Poland, Hungary, Romania, Bulgaria, the Czech Republic, Slovakia, Bosnia, Serbia—have** for centuries been in the middle of an East-West tug-of-war.

Use parentheses when you want readers to hear your comment as a *sotto voce* aside:

✓ The brain **(at least that part that controls nonprimitive functions)** may comprise several little brains operating simultaneously.

Or use it as an explanatory footnote inside a sentence:

✓ Lamarck **(1744–1829)** was a pre-Darwinian evolutionist.

✓ The poetry of the *fin de siècle* **(end of the century)** was characterized by a world-weariness and fashionable despair.

When loose commentary is at the end of a sentence, use a comma to separate it from the first part of the sentence. Be certain, however, that the meaning of the comment is not crucial to the meaning of the sentence. If it is, do not use a comma. Contrast these:

✓ I wandered through **Europe, seeking a place** where I could write undisturbed.

✓ I spent my **time seeking a place** where I could write undisturbed.

✓ Offices will be closed July **2–6, as announced in the daily bulletin.**

✓ When closing offices, secure all safes **as prescribed in the manual.**

✓ Historians have studied social changes, **at least in this country.**

✓ These records must be kept **at least until the IRS reviews them.**

PUNCTUATING COORDINATED ELEMENTS

Punctuating Two Coordinated Elements

Generally speaking, do not put a comma between just two coordinated elements. Compare these:

As computers have become **sophisticated, and** powerful they have taken over more **clerical, and** bookkeeping tasks.

✓ As computers have become **sophisticated and** powerful they have taken over more **clerical and** bookkeeping tasks.

Four Exceptions

1. **For a dramatic contrast, put a comma after the first coordinate element to emphasize the second (keep the second short):**

   ✓ The ocean is nature's most glorious **creation, and** its most destructive.

   To emphasize a contrast, use a comma before a *but*, again keeping the second part short:

   ✓ Organ transplants are becoming more **common, but** not less expensive.

2. **If you want your readers to feel the cumulative power of a coordinated pair (or more), drop the *and* and leave just a comma. Compare:**

   ✓ Lincoln never had a formal **education and** never owned a large library.

   ✓ Lincoln never had a formal **education, never** owned a large library.

   ✓ The lesson of the pioneers was to ignore conditions that seemed difficult or even **overwhelming and** to get on with the business of subduing a hostile environment.

   ✓ The lesson of the pioneers was to ignore conditions that seemed difficult or even **overwhelming, to** get on with the business of subduing a hostile environment.

3. **Put a comma between long coordinated pairs only if you think your readers need a chance to breathe or to sort out the grammar.** Compare:

> It is in the graveyard that Hamlet finally realizes that the inevitable end of life is the **grave and clay and that the** end of all pretentiousness and all plotting and counter-plotting, regardless of one's station in life, must be dust.

A comma after *clay* signals a natural pause:

> ✓ It is in the graveyard that Hamlet finally realizes that the inevitable end of all life is the **grave and clay, and that the** end of all pretentiousness and all plotting and counter-plotting, regardless of one's station in life, must be dust.

More important, the comma after *clay* sorts out the grammatical structure of a potentially confusing sequence *grave and clay and that.*

In this next sentence, the first half of a coordination is long, so a reader might have a problem connecting the second half to its origin:

> Conrad's *Heart of Darkness* brilliantly dramatizes those primitive impulses that lie deep in each of us and stir only in our darkest **dreams but asserts** the need for the values that control those impulses.

A comma after *dreams* would clearly mark the end of one coordinate member and the beginning of the next:

> ✓ Conrad's *Heart of Darkness* brilliantly dramatizes those primitive impulses that lie deep in each of us and stir only in our darkest **dreams, but asserts** the need for the values that control those impulses.

On the other hand, if you can make sense out of a complicated sentence like that only with punctuation, you need to revise the sentence.

4. **If a sentence begins with a phrase or subordinate clause modifying two following clauses that are independent and coordinated, put a comma after the introductory phrase or clause but do not put a comma between the two coordinated independent clauses:**

> ✓ Once the financial crisis ended, the stock market rebounded **[no comma here]** but unemployment persisted.

Punctuating Three or More Coordinated Elements

Finally, there is the matter of punctuating a series of three or more coordinated elements. Writers and handbooks disagree on this one. A few omit it, but most insist a comma must always precede the last one:

✓ His wit, his **charm and his loyalty** made him our friend.
✓ His wit, his **charm, and his loyalty** made him our friend.

Both are correct, but be consistent.

If any of the items in the series has its own internal commas, use semicolons to show readers how they should group the coordinated items:

✓ In mystery novels, the principal action ought to be economical, organic, and **logical; fascinating,** yet not **exotic; clear,** but complicated enough to hold the reader's interest.

APOSTROPHES

There are few options with apostrophes, only rules, and they are Real Rules (review pp. 11–12). Those who violate them are derided by those who police such matters.

Contractions

Use an apostrophe in all contracted words:

don't   we'll   she'd   I'm   it's

Writers in the academic world often avoid contractions in their professional writing because they don't want to seem too casual. I've used them in this book because I wanted to avoid a formal tone. Check with your teacher before you experiment.

Plurals

Except for two cases, *never use an apostrophe to form a plural.* Never this: *bus's, fence's, horse's.* That error invites withering abuse.

Use an apostrophe to form plurals in only two contexts: (1) with all lower-case single letters and (2) with the single capital letters *A, I,* and *U* (the added *s* would seem to spell the words *As, Is,* and *Us*):

Dot your i's and cross your t's.   many A's and I's

But when a word is unambiguously all numbers or multiple capital letters, add just *s*, with no apostrophe:

The ABCs	the 1950s	767s
CDs	URLs	45s

Possessives

With a few exceptions, form the possessive of a singular common or proper noun by adding an apostrophe + *s*.

FDR's third term   the U.S.'s history   a 747's wingspan

The exceptions include singular nouns that already end in *s*. For these, add the apostrophe only:

politics' importance   the United States' role

Some handbooks also recommend omitting the s when forming the possessive of proper nouns that end in *s*, especially when they are biblical or classical:

Moses' tablets   Sophocles' plays

Others, though, give different advice, recommending an apostrophe + *s* in all cases. Whatever you choose, be consistent.

For plural common and proper nouns that end in *s*, form the possessive by adding an apostrophe only.

workers' votes   the Smiths' house

Form the possessive of a singular compound noun by adding an apostrophe + *s* to the last word:

the attorney general's decision   his sister-in-law's business

SUMMING UP

There are some Real Rules governing punctuation, but you also have a wide range of choices. Use your judgment, and punctuate in ways that help your readers see the connections and separations that they have to see to make sense of your sentences.

1. Always signal the end of a grammatical sentence. You can do so in ten ways. Three are conventional and common:

1. Period	*I win. You lose.*
2. Semicolon	*I win; you lose.*
3. Comma + coordinating conjunction	*I win, and you lose.*

Four are debatable, but good writers do sometimes use them, especially the first:

4. Period + coordinating conjunction   *I win. And you lose.*
5. Semicolon + coordinating conjunction *I win; and you lose.*
6. Coordinating conjunction alone   *I win and you lose.*
7. Comma alone   *I win, you lose.*

Three are for writers who want to be a bit stylish in their punctuation:

8. Colon   *I win: you lose.*
9. Dash   *I win—you lose.*
10. Parentheses   *I win (you lose).*

2. These are reliable rules of punctuation. Observe them.

   1. Always separate an introductory element from the subject if a reader might misunderstand the structure of the sentence.
   2. Never end an introductory clause or phrase with a semicolon.
   3. Do not put a comma after a subordinating conjunction if the next element of the clause is its subject.
   4. Do not put a comma after a coordinating conjunction if the next element of the clause is its subject.
   5. Put a comma after a short introductory word or phrase if it comments on the whole of the following sentence or if it connects one sentence to another.

3. These are strong principles:

   1. Put a comma after a short introductory phrase or not, as you choose.
   2. Readers need a comma after a long introductory phrase or clause.

4. These are reliable rules of internal punctuation. Observe them.

   1. Do not interrupt a subject and verb or verb and object with any punctuation, unless absolutely necessary for clarity.
   2. Inside a clause, always set off long interruptions with paired marks of punctuation commas, parentheses, or dashes. Never use semicolons.
   3. Put a comma at the end of an independent clause before a tacked-on subordinate clause when that clause is not essential to the meaning of the sentence.

5. Use commas to separate items in a series if the items have no internal punctuation. Use semicolons to set off items in a series if they do.

6. Know and follow the rules governing apostrophes, and where you have choices, be consistent.

APPENDIX II
Using Sources

Everything of importance has been said before by somebody who did not discover it.
—ALFRED NORTH WHITEHEAD

There is not less wit nor less invention in applying rightly a thought one finds in a book, than in being the first author of that thought.
—PIERRE BAYLE

USING SOURCES PROPERLY

Few writers can get by on their own thoughts alone, and a researcher never can. We all write better when our thinking is enriched by what we learn from others. But there are rules for using the words and ideas of others, and your first obligation is to understand and follow them. Mistakes here can damage your credibility, your grade, and even your reputation for honesty.

But as with other aspects of style, you also have choices, and in this lesson, as in our others, I focus less on what you *must* do to use sources properly than on what you *can* do to use them effectively.

Avoiding Plagiarism

Plagiarism means using the words or ideas of others in ways that suggest they are one's own. It is among the most serious transgressions a writer can commit. Only a few—for example, fabricating evidence or outright lying—are worse. I begin with this issue not because I think you are dishonest but to emphasize its seriousness and then to put it behind us, so that we can attend to the *choices* you have when using sources.

Honest writers sometimes think they don't have to worry about plagiarism. But even honest writers can plagiarize inadvertently, and even inadvertent plagiarism can damage a writer's credibility and reputation or bring disciplinary consequences. Yet just as you can't write well if, with every word you set down, you worry about violating some rule of correctness, so you can't write well if, with every source you use, you worry about committing an act of plagiarism. You need to fear plagiarizing only if you fail to understand and follow reliable practices that ensure you will avoid it.

Plagiarists steal more than words. They also steal the respect and recognition due to others for their work. And student plagiarists also steal acknowledgment and even grades due to their peers by making their peers' work seem worse in comparison to their own. When such theft becomes common, the community grows suspicious, then distrustful, then cynical: *So who cares? Everyone does it.* Teachers then have to be concerned less with teaching and learning and more with detecting dishonesty. Those who plagiarize thus fray the ethical fabric of their entire community.

The overriding principle is this: *avoid doing anything that might lead an informed reader to think that you are taking credit for words or ideas not your own.* This principle applies to sources of any kind: print, online, recorded, or oral. Some writers think that if something is freely circulated online, they are free to treat it as their own. They are wrong: cite everything you borrow.

In particular, follow these practices:

1. **When you quote from a source:** cite the source according to the conventions of your field, and put those words in quotation marks or in a block quotation.

2. **When you paraphrase a passage from a source:** cite the source according to the conventions of your field, and recast the passage entirely in your own words in a new sentence structure.

3. **When you use an idea or method you found in a source:** cite the source according to the conventions of your field. If the entire source concerns the idea or method, do not add page numbers.

Of course, you can't follow these good practices if you take sloppy notes or if you don't know how to properly quote from and cite your sources.

Take Good Notes

To use and cite sources correctly, you must start by taking good notes. Since the work can be tedious, set up a system to get things right the first time so that you don't have to check and recheck, again and again.

1. **Record bibliographical information the first time you touch a source.** Do this early, not when you are rushing to meet a deadline.

   For books, record
   - ❑ author(s)
   - ❑ title (and subtitle)
   - ❑ title of series (if any)
   - ❑ edition or volume (if any)
   - ❑ city and publisher
   - ❑ year published
   - ❑ pages for chapter (if any)

   For articles, record
   - ❑ author(s)
   - ❑ title (and subtitle)
   - ❑ journal, magazine, etc.
   - ❑ volume and issue number
   - ❑ online database (if any)
   - ❑ date published
   - ❑ pages for article

   Online sources are less predictable. In addition to the above information, record at least the URL and the access date, as well as any other information that might help you identify the source for readers.

2. **Record quotations exactly.** Copy quotations *exactly* as they appear in the original, down to every comma and semicolon. If the quotation is long, photocopy it, cut-and-paste it, or download the entire source.

3. **Mark quotations and paraphrases unambiguously as the words of others.** This is crucial: take notes so that weeks or months later you *cannot possibly* think that words and ideas from a source are your own. Whether you take notes longhand or on a computer, *always* highlight, underline, or use a different font to distinguish direct quotations. Then use another way to distinguish paraphrases and summaries. Prominent scholars have been humiliated by accusations of plagiarism because, they claimed, they did not clearly mark words they copied or paraphrased, then "forgot" they were not their own.

4. **Don't paraphrase too closely.** When you paraphrase a source in your notes, you must do more than merely replace words in the source with synonyms. That is also considered plagiarism, even if you cite the source. You must recast the entire passage

in your own language. For example, the first paraphrase below is plagiarism because it tracks its sentence structure almost word for word. The second paraphrase is paraphrased appropriately.

Original: At the heart of the argument culture is our habit of seeing issues and ideas as absolute and irreconcilable principles continually at war. To move beyond this static and limiting view, we can remember the Chinese approach to yin and yang. They are two principles, yes, but they are conceived not as irreconcilable polar opposites but as elements that coexist and should be brought into balance as much as possible.
—Deborah Tannen, *The Argument Culture: Stopping America's War of Words*

Plagiarized: At the center of our culture of argument is our tendency to regard positions and ideas as entirely and irresolvably in conflict. To get past this rigid and narrow understanding, we need to see our concepts not as completely opposed but as perspectives that exist simultaneously and that should be harmonized to the fullest possible extent.

Appropriate: Our society's approach to argument is based on an assumption that competing positions and ideas must always be in conflict. To transcend it, we need to recognize that these competing positions and ideas can often be reconciled.

Punctuating Quotations

Here are three rules for using punctuation with quotation marks:

1. **If the quotation ends in a period, comma, semicolon, or colon, replace it with the punctuation you need in your own sentence.**

   - If your punctuation is a period or comma, put it *before* a final quotation mark:

     President Nixon said, "I am not a crook."
     Falwell claimed, "This is the end," but he was wrong.

   - If your punctuation is a question mark, colon, or semicolon, put it *after* the final quotation mark:

     My first bit of advice is "Quit complaining"; my second is "Get moving."

The Old West served up plenty of "rough justice": lynchings and other forms of casual punishment were not uncommon.

How many law professors believe in "natural law"?

Why does Keats write, "Beauty is truth, truth beauty"?

2. **If the quotation ends with a question mark or exclamation point and your punctuation is a period or comma, drop your punctuation and put the question mark *before* the quotation mark:**

   Freud famously asked, "What do women want?"

3. **If you use quotation marks inside a quotation, put your comma or period before both of the marks:**

   She said, "I have no idea how to interpret 'Ode to a Nightingale.'"

Citing Sources Appropriately

Your last task is to cite your sources fully, accurately, and appropriately. No one will accuse you of plagiarism for a misplaced comma, but some will conclude that if you cannot get these little matters right, you cannot be trusted on the big ones. There are many styles you can use for your citations, so find out which one your readers expect. Three are most common:

- Chicago style, from *The Chicago Manual of Style*, common in the humanities and some social sciences

- MLA style, from the Modern Language Association, common in literary studies and in high-school and college writing classes

- APA style, from the American Psychological Association, common in the social sciences

You can find guides to citation in most bookstores or online.

USING SOURCES EFFECTIVELY

Again, to use sources ethically, you must quote accurately, paraphrase appropriately, and follow the citation conventions of your field. But to use sources effectively, you must do more than follow sound rules and practices. As with other aspects of style, you have choices in how you incorporate sources into your writing, and you can shape the responses of your readers through the choices you make. To use a source in your writing, you have to make at least three decisions:

- **How much of the source to include:** will you use just a word or phrase, a sentence, a passage, or a summary of the whole?
- **How to include it:** will you use the source's exact words or put the source's ideas into your own words?
- **How to attribute it:** will you explicitly attribute it to the source's author?

Before I discuss these choices, a word of caution: like citation conventions, ways of using sources vary from field to field. In some fields, writers quote extensively; in others, they quote rarely, relying instead on summary and paraphrase. The best way to learn the typical practices of your field is to read writers who are recognized authorities in it.

Here then, in general terms, are your options. (Note: in my illustrations, I use parenthetical citations; in your own writing, you should follow the conventions of your field.)

How Much of a Source to Include?

To use a source in your writing, you must first decide how much of it to include through quotation, paraphrase, or summary: just a few words, a single sentence, a longer passage, a summary of the whole? There are no hard-and-fast rules that answer this question, but here are three principles to help you choose:

1. **Include just as much of a source as you need.** If you don't quote or paraphrase enough, your writing can seem thin and disconnected from the larger conversation to which it contributes; if you quote or paraphrase too much, your writing can seem slow, plodding, or insecure. It is hard to know what's "just right": that sense of proportion is something you must acquire slowly, through instruction, reading, and practice. But you have to try. The best advice I can give is this: make your choice not to ease your anxieties but to enhance your argument.

2. **Include a source in proportion to the attention you want to give it.** If a source is especially important to your thinking, or if you discuss it in detail, include more of it; if you acknowledge it only in passing, include less of it.

3. **Include a source in proportion to your stance toward it.** This principle is a matter of *ethos*, or the character you project as a writer (see p. 177). When you agree with a source, you can include

it less prominently in your writing, because readers assume you are representing it accurately and fairly. When you challenge a source, you need to include more of it, to assure your readers that you are giving it its due. You cannot risk even the appearance that you are distorting its meaning to make it easier to question.

How to Include a Source: Summary, Paraphrase, or Quotation?

Once you've decided *how much* of a source to include, you have to choose *how* you will include it. You can summarize, paraphrase, or quote. To *summarize* is to briefly present a source's main points in one's own words; to *paraphrase* is to recast a specific passage from a source in one's own words; to *quote* is to repeat words from a source exactly. A good rule of thumb is to quote only when you need a source's exact words; otherwise, summarize or paraphrase. Here, in detail, are your options.

Summarize. You can summarize a whole source, a section of it, or even an aspect of it. Use summary to give your readers a *general* understanding of what a source says; do not rely on summary to communicate the details of a source's argument or if you want to use a source as evidence (for example, if you want to discuss a passage from a novel, or if you want to analyze data from a re-search report). Summaries can vary in length from a single clause or sentence to several paragraphs. How long a summary should be depends on how you want to use it. Choose in light of the three principles above.

When you summarize, you ask your readers to trust that you are representing your source accurately and fairly. Some novice writers are reluctant to accept this responsibility, either because they are un-sure they fully understand their source or because they worry that in summarizing it they will distort it. These worries reflect important truths. Summarizing is difficult, because it involves not just repeat-ing or recasting passages from a source but distilling a sense of the whole. Nevertheless you must try, because summary is fundamen-tal to most forms of academic and professional writing. Likewise, strictly speaking, no summary can capture the *exact* meaning of the original source. Every decision about what to include or leave out is also an interpretation, a decision about what you understand a source to mean and about what you want it to mean for your readers.

Skilled writers, however, see this situation not as an insur-mountable problem but as an opportunity to *shade* a source, to emphasize some of its aspects over others. In fact, knowing how far one can go in shading a source without *misrepresenting* it is a mark of true skill and expertise: it is a powerful way to demonstrate command of a topic and to guide the attention of your readers. Unfortunately, I can't tell you where the line is. You have to learn for yourself by reading respected writers in your field. I can offer two bits of advice. The first is to be cautious. It is much better to be seen as too fastidious than as cavalier. The second is to be doubly cautious when you disagree with a source, because in that situation, you cannot risk seeming unfair.

Paraphrase. Earlier, I discussed paraphrase in the context of plagiarism. Now, I want to approach it from the perspective of style. When you paraphrase, as when you summarize, you inevitably shade the meaning of your source. How could you not? Every change in grammar or vocabulary also involves a change in meaning, however slight. Your challenge is to manage these small shifts in meaning deliberately and responsibly. Look again at Tannen's original passage and my paraphrase of it:

> At the heart of the argument culture is our habit of seeing issues and ideas as absolute and irreconcilable principles continually at war. To move beyond this static and limiting view, we can remember the Chinese approach to yin and yang. They are two principles, yes, but they are conceived not as irreconcilable polar opposites but as elements that coexist and should be brought into balance as much as possible. (284)
>
> —Deborah Tannen, *The Argument Culture: Stopping America's War of Words*

> Our society's approach to argument, notes linguist Deborah Tannen, is based on an assumption that competing positions and ideas must always be in conflict. To transcend it, we need to recognize that these competing positions and ideas can often be reconciled. (284)

My paraphrase doesn't convey the meaning of Tannen's original exactly; it expresses my own understanding of it, which also includes my sense of what aspects of it are most important. Could someone else paraphrase the passage differently? Of course. Even so, I believe my version to be accurate and fair.

When paraphrasing, you can't avoid these kinds of choices, but you can make them deliberately and ethically, which is to say in ways that are faithful to your source, that support your own line of thought, and that serve your readers.

I now turn to several ways of quoting.

Use a block quotation. If you quote five lines or more, put the quotation into a block quotation with no quotation marks around it. Indent the same number of spaces as you indent a paragraph. If the quotation begins with a paragraph indentation, indent the first line again:

> About our society's approach to argument, linguist Deborah Tannen offers this observation:
> At the heart of the argument culture is our habit of seeing issues and ideas as absolute and irreconcilable principles continually at war. To move beyond this static and limiting view, we can remember the Chinese approach to yin and yang. They are two principles, yes, but they are conceived not as irreconcilable polar opposites but as elements that coexist and should be brought into balance as much as possible. (284)

The most common practice, as in that example, is to introduce a block quotation with words that announce it, followed by a period or colon. You can also let the quotation complete the grammar of your introductory sentence. In that case, punctuate the end of your sentence as if you were running the block quotation into your text:

> Linguist Deborah Tannen observes that the core of our society's approach to argument
> is our habit of seeing issues and ideas as absolute and irreconcilable principles continually at war. . . .

Choose a block quotation if you need to quote at length and plan to address the quotation in detail.

Drop in a quotation. If you quote four or fewer lines, you can simply drop the quotation into your text, introducing it with a brief "tag" phrase:

> According to linguist Deborah Tannen, "At the heart of the argument culture is our habit of seeing issues and ideas as absolute and irreconcilable principles continually at war" (284).
> As Tannen says/asserts/states/claims/comments/notes/observes/suggests, "At the heart . . ." (284).

The verb indicates your attitude toward the quotation, so choose it carefully.

If the author of the quotation isn't clear from context, provide it in your citation:

> According to one eminent linguist, "At the heart of the argument culture is our habit of seeing issues and ideas as absolute and irreconcilable principles continually at war" (Tannen 284).

You can insert the tag phrase into the quotation, like this:

> "At the heart of the argument culture," writes linguist Deborah Tannen, "is our habit of seeing issues and ideas as absolute and irreconcilable principles continually at war" (284).

You can also drop in a quotation as a subordinate clause. In that case, don't use a comma, and begin the quotation with a lowercase letter even if it was capitalized in the original:

> Linguist Deborah Tannen observes that "at the heart of the argument culture is our habit of seeing issues and ideas as absolute and irreconcilable principles continually at war" (284).

Drop in a quotation when you want to give your readers an author's full thought in his or her own words. But too many quotations dropped into a text can feel intrusive, and readers can question your thinking when they find bare quotations dropped in with little or no effort to connect them to your own points. So when you quote, be sure to indicate how the quotation contributes to *your* line of thought.

Weave in a quotation. Weaving a quotation into your own sentence, like this, can help you incorporate it into your own thinking:

> Linguist Deborah Tannen suggests that to change our "argument culture," we need to stop "seeing issues and ideas as absolute and irreconcilable principles continually at war" and to view them instead "as elements that coexist and should be brought into balance as much as possible" (284).

To make the quotation fit your sentence, you can modify it by adding, deleting, or even changing words. If you do, be sure not to change the quotation's meaning. Indicate added or changed words with square brackets, and indicate deletions with three spaced dots or *ellipses* (use four ellipses if you delete a sentence or more):

> Linguist Deborah Tannen suggests that to change our "argument culture," we need to stop "seeing issues and ideas as . . . continually at war" and, instead, to "[bring them] into balance as much as possible" (284).

You can also add emphasis to a quotation, but if you do, add *my emphasis, emphasis mine,* or *emphasis added* either in square brackets after the emphasis or in the parenthetical citation:

> Linguist Deborah Tannen challenges us to view our different concepts "as *elements that coexist* [my emphasis] and should be brought into balance as much as possible" (284).

Linguist Deborah Tannen challenges us to view our different concepts "as elements that coexist and should be brought into *balance as much as possible*" (284, emphasis added).

Weaving a quotation into your own sentence works like a spotlight, focusing your readers' attention on particular words or phrases. The fewer words you quote, the tighter and brighter the beam. Compare:

> Linguist Deborah Tannen suggests that "at the heart of the argument culture is our habit of seeing issues and ideas as absolute and irreconcilable principles continually at war," and she challenges us to view them instead "as elements that coexist and should be brought into balance as much as possible" (284).

> Linguist Deborah Tannen suggests that our "argument culture" is based on our tendency to regard "issues and ideas as absolute and irreconcilable principles continually at war," and she challenges us to "[bring them] into balance as much as possible" (284).

> Linguist Deborah Tannen suggests that our "argument culture" is based on our tendency to regard different positions and concepts as "continually at war," and she challenges us to seek a "balance" instead (284).

The fewer words you quote, the more emphasis they receive. But you sacrifice the context of the original and limit your readers' ability to independently verify your interpretation of your source. When you quote isolated words or short phrases, you implicitly ask your readers to trust that you are representing your source accurately and fairly.

Use just a few words from a source. When you repeat just a few words from a source, you have to decide whether or not to quote them. If they are words anyone might use, treat them as your own. If they are strikingly original or especially important, put them in quotation marks and cite their source. Consider our sentence from Tannen:

> At the heart of the argument culture is our habit of seeing issues and ideas as absolute and irreconcilable principles continually at war.

The phrase "issues and ideas" is so ordinary that it requires neither citation nor quotation marks. The term "argument culture," though, is Tannen's coinage and should be quoted and cited. Once you cite those words, you can use them again without quotation marks or citation.

How to Attribute a Source: Explicitly or Not?

When summarizing, quoting, or paraphrasing, you have to choose whether or not to explicitly name your source's author. Compare the following:

> Linguist Deborah Tannen observes that our society's approach to argument is based on an assumption that competing positions and ideas must always be in conflict (284).

> Our society's approach to argument is based on an assumption that competing positions and ideas must always be in conflict (Tannen 284).

Which you should choose depends on your purpose. When you explicitly attribute an idea to another writer, as in the first version, you hold it at arm's length. When you acknowledge an author only parenthetically, as in the second version, you seem to embrace her idea as your own. If you want to agree with Tannen, you could choose either version:

> Linguist Deborah Tannen observes that our society's approach to argument is based on an assumption that competing positions and ideas must always be in conflict (284). **This view helps us understand the shrill tone of much talk radio today.**

> Our society's approach to argument is based on an assumption that competing positions and ideas must always be in conflict (Tannen 284), **an assumption that helps us understand the shrill tone of much talk radio today.**

If you want to disagree with Tannen, you would probably choose the first version (note also the different verb):

> Linguist Deborah Tannen **claims** that our society's approach to argument is based on an assumption that competing positions and ideas must always be in conflict (284). **But in fact, many in our society recognize that different perspectives on an issue can be valuable.**

You need to attribute that first idea to someone else so you can disagree with it. If you don't, you might sound like you are contradicting yourself:

> Our society's approach to argument is based on an assumption that competing positions and ideas must always be in conflict (Tannen 284). **But in fact, many in our society recognize that different perspectives on an issue can be valuable.**

If you don't want to identify the author of your source by name, you can still attribute an idea generically:

> **Some linguists claim** that our society's approach to argument is based on an assumption that competing positions and ideas must always be in conflict (Tannen 284). **But in fact, many in our society recognize that different perspectives on an issue can be valuable.**

SUMMING UP

You have ethical obligations to acknowledge words and ideas you borrow from others and to represent your sources accurately and fairly.

Plagiarism, or using the words or ideas of others in ways that suggest they are one's own, is a serious transgression. To avoid the appearance of plagiarism, follow this principle:

- Avoid doing anything that might lead an informed reader to think that you are taking credit for words or ideas not your own.

Follow these three reliable practices for giving credit to your sources:

- When quoting from a source, put those words in quotation marks, and cite the source according to the conventions of your field.
- When paraphrasing a passage from a source, recast the passage entirely in your own words, and cite the source according to the conventions of your field.
- When taking an idea or method from a source, cite the source according to the conventions of your field.

Take notes in a way that ensures you will not mistake words or ideas taken from a source for your own words or ideas.

Punctuate and cite sources according to the conventions of your field.

Understand the choices you have to make to use sources effectively:

- How much of the source to include: Will you use just a word or phrase, a sentence, a passage, or a summary of the whole?
- How to include it: Will you use the source's exact words or put the source's ideas into your own words?
- How to attribute it: Will you explicitly attribute it to the source's author?

Summarize or paraphrase if you do not need a source's exact words; otherwise quote.

When quoting, you have these options:

- use a block quotation when quoting five lines or more
- drop a quotation into your text
- weave a quotation into your text
- take just a few words from a source

Choose based on how you want your readers to respond to the quotation.

When you attribute a quotation or idea to its author, you hold it at arm's length, which allows you to agree or disagree with it. When you quote or paraphrase a passage without attributing it to its author, you seem to embrace it as your own.

GLOSSARY

Grammar is the ground of all.
—WILLIAM LANGLAND

*Most of the grounds of the world's troubles are
matters of grammar.*
—MONTAIGNE

*There is a satisfactory boniness about grammar which the flesh of
sheer vocabulary requires before it can become vertebrate and walk
the earth. But to study it for its own sake, without relating it to
function, is utter madness.*
—ANTHONY BURGESS

*Thou hast most traitorously corrupted the youth of the
realm in erecting a grammar school. . . . It will be proved to
thy face, that thou hast men about thee that usually talk of
a noun and a verb, and such abominable words as no christian
ear can endure to hear.*
—WILLIAM SHAKESPEARE, *2 HENRY VI, 4.7*

What follows is no tight theory of grammar, just definitions useful for the terms in this book. Where the text discusses something at length, I refer you to those pages. If you want to do a quick review to get started, read the entries on SUBJECT, SIMPLE SUBJECT, WHOLE SUBJECT, and VERB.

Action: Prototypically, action is expressed by a verb: *move, hate, think, discover.* But actions also appear in NOMINALIZATIONS: *movement, hatred, thought, discovery.* Actions are also implied in some adjectives: *advisable, resultant, explanatory,* etc.

Active Voice: See p. 53.

Adjectival Clause: Adjectival clauses modify nouns. Also called RELATIVE clauses, they usually begin with a relative pronoun: *which, that, whom, whose, who.* There are two kinds: RESTRICTIVE and NONRESTRICTIVE. See p. 15.

Restrictive	The book **that** *I read* was good.
Nonrestrictive	My car, **which** *you saw*, is gone.

Adjective: A word you can put *very* in front of: *very old, very interesting.* There are exceptions: *major, additional,* etc. Since this is also a test for ADVERBS, distinguish adjectives from adverbs by putting them between *the* and a noun: *The **occupational** hazard, the **major** reason,* etc. Some nouns also appear there—*the **chemical** hazard.*

Adjectival Phrase: A phrase that functions like an adjective: *the jar **in the refrigerator**.*

Adverb: Adverbs modify all parts of speech except NOUNS:

Adjectives	**extremely** large, **rather** old
Verbs	**frequently** spoke, **often** slept
Adverbs	**extremely** carefully, **incredibly** rudely
Articles	**precisely** the man I meant, **just** the thing I need
Sentences	**Fortunately,** we were on time.

Adverbial Phrase: A phrase that functions like an adverb: *I came **as soon as I could**.*

Adverbial Clause: This is a kind of SUBORDINATE CLAUSE. It modifies a VERB or ADJECTIVE, indicating time, cause, condition, etc. It usually begins with a SUBORDINATING CONJUNCTION such as *because, when, if, since, while, unless:*

If you leave, I will stop.	**Because he left**, I did too.

Agent: Prototypically, agents are flesh-and-blood sources of an ACTION, but for our purposes, an agent is the *seeming* source of any action, an entity without which the action could not occur: ***She** criticized the program in this report.* Often, we can make the means by which we do something a seeming agent: ***This report** criticizes the program.* Do not confuse agents with SUBJECTS. Agents prototypically are subjects, but an agent can be in a grammatical OBJECT: *I underwent an interrogation by **the police**.*

Appositive: A noun phrase that is left after deleting **which** and **be:** *My dog, ~~which is~~ **a dalmatian**, ran away.*

Article: They are easier to list than to define: *a, an, and the.* An article is one kind of DETERMINER.

Character: See pp. 29–30.

Clause: A clause has two defining characteristics:

1. It has at least one subject and a verb.
2. The verb must agree with the subject in number and can be made past or present.

By this definition, these are clauses:

| She left | that they leave | if she left | why he is leaving |

These next are not, because the verbs cannot be made past tense nor do they agree in number with the putative subject:

for them to **go**   her **having gone**

Comma Splice: You create a comma splice when you join two independent clauses with only a comma:

Oil-producing countries depend too much on oil revenues, they should develop their educational and industrial resources, as well.

See p. 199.

Complement: Whatever completes a VERB:

I am **home.**   You seem **tired.**   She helped **me.**

Compound Noun Phrase: See p. 60.

Conjunction: Usually defined as a word that links words, PHRASES, or CLAUSES. They are easier to illustrate than define (the first two are also categorized as SUBORDINATING conjunctions):

adverbial conjunctions	because, although, when, since
relative conjunctions	who, whom, whose, which, that
sentence conjunctions	thus, however, therefore, nevertheless
coordinating conjunctions	and, but, yet, for, so, or, nor
correlative conjunctions	both X and Y, not only X but Y, (n)either X (n)or Y, X as well as Y

Coordination: Coordination joins two grammatical units of the same order with *and, or, nor, but, yet:*

same part of speech	you **and** I, red **and** black, run **or** jump
phrases	in the house **but** not in the basement
clauses	when I leave **or** when you arrive

Dangling Modifier: See p. 155.

Dependent Clause: Any CLAUSE that cannot be punctuated as a MAIN CLAUSE, one beginning with a capital letter and ending with a period or question mark. It usually begins with a subordinating conjunction such as *because, if, when, which, that:*

why he left	because he left	which he left

Determiner: A word that precedes and comments on a noun but is not an ADJECTIVE: *the, this, some, first, one, once,* etc.

Direct Object: The NOUN that follows a TRANSITIVE VERB and can be made the SUBJECT of a PASSIVE verb:

I found **the money.** → **The money** was found by me.

Finite Verb: A VERB that can be made past or present. These are finite verbs because we can change their tense from past to present and vice versa:

She **wants** to leave. → She **wanted** to leave.

These are not finite verbs because we cannot change the INFINITIVE to a past tense:

She wants to **leave.** → She wanted to **left.**

Fragment: A PHRASE or DEPENDENT CLAUSE that begins with a capital letter and ends with a period, question mark, or exclamation mark:

Because I left.	Though I am here!	What you did?

These are complete sentences:

He left because I did.	Though I am here, she is not!	I know what we did.

Free Modifier: See pp. 147–148.

Genre: A class of texts that bear a family resemblance to one another and that function in context to facilitate specific kinds of communication.

Gerund: A NOMINALIZATION created by adding -*ing* to a VERB:

When she **left** we were happy. → Her **leaving** made us happy.

Goal: That toward which the ACTION of a VERB is directed. In most cases, goals are DIRECT OBJECTS:

I see **you**.   I broke **the dish**.   I built **a house**.

But in some cases, the literal goal of an action can be the SUBJECT of an ACTIVE VERB:

I underwent an interrogation.   **She** received a warm welcome.

Grammatical Sentence: See p. 194.

Hedge: See pp. 129–130.

Independent Clause: A CLAUSE that that can be punctuated as a grammatical sentence.

Infinitive: A VERB that cannot be made past or present. It often is preceded by the word to: *He decided to **stay**.* But sometimes not: *We helped him **repair** the door.*

Intensifier: See pp. 131.

Intransitive Verb: A verb that does not take an OBJECT and so cannot be made PASSIVE. These are not TRANSITIVE verbs:

He **exists**.   They **slept** soundly.   She **became** a doctor.

Linking Verb: A VERB with a COMPLEMENT that refers to its SUBJECT.

He **is** my brother.   They **became** teachers.   She **seems** reliable.

Main Clause: A main or independent clause has at least a SUBJECT and VERB (imperatives are the exception) and can be punctuated as an independent sentence:

I left.   Why did you leave?   We are leaving.

A SUBORDINATE or DEPENDENT CLAUSE cannot be punctuated as an independent sentence. These are incorrectly punctuated:

Because she left.   That they left.   Whom you spoke to.

Main Subject: SUBJECT of the MAIN CLAUSE.

Metadiscourse: See pp. 58.

Nominalization: See pp. 32–33.

Nonrestrictive Clause: See pp. 14–15.

Noun: A word that fits this frame: *The* [ ] *is good.* Some are concrete: *dog, rock, car;* others are abstract: *ambition, space, speed.*

The nouns that most concern us are NOMINALIZATIONS, nouns derived from VERBS or ADJECTIVES: *act* → *action, wide* → *width.*

Noun Clause: A noun clause functions like a noun, as the SUBJECT or OBJECT of a VERB: *That you are here* proves *that you love me.*

Object: There are three kinds:

1. DIRECT object: the NOUN following a TRANSITIVE VERB:

    I *read* the **book.** We *followed* the **car.**

2. PREPOSITIONAL object: the noun following a preposition:

    in the **house**   *by* the **walk**   *with* **fervor**

3. INDIRECT object: the noun between a VERB and its direct object:

    I *gave* **him** a tip.

Parallel: Sequences of COORDINATED words, PHRASES, or CLAUSES are parallel when they are of the same grammatical structure. This is parallel:

    I decided to work hard and do a good job.

This is not:

    I decided to work hard and that I should do a good job.

Passive Voice: See pp. 53–56.

Past Participle: Usually the same form as the past tense -*ed: jumped, worked.* Irregular VERBS have irregular forms: *seen, broken, swum,* etc. It follows forms of *be* and *have: I have **gone**. It was **found**.* It sometimes serves as a modifier: ***found** money.*

Personal Pronoun: Easier to list than define: *I, me, we, us, my, mine; our, ours; you, your, yours; he, him, his; she, her, hers; they, them, their, theirs.*

Phrase: A group of words constituting a unit but not including a SUBJECT and a FINITE VERB: *the dog, too old, was leaving, in the house, ready to work.*

Possessive: *my, your, his, her, its, their* or a NOUN ending with -*'s* or -*s': the **dog's** tail.*

Predicate: Whatever follows the whole SUBJECT, beginning with the VERB PHRASE, including the COMPLEMENT and what attaches to it: He *left yesterday to buy a hat.*

Preposition: Easier to list than to define: *in, on, up, over, of, at, by,* etc.

Prepositional Phrase: The preposition plus its OBJECT: *in + the house.*

Present Participle: The *-ing* form of a VERB: *running, thinking.*

Progressive: The PRESENT PARTICIPLE form of the VERB: *Our team is **winning** the game.*

Punctuated Sentence: See p. 194.

Relative Clause: A clause beginning with a relative pronoun. See pp. 141–142.

Relative Pronoun: *who, whom, which, whose, that* when used in a relative clause.

Restrictive Clause: See pp. 14–15.

Resumptive Modifier: See pp. 146–147.

Run-on Sentence: A PUNCTUATED SENTENCE consisting of two or more GRAMMATICAL SENTENCES not separated by either a COORDINAT-ING CONJUNCTION or any mark of punctuation this entry illustrates a run-on sentence.

Simple Subject: The simple subject (italicized and boldfaced) is the smallest unit inside the WHOLE SUBJECT (italicized) that determines whether a VERB (boldfaced) is singular or plural:

*The **books** that are required reading* **are** listed.

The simple subject should be as close to its verb as you can get it.

If **a book** is required reading, **it** is listed.

Stress: See pp. 82–86.

Subject: The subject is what the VERB agrees with in number:

Two men *are* at the door.   **One man** *is* at the door.

Distinguish the WHOLE SUBJECT from its SIMPLE SUBJECT.

Subjunctive: A form of the VERB used to talk about events that are contrary to fact:

If he **were** President . . .

Subordinate Clause: A clause that usually begins with a SUBORDINATING CONJUNCTION such as *if, when, unless,* or *which, that, who.* There are three kinds of subordinate clauses: NOUN, ADVERBIAL, and ADJECTIVAL.

Subordinating Conjunction: *because, if, when, since, unless, which, who, that, whose,* etc.

Summative Modifier: See p. 147.

Thematic Thread: A sequence of THEMES running through a passage.

Theme: See pp. 87–89.

Topic: See pp. 69–72.

Topic String: The sequence of TOPICS through a series of sentences.

Transitive Verb: A VERB with a DIRECT OBJECT. The direct object prototypically "receives" an ACTION. The prototypical direct object can be made the SUBJECT of a PASSIVE verb:

We **read** the book. → The book **was read** by us.

By this definition, *resemble, become,* and *stand* (as in *He stands six feet tall*) are not transitive.

Verb: The word that must agree with the SUBJECT in number and that can be inflected for past or present:

The book **is** ready.   The books **were** returned.

Whole Subject: You can identify a whole subject once you identify its VERB: Put a *who* or a *what* in front of the verb and turn the sentence into a question. The fullest answer to the question is the whole subject:

The ability of the city to manage education is an accepted fact.

Question: **What** is an accepted fact?

Answer (and whole subject): the ability of the city to manage education

Distinguish the whole subject from the SIMPLE SUBJECT:

The **ability** *of the city to manage education* is an accepted fact.

SUGGESTED ANSWERS

You will almost certainly come up with answers different from these, many much better. Don't worry whether yours match mine word-for-word; focus only on the general principle of the lesson and exercise.

EXERCISE 3.2

Subjects are <u>underlined</u>, verbs CAPITALIZED, characters *italicized,* and actions **boldfaced.**

1a. <u>There</u> IS **opposition** among many *voters* to *nuclear power plants* BASED on a **belief** in their **threat** to human health.

1b. Many <u>*voters*</u> OPPOSE nuclear power plants because *they* BELIEVE that such *plants* THREATEN human health.

3a. <u>There</u> IS a **belief** among some *researchers* that *consumers'* **choices** in fast food *restaurants* ARE healthier because <u>there</u> ARE **postings** of nutrition information in their menus.

3b. Some <u>*researchers*</u> BELIEVE that <u>*consumers*</u> ARE **CHOOSING** healthier foods because fast food <u>*restaurants*</u> ARE **POSTING** nutrition information in their menus.

5a. Because the *student's* **preparation** for the exam WAS thorough, <u>none</u> of the questions on it WERE a **surprise.**

5b. Because the <u>*student*</u> PREPARED thoroughly for the exam, <u>*she*</u> WAS not **SURPRISED** by any of the questions on it.

EXERCISE 3.4

1a. Verbs: *argue, elevate.* No nominalizations.

1b. Verbs: *has been.* Nominalizations: *speculation, improving, achievement.*

3a. Verbs: *have identified, have failed, to develop, to immunize.* Nominalizations: *risk.*

3b. Verbs: *met.* Nominalizations: *attempts, defining, employment, failure.*

5a. Verbs: *resulted.* Nominalizations: *loss, share, disappearance.*

5b. Verbs: *embrace, teach.* No nominalizations.

EXERCISE 3.5

1b. Some educators have speculated about whether families can improve educational achievement (help students achieve more).

3b. Economists have attempted but failed to define full employment.

5a. When domestic automakers lost market share to the Japanese, hundreds of thousands of jobs disappeared.

EXERCISE 3.6

1. Lincoln hoped to preserve the Union without war, but when the South attacked Fort Sumter, war became inevitable.

3. Business executives predicted that the economy would quickly revive.

5. Several candidates attempted to explain why more voters participated in this year's elections.

7. The business sector did not independently study why the trade surplus suddenly increased.

EXERCISE 4.1

1. We were required to explain the contradictions among the data.

3. In recent years, historians have interpreted the discovery of America in new ways, leading them to reassess the place of Columbus in Western history.

5. Medical professionals usually decide on-scene whether to forcibly medicate patients who are unable to legally consent.

7. Although critics panned the show's latest season, loyal fans still loved it.

EXERCISE 4.2

1. Young people gain independence when they learn skills valued by the marketplace. [Note how the passive here emphasizes "marketplace."]

3. In this article, I argue that the United States fought the Vietnam War to extend its influence in Southeast Asia and did not end it until North Vietnam made it clear that it could be defeated only if the United States used atomic weapons.

EXERCISE 4.3

1. We believe that students binge because they do not understand the risks of alcohol.

3. We suggest that Russia's economy has improved because it has successfully exported more crude oil for hard currency.

5. In Section IV, I argue that the indigenous culture overcultivated the land and thereby exhausted it as a food-producing area.

7. To evaluate how the flow rate changed, the current flow rate was compared to the original rate on the basis of figures collected by Jordan in his study of diversion patterns of slow-growth swamps. [This sentence technically has a dangling modifier, but it is so common that no reader of technical prose would balk. That last clump of nominalizations is acceptable, because it is a technical term.]

EXERCISE 4.4

1. Diabetic patients may reduce their blood pressure by applying renal depressors.

3. Based on these principles, we may now attempt to formulate rules for extracting narrative information.

5. The Federal Trade Commission must be responsible for enforcing the guidelines for the durability of new automobile tires.

EXERCISE 5.1

1. When the president assumed office, he had two aims—the recovery of . . . . He succeeded in the first as testified to by the drop in. . . . But he had less success with the second, as indicated by America's increased involvement. . . . Nevertheless, the American voter was pleased by vast increases in the military. . . .

EXERCISE 5.2

1. Except for those areas covered with ice or scorched by continual heat, the earth is covered by vegetation. Plants grow most richly in fertilized plains and river valleys, but they also grow at the edge of perpetual snow in high mountains. Dense vegetation grows in the ocean and around its edges as well as in and around lakes and swamps. Plants grow in the cracks of busy city sidewalks as well as on seemingly barren cliffs. Vegetation will cover the earth long after we have been swallowed up by evolutionary history.

EXERCISE 6.1

One can imagine different rationales for different stresses.

1. In my opinion, at least, America is most threatened by the President's tendency to rewrite the Constitution.

3. In large colleges and universities, opportunities for faculty to work with individual students are limited.

5. College students commonly complain about teachers who assign a long term paper and then give them a grade but no comments.

EXERCISE 6.2

1. Because the most important event in Thucydides's *History* is Athens's catastrophic Sicilian Invasion, Thucydides devotes three-quarters of his book to setting it up. We can see this anticipation especially in how he describes the step-by-step decline in Athenian society so that he could create the inevitability that we associate with the tragic drama.

EXERCISE 9.1

1. Critics must use complex and abstract terms to analyze literary texts meaningfully.

3. Most patients who go to a public clinic do not expect special treatment, because their health problems are minor and can be easily treated.

5. We can reduce the federal deficit only if we reduce federal spending.

EXERCISE 9.3

1. On the other hand, some TV programming will always appeal to our most prurient interests.

3. Schools transmit more social values than do families.

EXERCISE 10.1

1. To explain why Shakespeare had Lady Macbeth die off-stage, we must understand how the audience reacted to Macbeth's death.

3. A student's right to access his or her records generally takes precedence over an institution's desire to keep those records private, unless the student agrees to limits on those rights during registration.

5. Cigarette companies no longer claim that smoking does not cause heart disease and cancer.

7. Employers have had no difficulty identifying skilled employees, even though teachers, administrators, and even newspapers continue to debate grade inflation.

9. Parents and students need to understand how serious it is to bring to school anything that looks like a weapon, because, as school officials have said, principals may require students to pass through metal detectors before entering a school building.

EXERCISE 10.2

1. Many school systems are returning to the basics, basics that have been the foundation of education for centuries./... a change that is long overdue.../trying to stem an ever rising drop-out rate.

3. For millennia, why we age has been a puzzle, a puzzle that only now can be answered with any certainty./... a mystery that we can answer either biologically or spiritually./... hoping that one day we might stop our inevitable decline into infirmity and death.

EXERCISE 11.1

1. Those who argue stridently over small matters are unlikely to think clearly about large ones.

3. Some teachers mistake neat papers that rehash old ideas for great thoughts wrapped in impressive packaging.

EXERCISE 11.2

1. If we invest our sweat in these projects, we must avoid appearing to be working only for our own self-interest.

3. Throughout history, science has progressed because dedicated scientists have ignored the hostility of an uninformed public.

EXERCISE 12.1

As the State Utilities Commission has authorized, **you** will have to pay... **You** have not had to pay..., but **you** will now pay rates that have been restructured consistent with revised state policy, which lets us base what **you** pay on what it costs us to provide you with service.

As the State Utilities Commission has authorized, **we** are charging you... **We** have not raised rates... but **we** are restructuring the rates now... so that **we** can charge you for what **we** pay to provide you with service.

EXERCISE 12.2

Your car may have a defective part that connects the suspension to the frame. If you brake hard and the plate fails, you won't be able to steer. We may also have to adjust the secondary latch on your hood because we may have misaligned it. If you don't latch the primary latch, the secondary latch might not hold the hood down. If the hood flies up while you are driving, you won't be able to see. If either of these things occurs, you could crash.

ACKNOWLEDGMENTS

From "The Aims of Education" in *The Aims of Education and Other Essays* by Alfred North Whitehead. Copyright © 1929 by Macmillan Publishing Co., Inc., renewed © 1957 by Evelyn Whitehead. Reprinted by permission.

Strunk, William; White, E. B., ELEMENTS OF STYLE, THE, 3rd Ed., ©1979. Reprinted and Electronically reproduced by permission of Pearson Education, Inc., Upper Saddle River, New Jersey.

Cover: Odilion Dimier/Getty Images.

Front Matter Page v: Williams, Joseph: "College English", by Joseph M. Williams. Vol. 40, No. 6 (Feb., 1979), pp. 595–609. National Council of Teachers of English.

Chapter 1 Page **3**: Orwell, George, "Politics and the English Language," Horizon, Vol. 13, Issue 76, pp. 252–265, GB, London: April 1946. Print; p. **3**: Mulcaster, Richard, "The First Part of the Elementary." Scholar Press. Print. p. **4**: Sprat, Thomas, "History of the Royal Society." 1667. Print; p. **4**: Paine, Thomas, "Common Sense." 1776. Print; p. **4**: Cooper, James Fenimore, "The American Democrat." 1838. Print; p. **4**: Twain, Mark, "Fenimore Cooper's Literary Offenses." North American Review 161, July 1895. Print; p. **5**: Orwell, George, "Politics and the English Language," Horizon, Vol. 13, Issue 76, pp. 252–265, GB, London: April 1946. Print. p. **5**: Mills, C. Wright, "The Sociological Imagination." London: Oxford University Press, 1959; p. **5**: Crichton, Michael, "Medical Obfuscation: Structure and Function." New England Journal of Medicine, Dec. 11, 1975; p. **5**: Goldstein, Tom. "Lawyers Now Confuse Even the Same Aforementioned". New York Times (1923–Current file); Apr 1, 1977; ProQuest Histroical Newspapers: The New York Times (1851–2009) p. **23**; p. **6**: Chadwick, Douglas. "Our Unfortunate Cousins," New York Times Book Review, December 11, 1994; p. **7**: Kennedy, John F., Inaugural Address, January 20, 1961. Print; p. **8**: Mencken, H. L., "Literature and the School Ma'am," Prejudices, Fifth Series, Alfred Knopf, 1926.

Chapter 2 Page **9**: Erasmus, "Apologia to the Novum Instrumentum of 1516."; p. **9**: White, E .B., "English Usage," The Second Tree from the Corner, Harper & Row, 1954; p. **9**: Blair, Hugh. Lectures on Rhetoric and Belles

Lettres, 1783; pp. 10–11: Burns, Robert, "Address to the Inco Guid, or The Rigidly Righteous," 1786' p. **13**: Follett, Wilson, "Modern American Usage, A Guide." Edited and completed by Jacques Barzun et al., Hill & Wang, 1966; p. **14**: Ong, Walter J. "The Expanding Humanities and the Individual Scholar," Publication of the Modern Language Association, September 1967; p. **14**: Barzun, Jacques, "Simple and Direct." New York: Harper and Row, 1975; p. **15**: Fowler, Henry, "A Dictionary of Modern English Usage." Oxford University Press, 1926; p. **16**: Annan, Noel Gilroy. Lord Annan, "The Life of the Mind in British Universities Today," American Council of Learned Societies Newsletter, pp. **18–19**, 1969; p. **17**: MacDonald, Dwight, "The String Untuned," The New Yorker, March 10, 1962; p. **17**: Zinsser, William, "On Writing Well." HarperCollins Publishers, 1976; p. **17**: Gowers, Ernest, "The Complete Plain Words." HMSO, 1954; p. **18**: Orwell, George, "Politics and the English Language," Horizon, Vol. 13, Issue 76, pp. 252–265, GB, London: April 1946.

Chapter 3 Page **27**: Wittgenstein, Ludwig, "Tractatus Logico-Philosophicus (proposition 4.116)." Translated by C. K. Ogden, 1922; p. **29**: Gass, William H. "The Art of Fiction No. 65." Interview with Thomas LeClair. THE PARIS REVIEW.

Chapter 4 Page **51**: Brand, Miles, "Intending and Acting." Cambridge and London: The MIT Press/A Bradford Book, 1984; p. **57**: Nathan, Andrew J. and Tianjian Shi, "Cultural Requisites for Democracy in China: Findings from a Survey," Daedalus. Vol. 122, No. 2, Spring, 1993; p. **57**: Newton, Isaac, "New Theory of Light and Colors," 1672; p. **57**: Matthews, P. H. "Problems of selection in transformational grammar." Journal of Linguistics 1.01 (1965): 35-47; p. **58**: Gilbert, John P., Bucknam McPeek, and Frederick Mosteller, "Statistics and Ethics in Surgery and Anesthesia," Science, pp 684–689, 1977; p. **61**: Parsons, Talcott, "Essays in Sociological Theory." Simon & Schuster, 1954.

Chapter 6 Page **79**: Eliot, T.S., "East Coker" from Four Quartets. Originally published in New English Weekly, 1940; p. **81**: Rosenberg, Steven A. M.D., Ph.D., "Observations on the Systemic Administration of Autologous Lmphokine-Activated Killer Cells and Recombinant Interleukin-2 to Patients with Metastatic Cancer". New England Journal of Medicine, Vol 313, No. 23; p. **82**: Edmundson, Mark. "Why Teach? In Defense of a Real Education." Bloomsbury, USA. 2013.

Chapter 7 Page **94**: Dewey, John, "How We Think." 1910. Print; p. **94**: Einstein, Albert and Infeld, Leopold, "The Evolution of Physics." 1938.

Chapter 8 Page **109**: Marquez, Gabriel Garcia interviewed by Peter H. Stone; published as "Gabriel Garcia Marquez, The Art of Fiction," No. 69, The Paris Review, Winter 1981, No. 82.

Chapter 9 Page **121**: Sterne, Laurence, "The Works of Laurence Sterne: With an Account of the Life and Writings of the Author." Volume 4, 1790; **127**: Tannen, Deborah, "The Argument Culture." Ballantine Books, 1999; p. **130**: Watson, J. D. and F. H. C. Crick, "Molecular Structure of Nucleic Acids," Nature, 171, April 25, 1953; pp. 132–133: Strunk, William; White, E.B., "The Elements of Style", 3rd Ed., © 1979. Reprinted and Electronically reproduced by permission of Pearson Education, Inc., New York, NY.

Chapter 10 Page **137**: Stein, Gertrude, "Lectures in America." Beacon Press, 1935; p. **148**: Hoffman, Eva, "Minor art offers special pleasures," New York Times, February 27, 1983.

Chapter 11 Page **160**: Maugham, Somerset, "The Summing Up." 1938; p. **160**: Pearson, Hesketh, "George Bernard Shaw: His Life and Personality." London: Collins, 1942; p. **161**: Editorial Board, "Little League's Scapegoats." The Washington Post, 12 Feb 2015; p. **165**: Gibbon, Edward, "History of the Decline and Fall of the Roman Empire." 1776–1789; p. **166**: Gay, Peter, "Style in History." New York: W. W. Norton & Co., 1974; p. **167**: Fallows, James, "Breaking the News." New York, NY: Pantheon, 1996; p. **168**: Oates, Joyce Carol, "New Heaven and New Earth," Saturday Review, Nov. 4, 1972, 51–54; reprinted in Arts and Society, Spring-Summer 1973, 36–43; p. **170**: Wollstonecraft, Mary. "Letters Written During a Short Residence in Sweden, Norway, and Denmark." 1796; p. **172**: Sandel, Michael J. Justice: "What's the Right Thing To Do?" Farrar, Straus and Giroux. 2010.

Chapter 12 Page **175**: Russell, Bertrand, "Scientific Method in Philosophy." Clarendon Press, 1914; p. **176**: Gass, William, "Finding a Form: Essays." Knopf, 1996; p. **176**: Whitehead, Alfred North, "Aims of Education." New York: Macmillan Co., Free Press edition, 1967; p. **177**: Ochs, E., and B. Schieffelen, "Planned and Unplanned Discourse," Syntax and semantics, vol. 12: Discourse and syntax, ed. by T. Givon. New York: Academic Press, 1979; p. **178**: Newspaper advertisement copy, Sears, 1992; p. **182**: Babba, Homi K., "The Location of Culture." Routledge, 1994; p. **182**: Wittgenstein, Ludwig, "Tractatus Logico-Philosophicus (proposition 4.116)." translated by C .K. Ogden, 1922; p. **183**: Aronowitz, Stanley, and Henry Giroux, "Postmodern Education." University of Minnesota Press, 1991; p. **192**: Whitehead, Alfred North, "The Aims of Education." New York: Macmillan Co., Free Press edition, 1967.

Appendix I Page **193**: Stein, Gertrude, "Lectures in America." Beacon Press, 1935; p. **201**: Twain, Mark. Harper's Bazaar, XLIV, II8–II9. Feb.,1910.

Appendix II Page **213**: Whitehead, Alfred North, "Aims of Education." New York: Macmillan Co., Free Press edition, 1967; p. **216**: Tannen, Deborah, "The Argument Culture: Stopping America's War of Words." Ballantine Books, 1999.

INDEX